D1061909

SMITHSONIAN SCIENTIFIC SERIES

Editor-in-chief
CHARLES GREELEY ABBOT, D.Sc.
Secretary of the
Smithsonian Institution

Published by
SMITHSONIAN INSTITUTION SERIES, Inc.
NEW YORK

Sioux Indian warrior in full war costume, National Museum

THE NORTH AMERICAN INDIANS

AN ACCOUNT OF THE AMERICAN INDIANS NORTH OF MEXICO, COMPILED FROM THE ORIGINAL SOURCES

By

Rose A. Palmer

VOLUME FOUR
OF THE
SMITHSONIAN SCIENTIFIC SERIES

CONTENTS

ILLUSTRATIONS

LIST OF PLATES

LIST OF TEXT FIGURES

THE NORTH AMERICAN INDIANS

THE NORTH AMERICAN INDIANS

CHAPTER I

THE RED MEN DISCOVER THE NEW WORLD

When our fathers and mothers studied geography in the little red school house of old, they were taught that there are Five Races of men—the White, the Yellow, the Red, the Brown, and the Black—all derived from one primeval stock (presumably neutral in tint) by passing through the magic prism of "local variation." Today we dare not apply so simple a scheme of classification to the complex science of ethnology; anthropologists, like other scientists, have learned to proceed more cautiously from fact to theory than did their predecessors, whose imaginations were less hampered by exact knowledge.

Nevertheless, though discussed under many learned names and divided and recombined according to every conceivable plan—linguistic, geographical, cultural, historical—the several distinct types of mankind persist and still challenge us to reverse the prism and reconstruct the mother race. Gropingly ethnologists are feeling their way, through patient archeological and biological researches, back through the ages to the approximate time and place of the birth of the human species.

When we thus try to pierce the mists of prehistoric time and trace the origin of the Red race of America, we are led, by certain similarities of color and anatomy, to associate them with the peoples of eastern Asia. Noting the narrow sea which separates North America from

Siberia, we find it not hard to imagine the possibility of migrations across so slight a barrier. Indeed, if we had no other evidence to guide us, it would be difficult to say whether the Asiatic races gave birth to the American as an offshoot, or whether a primeval American race colonized northeastern Asia.

The vocabularies of the languages spoken by the American Indians, however, are now so utterly unlike those of Asiatic tongues that it is necessary to set the period of the migrations very far back in terms of centuries—certainly to a time more than 10,000 years ago. On the other hand, the human remains of western Europe represent a much earlier epoch than do those found thus far in America, which seems to be a comparatively recent home of human life, counting time in geological ages. From such considerations anthropologists are inclined to believe that the Indians are descended from the same ancestors as the reddish races of eastern Asia, and that they migrated from Asia to America, probably in several waves, many thousands, perhaps even tens of thousands, of years ago.

This theory gains added weight from the researches of Dr. Aleš Hrdlička, who has found in different parts of Asia living remnants of the older yellow-brown stock from which our Indians were probably derived. Particularly in the southern slopes of the Himalayas, among the Tibetan tribes, are types so closely resembling the American Indians that if they were transplanted into America nobody could possibly take them for anything but Indians "in physique, in behavior, in dress, and even in the intonations of their language." Despite their Asiatic origin, however, the red men have inhabited America for so long a time that they may justly be regarded as native to its soil.

Most people think of the aborigines of North America, excepting the Eskimo, as just "Indians," but the study of their languages shows that they represent more than fifty different families, whose vocabularies are often as distinct from one another as are ours from theirs. Doubtless, however, resemblances may in future be brought out which will diminish somewhat the number of Indian stocks now thought to be unrelated. It is the presence of these distinct types among the American Indians which points to the probability of their having reached the New World in several separate waves of migration. In this connection Doctor Hrdlička says:

The newcomers, though all belonging to the same main race, were evidently not strictly homogeneous, but represented several distinct sub-types of the yellow-brown people, with differences in culture and language.

The first of these sub-types to come over was, according to many indications, the dolichocephalic Indian [*i.e.*, those having relatively narrow heads] represented in North America today by the great Algonquian, Iroquoian, Siouan, and Shoshonean stocks, farther south by the Piman-Aztec tribes, and in South America by many branches extending over large parts of that continent from Venezuela and the coast of Brazil to Tierra del Fuego.

Next came, it seems, what Morton called the "Toltec" type, quite as Indian as the other, but marked by brachycephaly [*i.e.*, with relatively broad heads]. This type settled along the northwest coast, in the central and eastern mound region, in the Gulf states, the Antilles, Mexico (including Yucatan), over much of Central America, reaching finally the coast of Peru and other parts of northern South America.

Still later, and when America was already well peopled, there came, according to all indications, the Eskimo and the Athapascan Indians. The former, finding resistance in the south which he could not overcome, remained in and spread over the far-north land, developing various environmental physical modifications that have removed him, on the whole, farther from the Indians than is the case with any other branch of the yellow-brown people. The Athapascans, a virile brachycephalic type, on the one side closely allied physically to the prevailing Mongolian type of northeastern Asia and on the other to the earlier American brachycephals, may have reached the continent before the Eskimo. However this may be, their progress south was evidently also blocked, compelling the body of the enlarging tribe to remain in Alaska and northwestern Canada; but along the western coast some contingents succeeded in penetrating as far as California, where they left the Hupa, and to Arizona, New Mexico, Texas, and parts of northern Mexico, where we know them to this day as the Lipan and the Apache.

Of the more than fifty distinct families composing the American Indians at the time of the coming of the white men, nine predominated over great areas of North America. Farthest north, on the Atlantic and Pacific coasts and along the shores which fringe the Arctic Ocean, lived then, as now, the tribes of the Esquimauan family, who may be regarded as Indians only in the broadest meaning of the word. In the interior of Alaska and the great northwest of Canada were the Athapascans, whose offshoots were widely scattered throughout the West. Two smaller families disputed part of this territory with the Athapascans: the Salishan of British Columbia, and the northwestern United States; and the Siouan, whose chief habitat was the northwest, centering in Dakota, but who had a strong offshoot in the eastern Carolinas, and were also represented on the coast of the Gulf of Mexico.

The East was divided chiefly between two mighty families: the Algonquian, who occupied most of eastern Canada and extended in the United States from Maine to the Mississippi River and as far south as North Carolina; and the Iroquoian, who held the valley of the St. Lawrence, most of New York, and Pennsylvania, with offshoots in eastern North Carolina and the southern Appalachian Mountains.

Of the three remaining great families, the Shoshonean occupied the Great Plateau and extended into California, and were represented on the Plains by one tribe, the Comanche; the Caddoans were found chiefly in Louisiana, Texas, and Nebraska; while the Muskhogeans held the eastern Gulf States.

In addition to these there were over forty smaller but distinct families, mostly fringing the Pacific Ocean from Alaska to Mexico. Each family included one or more tribes or confederations of tribes, the names of some of which, as the Iroquois, Powhatan, and Apache, have become household words through traditions of the Colonial and later Indian wars.

While not nomads in the ordinary sense of the word, all

PLATE 1

Kinugumiut Eskimo of Cape Prince of Wales

Flathead or Salish man in native dress

PLATE 2

Yakima woman of the Shahaptian Family in native dress. Washington

Wasco man of the Chinookan Family in native dress. Arizona

the tribes were forced into seasonal migrations in search of food. These movements were greatest with the hunting tribes of the colder regions of the north and with those of the arid Western plains and plateaus, where agriculture was impracticable and game animals and edible plants were thinly distributed. The corn-raising tribes of the South supported themselves at home by their crops during a greater part of the year, but even they were forced to go long distances for their supplies of meat. The fishing tribes of the coasts possessed a fairly constant food supply, but they too shifted from point to point, following the runs of different species of fish, and in winter they usually went into the interior to hunt.

The lack of domestic animals prevented the population in the North and West from becoming as large and as dangerous to its neighbors as the pastoral tribes of the Old World; but for the same reason the corn-raising peoples had to move about more, partly to obtain meat and partly because they had no fertilizer with which to maintain the fertility of their fields. These conditions tended to keep down the increase of population in that part of North America now occupied by the United States and Canada. In southern Mexico and Central America a more favorable climate and a more abundant food supply gave rise to a denser population which culminated still farther south in the Andean section of South America; but nowhere was anything approaching the swarming populations of the warmer parts of Europe and Asia.

The question of the number of the native population of America at the coming of the white man has been the subject of much speculation. Extremists on the one hand have imagined a population of millions, while on the other hand the claim has been made, and persistently repeated, that there has been no decrease, but that on the contrary the Indians have thriven under misfortune and are more numerous today than at any former period.

The first error is due in part to the tendency to magnify

the glory of a vanished past and in part to the mistaken idea that the numerous ancient remains scattered over the country were built or occupied at practically the same period. The contrary error—that the Indian has increased—is due to several causes, chief of which is the mistake of starting the calculation at too recent a period, usually at the establishment of treaty relations. Prior to that time, however, the natives had been subjected to nearly three centuries of destructive influences which had wiped out many tribes entirely and reduced others to mere remnants. Moreover, the Indian of the discovery period was a full-blood; the Indian of today is very often a mongrel, with not enough of aboriginal blood to be distinguishable in the features; yet, excepting in a few tribes, no official distinction is made.

Among the chief causes of decrease since the coming of the white man may be mentioned smallpox and other epidemics; tuberculosis; sexual diseases; whiskey and attendant dissipation; removals, starvation, and subjection to unaccustomed conditions; low vitality due to mental depression under misfortune; and wars.

The destruction by disease and dissipation has been greatest along the Pacific Coast, where also the original population was most numerous. In California, the enormous decrease from about a quarter of a million to less than 20,000, is due chiefly to the cruelties and wholesale massacres perpetrated by the miners and early settlers. The almost complete extermination of the Aleut of the Northwest is attributable to the same causes during the early Russian period. Confinement in mission establishments has also been fatal to the Indian, in spite of increased comfort in living conditions. Wars in most cases have not greatly diminished the number of Indians. The tribes were in chronic warfare among themselves, so that the balance was nearly even until, as in the notable case of the Iroquois, the acquisition of firearms gave one body an immense superiority over its neighbors.

PLATE 3

"Drawings of Savages of Several Nations, New Orleans, 1735."
By A. de Batz, French engineer and painter. Courtesy of
Mr. David I. Bushnell, Junior

A careful study of the whole territory north of Mexico, taking each geographic section separately, indicates a total population, at the time of the coming of the white man, of nearly 1,150,000 Indians, which is believed to be within ten per cent of the actual number. Of this total 846,000 were within the limits of the United States proper, 220,000 in British America, 72,000 in Alaska, and 10,000 in Greenland. The number of Indians in the United States is now less than 400,000, but is gradually increasing.

None the less is the modern Indian a representative of a vanishing race. Vanishing as are the buffalo, the deer, and the other native wild creatures of America, because of the resistless march of the white man's civilization. It is this inevitable evanishment of the Indians as a distinct race which gives such importance and significance to the work of the Bureau of American Ethnology. The case was eloquently stated in an editorial in the Washington *Evening Star* of August 14, 1928:

There is a general assumption that when Europeans first came to the Americas they found a nomadic population of naked savages with turkey feathers in their hair. That, in fact, was what many of the white pioneers themselves, as well as their present-day descendants, assumed that they had found. They set about cheerfully, with flintlocks and scriptural tracts, to civilize the poor, bronze-skinned wretches.

The assumption, of course, was not altogether valid. What the white men actually found, even if they didn't know it at the time, was a people with a culture little inferior to their own. But to the Europeans it was a strange, incomprehensible culture expressed in symbols foreign to their minds.

The American Indian, in fact, had advanced a long way from savagery. He had developed an agriculture, a textile art, religions, literatures, and political organizations of his own from which the newcomers had much to learn. But these had been developed independently of European influences. Europeans did not feel at home in such a culture. Consequently they assumed that it either did not exist or was worthless.

The Indian was offered his choice, for all practical purposes, between extinction and adapting himself to a culture which was as foreign to his processes of thinking as his own civilization was to the minds of the newcomers.

Certain definite things which the Europeans brought with them were new to the Americas. The Indian had no gunpowder. He had no printing press. He had no facile system of writing. He was not familiar with those two fundamental inventions of the Old World, the wheel and the arch. He had domesticated few animals. Outside of these the white man had very little to give the red man.

From the culture of the "naked savages" the invaders took immediately a few things that have had a very important effect on the history of the world, notably corn and potatoes. They had much more to learn, but deferred the lessons until they had killed off their prospective teachers.

It was not until the middle of the last century that the white man, so far as he was represented by the United States Government, set about to find out what was to be learned from the Indians. Already it was almost too late. Much of the native culture was dead and forgotten. Much of the remainder was dying and half forgotten. The mind of the red man was changing into the mind of a white man. He himself was turning his back on the civilization of his ancestors for the more material civilization of his conquerors.

At the very time when Indian tribes were making their last stands for independence the Bureau of American Ethnology was organized as a Government institution, under the direction of the Smithsonian Institution. Its object was to preserve at least a record of the native cultures, to collect the inventions, the laws, the faiths and the songs of the vanishing peoples.

Few Government bureaus have operated with less public attention. The staff consists of a small group of scholars who are working for the future. They are trying to preserve, until such time as it will be appreciated, one of the world's great cultures. It is a priestly task.

It is a task which has a threefold aspect—linguistic, archeological, and anthropologic. The first two of these may be regarded as important in proportion as they have supplied the tools for the anthropological work. Therefore we will briefly sketch the more striking peculiarities of the languages and the chief characteristics of the material culture, together with certain fundamental beliefs and customs, before proceeding to an account of some of the typical Indian tribes.

PLATE 4

Yankton Sioux in full regalia

Cayuga man of the Iroquois confederation

PLATE 5

A typical Zuñi man, New Mexico

A chief of the Acoma, New Mexico

REFERENCES

Brinton, Daniel G. The American race. New York, 1891.

Holmes, William H. On the race history and facial characteristics of the aboriginal Americans. Smithsonian Inst. Ann. Rep., 1919, pp. 427–432. Washington, 1921.

Hrdlička, Aleš. The genesis of the American Indian. Proc. 19th Cong. Americanists, 1915, pp. 559–568. Washington, 1917.

—— The origin and antiquity of the American Indian. Smithsonian Inst. Ann. Rep. 1923, pp. 481–494. Washington, 1925.

—— The peopling of the earth. Proc. Amer. Philos. Soc. Vol. 65, pp. 150–156, 1926.

Mason, Otis T. Migration and the food quest: a study in the peopling of America. Smithsonian Inst. Ann. Rep. 1894, pp. 523–539. Washington, 1896.

Mooney, James. The aboriginal population of America north of Mexico. Smithsonian Misc. Collect. Vol. 80, No. 7. Washington, 1928.

CHAPTER II

THE STONE AGE OF NORTH AMERICA

In a population of about a million people speaking more than two hundred distinct languages it was necessary to have some means of communication other than words. It is not surprising, therefore, that sign languages were gradually evolved by means of which it became possible for members of different tribes, notably among the Plains Indians, to converse with surprising ease. This was partly due to the innate dramatic instinct of the Indians and their customary use of effective gestures even in ordinary speech. While many of the signs which constituted such wordless languages crystallized into convenient symbols, still more were devised at need as a sort of pantomime by which a narrative was acted out instead of spoken.

Certain individuals were, of course, more expert than others in the use and interpretation of signs. Their services were always in demand on those rare occasions when a tribe might be visited by "foreign" Indians and this occasionally resulted in a very roundabout method of communication, as is well illustrated in Ivan Petroff's ccount of a "Sign Dialogue Between Alaskan Indians":

In the month of September, 1866, there arrived on the Lower Kinnik River, a stream emptying its waters into Cook's Inlet, two Indians from a distant region, who did not speak the Kenaitze language. The people of the settlement at which the strangers made their first appearance were at a loss to understand the visitors. At last a chief of great age, bearing the name of Chatidoolts (mentioned by Vancouver as a youth), was found to be able to interpret some of the signs made by the strangers, and after a little practice he entered into conversation with them in a rather roundabout way, being himself blind. He informed me that it was the second or third time within his recollection that strangers like those then present had come to Kinnik from the northeast, but that in his youth he had frequently "talked with his hands" to visitors from the west and east. He also told me that he had acquired this art from his father, who, as the old man expressed himself, had "seen every country, and spoken to all the tribes of the earth." The conversation was carried on with the help of the old man's sons, who described to their blind parent the gestures of the strangers, and were instructed in turn by him with what gestures to reply.

The two Indians wore the pointed hunting shirt of tanned moose-skin, ornamented with beads and fringes, which is still common to the Kutchin tribes. They were not tattooed, but their ears and noses were encumbered with pendants of dentalium and a small red glass bead. Their feet were clothed in moccasins. One of them had a rifle of English manufacture, and his companion carried two huge knives, one of them of copper evidently of native manufacture.

Kenaitze.—Left hand raised to height of eye, palm outward, moved several times from right to left rapidly; fingers extended and closed; pointing to strangers with left hand. Right hand describes a curve from north to east—*Which of the northeastern tribes is yours?*

Tennanah.—Right hand, hollowed, lifted to mouth, then extended and describing waving line gradually descending from right to left. Left hand describing mountainous outline, apparently one peak rising above the other, said by Chatidoolts to mean—*Tenan-tnu-kohtana, Mountain-river-men.*

Kenaitze.—Left hand raised to height of eye, palm outward, moved from right to left, fingers extended. Left index finger describes curve from east to west. Outline of mountain and river as in preceding sign—*How many days from Mountain-river?*

Tennanah.—Right hand raised toward sky, index finger and thumb forming first crescent and then ring. This repeated three times—*Moon, new and full three times.* Continuing his narrative:

Right hand raised, palm to front, index finger raised and lowered at regular intervals—*Walked.*

Both hands imitating paddling of canoe, alternately right and left—*Traveled three months on foot and by canoe.*

Both arms crossed over breast, simulating shivering—*Cold, winter.* Right index finger pointing toward speaker—*I.* Left hand pointing to the west—*Traveled westward.*

Right hand lifted cup-shaped to mouth—*Water.* Right hand describing waving line from right to left gradually descending, pointing to the west—*River running westward.*

Right hand gradually pushed forward, palm upward from height of breast. Left hand shading eyes; looking at great distance—*Very wide.*

Left and right hands out together in shape of sloping shelter—*Lodge, camp.*

Both hands lifted, height of eye, palm inward, fingers spread—*Many times.*

Both hands closed, palm outward, height of hips—*Surprised.*

Index finger pointing from eye forward—*See.*

Right hand held up, height of shoulder, three fingers extended, left hand pointing to me—*Three white men.*

. . . .

Left hand upholding one finger, right pointing to me—*One white man.*

Right hand held horizontally, palm downward, about four feet from ground—*Small.*

Forming rings before eyes with index finger and thumb—*Eye-glasses.*

Right hand clinched, palm upward, in front of chest, thumb pointing inward—*Gave one.*

Forming cup with right hand, simulating drinking—*Drink.*

Right hand grasping chest repeatedly, fingers curved and spread—*Strong.*

Both hands pressed to temple and head moved from side to side—*Drunk, headache.*

By means of such simple but expressive pantomime, described to the blind interpreter and recounted in detail in Petroff's account, the traveler managed to relate a narrative which may be freely rendered in words as follows:

For three months I journeyed westward from the Mountain-river country, on foot and by canoe, through the cold of winter, until I reached a great river flowing westward. There to my surprise, I found the camp of three white men. One of these, a small man wearing eyeglasses, gave me a drink of strong liquor which made me drunk. Another, a Russian, had shot a moose. For two days I stayed with them, feasting gratefully on the good moose meat. Then we parted company, the three white men going westward and I eastward, on snow shoes over the deep snow, in the bitter cold. Cutting down a birch tree I peeled the bark and fashioned a canoe in which I poled upstream for one month, until I came to the high mountains where I camped for a month on the shore of a great lake. An old man lived there, with two women. One day a great tree fell on the head of the old man and killed him. Then the women built a lodge, cut off their

PLATE 6

Ancient Pueblo water jars, New Mexico. In National Museum

hair, blackened their faces, and began to weep and mourn. I shot a moose and gave part of it to the women, who received it gratefully. This man with me came to me in a canoe from the northeast. Together we paddled to this place.

Anyone who has tried to make himself understood in a foreign land without the aid of words will appreciate the value of this wordless Indian Esperanto.

Sometimes, of course, an Indian might acquire the language of a tribe other than his own, particularly if he was made a captive and "adopted" by the foreigners. But when the white men came to the Indians' land they found the native languages puzzling in the extreme and as difficult to master as the higher mathematics. Moreover, Indian tongues differ from one another almost as much as they do from ours and to us they are no less strange than are the many dialects of China. Yet from these sometimes harsh and apparently meaningless syllables linguists have worked out, little by little, through long and patient study, the vocabularies and grammatical structure of hundreds of different languages and dialects, distributed among the more than fifty linguistic families that are seemingly unrelated to one another.

Despite this diversity however, there are certain characteristics which serve to distinguish the Indian languages from the languages of other races. In this connection Dr. Truman Michelson has said:

> I do not know of a single feature that may be said to be characteristic of all American Indian languages. Even so, a combination of certain features is quite sufficient to determine whether any given language is an American Indian language or not. It is this which enables us to say without any hesitation that Chuckchee, Koryak, and Yukaghir (which are spoken in northeastern Asia) are Americanoid languages. If they were spoken in America we would call them American Indian languages.

In order to appreciate better the difficulties of the pioneer students of the Indian tongues, we must remember that, before these scholars began their work, our Indians had no written language. Moreover, a number of intertribal jargons had sprung up and spread rapidly among both the Indians and the first white settlers, increasing the complexities of the task a hundredfold.

In studying any new language, the two fundamental elements to consider, aside from its phonetics, are the lexic, relating to the words themselves; and the grammatic, dealing with the manner in which words are combined or changed in the building up of sentences.

While some Indian words seem melodious to our ear because the vowel sounds predominate, others contain many consonant sounds to which we are unaccustomed and which give them a harsh character. Particularly frequent are sounds similar to the Scotch *ch* in *loch*, and a number of explosive *l*'s. Harshness is characteristic of the languages of the northwest coast; sonorous languages are found in a large part of the Mississippi basin and in California.

A peculiarly picturesque quality is given to many words through the Indian custom of naming a thing from its most striking characteristic. The Chinook may say, *He runs into the water*, meaning *the mink*. The Hupa may say, *They have been laid together*, meaning *a fire* (of sticks). The Kwakiutl call a steamboat *fire on its back moving on the water*. Such descriptive phrases were a favorite means of providing terms for new objects.

Contrary to the prevalent notion, the vocabularies are rich and highly inflected. Owing to the wealth of derivatives it is difficult to estimate the number of words in any Indian language; but it is certain that in every one there are at least two thousand stem words, and, when derivatives are counted, many thousands of words as that term is defined in English dictionaries.

There is considerable variety in grammatical structure, but as already pointed out, a few common traits seem to be characteristic of most Indian languages. The complexity of grammar is often great because of the number of ideas expressed by grammatical processes alone. The Eskimo,

PLATE 7

Western Indians communicating by the sign language

PLATE 8

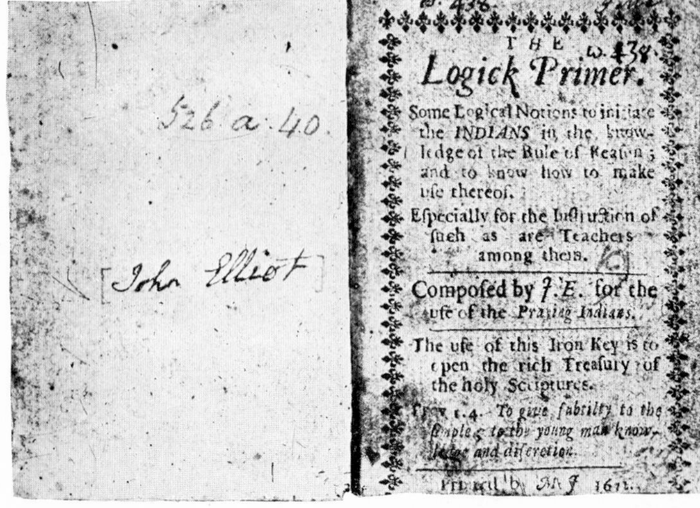

526 a. 40

[John Elliot]

THE

Logick Primer.

Some Logical Notions to initiate the *INDIANS* in the knowledge of the Rule of Reason; and to know how to make use thereof.

Especially for the Instruction of such as are Teachers among them.

Composed by *J. E.* for the use of the *Praying Indians.*

The use of this Iron Key is to open the rich Treasury of the holy Scriptures.

Prov. 1. 4. *To give subtilty to the simple; to the young man knowledge and discretion.*

Printed by M. J. 1672.

The Logick Primer.

In beginning created
1. Weske kutchissik ayum God
heaven earth This affirmative
kesuk kah ohke. Ne noowae
general Proposition.
wameyeue pakodtittumooonk.

Earth was not formed
2. Ohke mo matta kuhkenauin-
nothing in it.
neunkquttinno, & monteagwun-
This Negative special
inno. Ne quenoowae hanasiyeue
compound Proposition.
neesepiskue pakodtittumóonk.

Darkness upon deep
3. Pohkenum woskeche moonói.
This Affirmative general Pro-
Ne noowae wameyeue pakodtit-
position.
tumooonk.

4. Nashauanit

The Logick Primer.

Spirit moved
4. Nashauanit popomshau wos-
upon waters. This Affirmative
keche nippekontu. Ne noowae
general Proposition.
wameyeue pakodtittumooonk.

All single Notions are
Wame siyeumooe wahittumoo-
Pairs which in-
ash nequtayittumooash nish we-
lighten each other, them onely.
quohtoadtumooash, & nish webe.

Twenty Notional
Neesneechagquottash wahittum-
Pairs,
ooe nequtayittumooash, kah
two parts.
neese chippissuash.

1. Na-

Pages from John Eliot's "Logick Primer" printed in 1672 in the Algonquian language of the Massachusetts Indians. Eliot, a missionary, was the first to translate the Bible into an Indian language

for instance, by combining other elements with the stem *to see*, may express, *He only orders him to go and see;* a Chimmesyan combination with the verb *to go* is, *He went with him upstairs in the dark and came against an obstacle.*

Indian languages thus tend to express ideas with much graphic detail. For example, a Ponca Indian, in saying that a man killed a rabbit, would have to say: "The man, he, one, animate, standing, in the nominative case, purposely killed by shooting an arrow, the rabbit, he, one, animate, sitting, in the objective case." All these shades of meaning would be included in the form of the verb, which changes, by inflection and incorporated particles, to denote the person, number, and case of both its subject and its object, together with their "gender," by which is meant not merely feminine, masculine, and neuter forms, as in European tongues, but also forms indicating position, size, shape, and many other "corroborative details." Moreover the form of the verb in the example just given would have to express whether the killing was done accidentally or purposely, and whether it was by shooting or some other process, and if by shooting, whether by bow and arrow, or with a gun.

Indian languages are, therefore, not so well adapted to generalized statements as to lively description. The power to form abstract ideas is nevertheless not lacking, and the development of abstract thoughts would find in every one of the languages a ready means of expression. Yet, since the Indian is not given to purely abstract speculation, such ideas always appear in close connection with concrete thought. On the other hand, concrete objects are sometimes indicated by their qualities. For instance, the Chinook will say, *The man's badness killed the child's poverty*, meaning that *the bad man killed the poor child.* The lack of differentiation between verb and noun, too, may lead to such a roundabout expression as *it was the man it the coming* for so simple a thought as *the man came.*

There is a great difference in the number of dialects found in the various languages, some comprising only one dialect, while others embrace many that are mutually unintelligible. While the Eskimo, for example, have retained their language in all its minor features for centuries, that of the Salish, who are confined to a small area in the north Pacific region, is split up into more than thirty dialects. There is, however, no historical proof that any Indian language has changed as much since the time of the discovery as the language of England changed in the three centuries following the Norman conquest.

The North American Indians made up for their lack of a written language by an ingenious use of certain conventional symbols and pictures which sometimes approached the nature of hieroglyphics, as in the wampum belts used by the Iroquois and other Indians of the East. Stones and other objects were also employed for communicating ideas. In regard to such devices, Gregg says of the Plains tribes:

> When traveling, they will also pile heaps of stones upon mounds or conspicuous points so arranged as to be understood by their passing comrades; and sometimes they set up the bleached buffalo heads which are everywhere scattered over those plains, to indicate the direction of their march and many other facts which may be communicated by those simple signs.

A more ingenious but still arbitrary mode of giving information is practiced by the Abnaki. When they are in the woods, to say "I am going to the east" a stick is stuck in the ground pointing to that direction; "Am not gone far," another stick is stuck across the former, close to the ground; "Gone far" is the reverse. The number of days of proposed absence is shown by the number of sticks across the first. Cutting the bark from a tree on one, two, or three sides near the butt means "Have had poor, poorer, poorest luck." Cutting it off all around the tree means "I am starving." Smoking a piece of birch bark and hanging it on a tree means "I am sick."

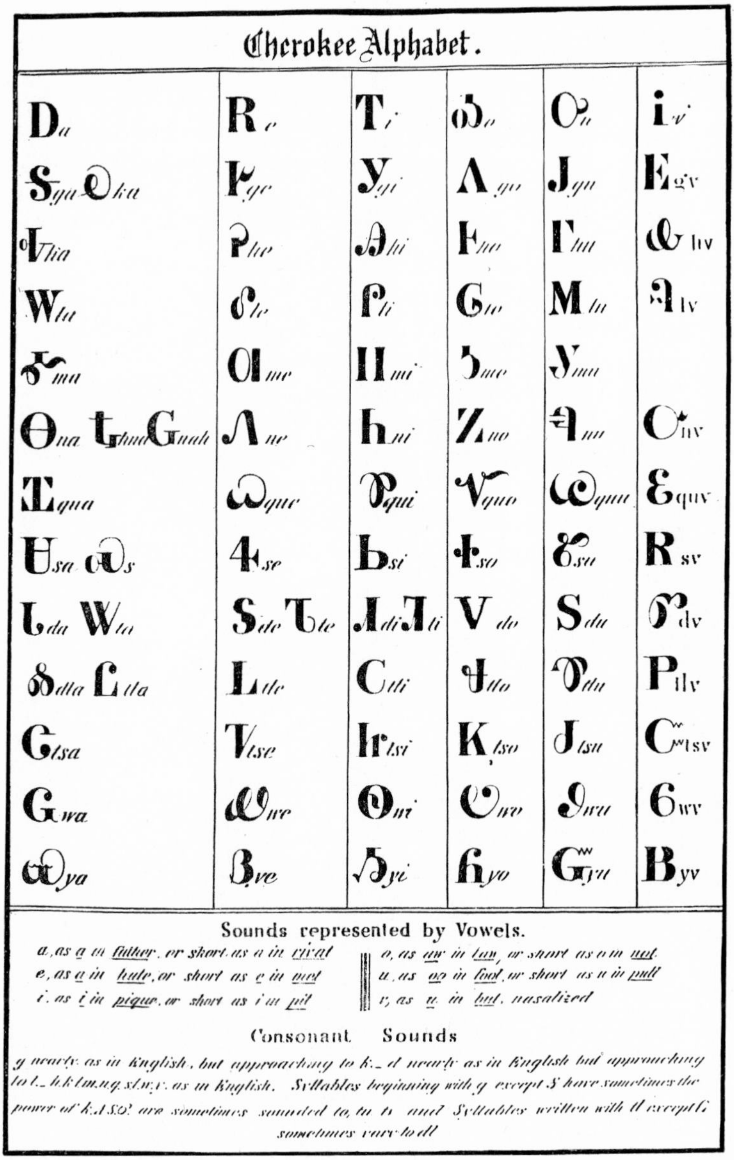

Cherokee Alphabet.

Ꭰ a	Ꭱ e	Ꭲ i	Ꭳ o	Ꭴ u	Ꭵ v
Ꭶ ga Ꭷ ka	Ꭸ ge	Ꭹ gi	Ꭺ go	Ꭻ gu	Ꭼ gv
Ꭽ ha	Ꭾ he	Ꭿ hi	Ꮀ ho	Ꮁ hu	Ꮂ hv
Ꮃ la	Ꮄ le	Ꮅ li	Ꮆ lo	Ꮇ lu	Ꮈ lv
Ꮉ ma	Ꮊ me	Ꮋ mi	Ꮌ mo	Ꮍ mu	
Ꮎ na Ꮏ hna Ꮐ nah	Ꮑ ne	Ꮒ ni	Ꮓ no	Ꮔ nu	Ꮕ nv
Ꮖ qua	Ꮗ que	Ꮘ qui	Ꮙ quo	Ꮚ quu	Ꮛ quv
Ꮜ sa Ꮝ s	Ꮞ se	Ꮟ si	Ꮠ so	Ꮡ su	Ꮢ sv
Ꮣ da Ꮤ ta	Ꮥ de Ꮦ te	Ꮧ di Ꮨ ti	Ꮩ do	Ꮪ du	Ꮫ dv
Ꮬ dla Ꮭ tla	Ꮮ tle	Ꮯ tli	Ꮰ tlo	Ꮱ tlu	Ꮲ tlv
Ꮳ tsa	Ꮴ tse	Ꮵ tsi	Ꮶ tso	Ꮷ tsu	Ꮸ tsv
Ꮹ wa	Ꮺ we	Ꮻ wi	Ꮼ wo	Ꮽ wu	Ꮾ wv
Ꮿ ya	Ᏸ ye	Ᏹ yi	Ᏺ yo	Ᏻ yu	Ᏼ yv

Sounds represented by Vowels.

a, as a in father, or short as a in rival
e, as a in hate, or short as e in met
i, as i in pique, or short as i in pit
o, as aw in law, or short as o in not
u, as oo in fool, or short as u in pull
v, as u in but, nasalized

Consonant Sounds

g nearly as in English, but approaching to k. d nearly as in English but approaching to t. h, k, l, m, n, q, s, t, w, y, as in English. Syllables beginning with g except Ꭶ have sometimes the power of k. Ꭺ, Ꮪ, Ꮫ are sometimes sounded to, tu, tv and Syllables written with tl except Ꮭ sometimes vary to dl.

The Cherokee alphabet invented by Sequoya

A nearer approach to writing is to be found in the pictographs or petroglyphs, which were rude etchings or paintings on rocks, stones, and bark; on various weapons and implements; and sometimes on clothing. The use of pictographic signs reached its highest development with the Kiowa and the Dakota tribes in their so-called calendars, which were painted on deer, antelope, and buffalo hides, and constituted a chronology of past years. Our present knowledge of Indian pictographs, however, does not justify the belief that they record events of great importance, and there seems to be no basis for the widespread belief that a mine of information respecting the customs, origin, and migrations of ancient peoples is locked up in these generally undecipherable symbols.

In "Hiawatha" Longfellow has given us a very useful key to the meaning of some of the more common pictographic symbols:

From his pouch he took his colors,
Took his paints of different colors,
On the smooth bark of the birch-tree
Painted many shapes and figures,
Wonderful and mystic figures.
And each figure had a meaning,
Each some word or thought suggested.
  Gitche Manito the Mighty,
He, the Master of Life, was painted
As an egg, with points projecting
To the four winds of the heavens.
Everywhere is the Great Spirit,
Was the meaning of this symbol.
  Mitche Manito the Mighty,
He the dreadful Spirit of Evil,
As a serpent was depicted,
As Kenabeek, the great serpent.
Very crafty, very cunning,
Is the creeping Spirit of Evil,
Was the meaning of this symbol.
  Life and Death he drew as circles,
Life was white, but Death was darkened;
Sun and moon and stars he painted,

Man and beast and fish and reptile,
Forests, mountains, lakes and rivers.
For the earth he drew a straight line,
For the sky a bow above it;
White the space between for daytime,
Filled with little stars for night-time;
On the left a point for sunrise,
On the right a point for sunset,
On the top a point for noontide,
And for rain and cloudy weather
Waving lines descending from it.

Such symbolic drawings were the only writings the Indians north of Mexico possessed until after the coming of the white men. With the early missionaries, who sought to Christianize the natives, the chief motive for reducing their languages to writing was the desire to translate the Scriptures into the Indian tongues. The most famous example of this kind is the Rev. John Eliot's translation of the Bible, dated 1663, into the language of the Algonquian Indians of Massachusetts.

Very celebrated, too, was the invention of the "Cherokee Alphabet" about the year 1821 by Sequoya, an uneducated Cherokee half-breed. Mooney says of this:

> The invention of the alphabet had an immediate and wonderful effect on Cherokee development. On account of the remarkable adaptation of the syllabary to the language, it was only necessary to learn the characters to be able to read at once. No school-houses were built, and no teachers hired, but the whole nation became an academy for the study of the system, until in the course of a few months, without schools or expense of time or money, the Cherokee were able to read and write in their own language.

Similar astonishing results came from the Cree syllabary invented about 1841 by Rev. James Evans, a Methodist missionary. It is said that an Indian of average intelligence can learn the whole in a day, and within less than a week can read fluently any book written on this plan.

At the time of the discovery, however, the Indians of the section we are considering, after being in possession of the land for thousands of years were still without a native alphabet. Traditions were handed down from generation to generation by word of mouth alone. That being the case, it is little wonder that their civilization had not progressed beyond the stage characteristic of the so-called "Stone Age."

To say that a race existed in the Stone Age, however, is to assert merely that such a people had not yet learned the art of smelting and casting metals, which was a comparatively recent discovery in the history of the human race and seems to have had little relation to its progress in other and far more important matters. Accordingly we find almost as much difference between two representative Indian tribes, such as the Kwakiutl of the Northwest coast and the Zuñi of the Southwest, as one might observe between the Norman conquerors of England and the present inhabitants of France, were they separated from each other by fifteen degrees of latitude instead of some eight centuries of time.

But although so diverse in manners and customs, the tribes north of Mexico were on much the same plane as regards material culture. Their raw materials and what they chose to fashion from them might differ, but the instruments and processes they employed were fundamentally the same.

Stone was the substance from which the Indians made most of their implements. Of the processes employed Wissler says:

> In the main, the stone industry of every social group comprises the following different methods: chipping, or flaking; abrading or pecking; grinding and polishing; sawing and drilling.
>
> The process used is dependent upon the materials. Thus any stone like flint, which has the property of conchoidal fracture, is flaked. While the precise manipulations seem to differ according to locality, the essential procedure is everywhere the same. A pebble is first brought to a generalized or blank form, by striking with a hammerstone. From this the desired implement is worked out, the fine chipping being by hand pressure with an antler or bone blunt-pointed tool. Holmes, our leading experimental archeologist, has worked out

in his laboratory many of the necessary processes, which, in the main, agree with those observed among living peoples.

For pecking, our best data are from the Nootka of Vancouver Island, who occasionally resorted to it as late as twenty-five years ago. . . . Parallel grooves were battered in the pebble to be shaped, then the intervening ridges pecked away and so on. The battering tool was a long, oval pebble of tough, hard stone. When the approximate shape of the desired implement had been attained, it was finished by grinding on suitable stones.

This seems to have been the method employed wherever polished tools of similar materials have been found. But nephrite, the fine, green, jade-like stone found on the North Pacific Coast and in Central America, cannot be worked in this way. It can only be cut and ground. Again, our best data are from Canada and Alaska. The Eskimo successfully sawed off pieces of the required shape by the use of thongs and sand and water; in short, the same principle as is employed in modern stone cutting. From unfinished pieces in collections and the fine examples unearthed by Smith, it appears that the final separation of the block was by fracture produced by wedging.

As to drilling and perforating, our data are less complete. Soft stones, like slate, were drilled with stone points. By experimental methods Rau has reconstructed the process of drilling with a hollow reed and sand, which accounts for the unfinished borings with attached cores we sometimes find in museums. Again, the Nootka made large perforations by pecking. First, a pit was formed in the stone to be perforated, into which a hard pebble was laid and pounded upon until the hole reached the middle; then the stone was inverted and the process repeated.

The fine sculptures of the Maya were executed with stone tools. We can safely assume, therefore, that all the stone work of the New World belongs strictly to a stone age and was such as could, and in the main was, accomplished without the use of metal tools.

For grinding and polishing the Indians used any rough surface, whether of rock, or of dogfish skin, or of some smooth material coated with sand. Of all shapes and sizes were these primitive grindstones and rasps, from small fragments to exposed rock surfaces which are often found covered with grooves made by the grinding work.

By means of such simple tools, employed with surprising skill, the Americans of the Stone Age fashioned the bows and arrows, the lances, spears, tomahawks, and harpoons with which they met their enemies in warfare

PLATE 10

Series showing evolution from rough stone to arrowhead

PLATE 10

Series showing evolution from rough stone to arrowhead

135626.
Piney Branch.
D.C.
Holmes.
Bur. Eth.

or pursued the animals so essential to their existence. The flesh of fishes, birds, and beasts formed an important item of the Indian's daily food; the skins of animals large and small supplied the material for his clothing, his tent, and even his boat; their fat was his fuel; their sinews his thread; their bones, horns, and tusks furnished many useful tools; their feathers and fur were greatly prized as ornaments and as symbols of wealth and power. Since in most cases, an Indian's resourcefulness and skill as a hunter were his chief means of livelihood, while his bravery and cunning in overcoming his foes were his sole guarantees of safety, it is small wonder that war and the chase were usually the only activities considered worthy of a man and most other occupations left to the women.

In order to supply the material for the necessary implements of peace and war, great quarries of flint and other rocks were worked, the remains of which are still found in many parts of the United States. Besides flint and obsidian, soapstone or steatite was much used, especially for cooking vessels and for tobacco pipes. Mica was quarried in many places in Virginia and North Carolina, and used for mirrors and for ornaments. Turquoise was extensively mined at Los Cerrillos, near Santa Fé, New Mexico, and at Turquoise Mountain, Arizona. Silliman speaks of finding many stone hammers in the mines at Los Cerrillos. With these rude tools, and without iron or steel, using fire in place of explosives, the patient workers of old managed to break down and remove the incredible masses of rock which form the mounds still to be seen at the ancient sites.

Although the use of stone was so very extensive, metals were by no means unknown to the Indians, even before the coming of the white man. Gold, silver, and copper were used by many of the more progressive American tribes before the discovery; but copper was the only metal extensively used north of Mexico. The smelting of ores was probably imperfectly understood, even by the most advanced tribes, and was not practiced at all north of Mexico; and iron, except in meteoric form or in the ore, was unknown. The mining operations consisted in removing the superficial earth and *dêbris* and in breaking up the rock with stone sledges, heating it, and then throwing cold water upon it, thus freeing the masses of metal, some of which were of large size.

These metals—copper, gold, silver, and meteoric iron—were worked into shape mainly by cold-hammering and grinding, but heat was sometimes used in the hammering process and in annealing. It can hardly be doubted that copper, gold, and silver were sometimes melted and that bits of native copper were freed from the matrix of rock by this means. Casting processes, however, seem to have been totally unknown. It is a remarkable fact that up to the present time no prehistoric crucible, mold, pattern, or metal-working tool of any kind whatsoever has been identified.

The implements used in cultivating the ground are described as "wooden howes" and "spades made of hard wood." In some localities, shells, in others shoulder-blades of large animals were used as hoes. However, certain stone implements have been found in vast numbers which are believed to have been used in breaking the soil. Of these the most characteristic are the hoes and spades of the middle Mississippi valley. It was a general custom to burn over the ground before planting in order to free it from weeds and rubbish. In the forest regions patches were cleared by first girdling the trees, thus causing them to die, and afterwards burning them down.

This, however, was a very wasteful process to forest dwellers who were acquainted with the many uses to which the bark of living trees might be put. Bark could be wrought into yarn, twine, rope, wallets, baskets, mats, and canoes, as well as cooking pots for hot stones, dishes for serving, vessels for storing, and many other utensils connected with the preparation and serving of food. Among some tribes, indeed, bark was itself eaten during the spring, the season of greatest need. Clothing was made from bark; houses were roofed and sometimes wholly covered with it; cradles and coffins were fashioned of it. The hunter made all sorts of apparatus from bark, even his bow string. The fisher wrought implements out of it and poisoned fishes with its juices, which were also used for medicines and dyes. The beginnings of writing in some localities were favored by bark, and cartography, winter counts, medical formulas, and tribal history were inscribed thereon. Finally it comes into the service of ceremony and religion. Masks and dance regalia such as Boas and others found among the Kwakiutl illustrate how obligingly bark lends itself to such occasions. There were also rites connected with gathering and working bark.

Other materials besides bark, such as feathers, goat's hair, and skins, were woven into blankets and garments, while cotton cloth was used by the cotton-growing tribes of the Southwest. The arts of basketry and pottery were also well known and extensively practiced. Beadwork was especially characteristic, as was also shellwork, both beads and shells being much prized for ornamentation. Porcupine quills, often dyed with various brilliant tints, were used by many tribes as embroidery on leather garments. In the eastern part of North America it was common for a tribe to have its peculiar cut and decoration of the moccasin, so that a man's tribe was proclaimed by his footgear.

Paint—white, black, blue, and red—was used on the face, hair, and body, often with symbolic meanings, as: red for war; black for mourning; white or blue with religious significance; or a combination of two or more colors forming various symbolic patterns; or merely for adornment. The war shirt was frequently painted to represent the wearer's prayer, having a design on the back for protection and one on the breast for victory. The shirt was occasionally decorated with a fringe of human hair, locks being generally contributed by female relatives.

The most imposing article of the warrior's regalia was the bonnet with its crown of golden-eagle feathers. Song and ceremony accompanied the making of a war bonnet by warriors of the tribe, and a war honor was recounted upon each feather before it was placed in position. A bonnet could not be made without the consent of the warriors, each of whom contributed his own plumes of honor; so that the head-dress of a chief might serve as a record of tribal valor as well as a personal distinction.

As the Indians had not progressed in the arts of civilization to the point of domesticating animals for food, they had to rely for their supply of meats on their skill and good fortune in hunting and fishing. No purely hunter stage, however, can be found, if it ever existed, for while the capture of animals and fish devolved on the men and the preparation of food on the women, the latter added to the diet such vegetables and grains as could be most easily supplied. These were obtained by the gathering of self-sown fruits, nuts, seeds, and roots, or the raising of cereal products, consisting chiefly of maize. Besides this grain, better known to modern Americans as corn, most of the tribes cultivated beans, squashes, and pumpkins. Wild rice was also cultivated in the region of the Great Lakes, where a sort of semi-agriculture was practiced. But no purely agricultural stage existed, and no domestication of animals, except in the case of the turkey and the dog, is found among the Indians north of Mexico. The absence of cows, with the consequent lack of milk for growing children, resulted in markedly limiting the increase of the population.

Contrary to popular belief, the Indians preferred cooked food. Even the Eskimo ate raw meat only when they had no fuel, or as a side dish. All the edible portions

PLATE 11

Cahokia mound across the river from St. Louis. Largest aboriginal earthwork in the United States 1,000 feet in length, 100 feet high

PLATE 12

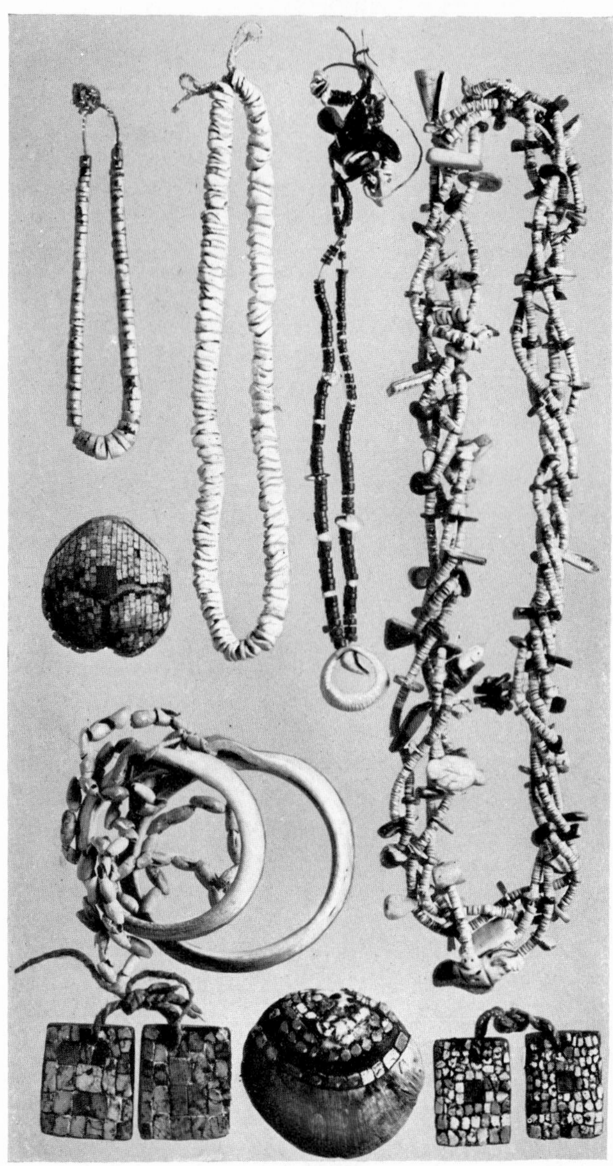

Ancient turquoise and shell bead ornaments from Tusayan, a Pueblo area which includes the Hopi

of an animal were put to use, and in many cases both animal and vegetable substances that were stale to the point of putrefaction were preferred. Thus salmon eggs were stored in sand by the Alaskans, and the Hurons soaked corn in water until it became putrid, when soup was made of it.

The Pueblo Indians were skillful cooks, and most Indian tribes knew how to prepare savory and nourishing dishes, some of which have been adopted by civilized peoples, such as hominy, samp, succotash, etc. The methods of cooking were broiling, roasting, and "stone boiling" by means of hot stones dropped into a pot of water.

Infusions of various herbs were used by the Indians as medicine, and they had several fermented drinks such as cider from Manzanita berries, and a beverage made from cactus fruit. "Carolina tea," or the "black drink," so named by British traders from its color, was a decoction made by parching and then boiling leaves of the *Ilex vomitoria*. It was employed by the tribes of the Gulf States and adjacent region for ceremonial purification. Among the Creeks the liquid was prepared and drunk before councils, in order, as they believed, to invigorate the mind and body and prepare for thought and debate. It was also used in the great "busk" or annual green-corn thanksgiving. The action of the drink in strong infusion is purgative, vomitive, and diuretic. It was long thought that this was the only effect, but recent investigation has shown that the plant contains caffeine, the leaves yielding a beverage with stimulating qualities like tea and coffee.

The cultivation and use of tobacco is one of the most important contributions to the world from the American Indians. The word "tobacco" is of Indian origin and has been introduced, with slight variations, into most foreign languages. Tobacco was cultivated in most tribes by the men alone, and was usually smoked by them only, although among some of the Carolina tribes the women are said to have been more inveterate smokers than the men. To the Indian the tobacco plant had a sacred character; it was almost invariably used on solemn occasions, accompanied by suitable invocations to their gods. It was also used to aid in disease or distress, to ward off danger, to bring good fortune, to generally assist one in need, and to allay fear.

Tobacco, after the whites had become accustomed to its use, was one of the few tastes that they and the red men had in common, many of the practices of the natives being abhorrent to civilized men. One custom regarded as particularly obnoxious was the characteristic Indian institution of the sweat-bath. Personal cleanliness, as understood by civilized peoples, seems to have been a luxury almost unknown to the American Indians, although among some of the tribes a daily bath was taken as a religious rite. The sweat-bath, however, was probably in use in every tribe north of Mexico, and the sweat-lodge is to this day common in most Indian villages and camps.

The type of the ordinary sweat-house, except among certain California tribes, seems to have been nearly everywhere the same. Willow rods or other pliant stems were stuck into the ground and bent and fastened with withes into a hemispherical or oblong framework, which generally was large enough to accommodate several persons. A hole was dug conveniently near the door, into which stones, usually heated outside, were dropped by means of forked sticks. These were sprinkled with water to generate steam. A temporary covering of blankets or skins made the inclosure tight. This was the sweat-house in its simplest form. In southern California, the heat of the sweat-house was produced by a wood fire, thus adding the choking fumes of the smoke to the discomfort of the victim. After a half hour or more spent in the steaming air of the sweat-house, the bather plunged into the cold water of a stream, when one was near, and thus the function was ended. Sweating was also important in medical practice for the cure of disease.

While there is every reason to believe that the Indian race was a comparatively healthy one, nevertheless they must have been subject to many of the same diseases that are found among civilized peoples. Although the exact nature of their special ills is not known, it is certain that they were sufficiently numerous to account for the existence of a powerful class of professed healers, who were honored, feared, and usually well paid. These healers, some of whom were women, were believed to possess supernatural powers that enabled them to recognize and cure disease; and there were others who, without the aid of such supernatural gifts, were better acquainted with actual remedies than most men.

As is common among primitive people, the Indian *shamans* professing magical powers soon became recognized as priests. They were regarded as having a special and intimate knowledge of natural forces and the potent but unseen agencies of the spiritual realm that made up the religious aspect of Indian life. The world of the savage is indeed of small extent, being limited to the few hundreds of miles within which his associations are all confined. Through this region travel for him the sun, moon, and stars, winds, meteors, and the aurora of the north. The Iroquois tribes believed that these were free, independent man-beings; and that trees and plants, hills, mountains, and whatsoever is immovably attached to earth, though once free, had suffered enchantment through powerful *orenda*, or magic powers, and so lost their former freedom.

Most revelations regarded by the Indians as coming from the supernatural powers were received in dreams or visions. Through them were bestowed on man magical abilities and the capacity to foresee future events, to control disease and to become able to fill the office of priest or of leader. It was the common belief of the Indians that these dreams or visions must be sought through the observance of some rite involving personal privation. In some tribes this initiation took place during the fast which occurred at puberty, and the thing seen at that time became the medium of supernatural help and knowledge. It was a man's most sacred object. It had no reference to his kindred, but was strictly personal in its efficacy, and he painted it on his person or his belongings as a prayer for assistance—a call for help in directing his actions. Any dream of ordinary sleep in which this object appeared had meaning for him and its suggestions were heeded.

The Indians, like other peoples, thought to approach the supernatural powers by prayer. Some prayers were ritualistic and of the nature of incantations. Not only spoken words but suitably placed symbolic objects were used in the act of praying. Such supplicatory objects are the feathered prayer sticks of the Pueblo Indians and others, which may be regarded as a symbolic substitute for human sacrifice. Prayer sticks, nearly always painted green or blue, are frequently found with the dead in ancient Pueblo cemeteries, and great deposits of them occur in ceremonial caves in southern Arizona.

The ritualistic prayers are very numerous and form considerable parts of the ceremonial dances which occupy so conspicuous a part in Indian life. They are addressed to different supernatural personages, for the Indians are by no means monotheistic in their religious beliefs. Yet there is a tendency to ascribe preeminent powers to some single deity. Thus the Pawnee invoke the father of powers for help to properly conduct their ceremony; the Arapahoe invoke the "Man-Above" for this purpose. While material benefits are naturally the object of prayer in by far the majority of cases, prayers for an abstract blessing and for ideal objects are not by any means absent. The Indians pray not only to those supernatural powers which are considered the protectors of

PLATE 13

Decorated pottery from ancient Indian mounds in Arkansas. In the National Museum

man—like the personal guardians or the powers of nature —but also to the hostile powers that must be appeased.

Closely associated with prayer is sacrifice. By far the greater number of sacrifices were offered by individuals, either male or female, as when bits of food were thrown into the fire during meals, or articles were laid upon sacred rocks or upon shrines. The offering of first-fruits among the Natchez was made by each father of a family; and on certain occasions, when a live stag was sacrificed by the Iroquois, it was the oldest man of the hut or village that gave the death-blow. Among the Muskhogean tribes a special sacrifice was offered by the war leader and his religious assistant before starting out upon an expedition, and in general it may be said that the leaders of war or hunting parties took the lead also in sacrifices and all other observances having in view the success of the enterprise.

Unless the customary immolation of a number of captives at the end of a war expedition may be considered sacrificial, human sacrifices do not seem to have been particularly common north of Mexico, though there are a number of instances. Perhaps the best known is that of the sacrifice of a female captive to the morning star by the Skidi Pawnee. In 1700 when Iberville was among the Taensa villages, their temple was struck by a thunderbolt and burned, upon which five women threw their infants into the flames as a sacrifice to the offended deity, and more would have done so had not the French interposed. On another occasion the Iroquois drove arrows into the body of a new-born babe, ground up its bones, and swallowed a little of the resultant powder before starting out to war; but this may have been a war-medicine rather than a true sacrifice.

Beliefs relating to the soul's existence after death are very uniform among primitive peoples, all over the world. The Indians believed that the souls live in the land of the dead in the form that they had in life, and continue their former occupations. Often the physical conditions in the land of the dead of which detailed descriptions are found among almost all American tribes, are the reverse of those in our world: when it is night here, it is day there; when it is summer here, it is winter there. The Eskimo tribes believe in several worlds of this kind. Those who suffer violent deaths go to the sky, while those who die of sickness go to another world. The Indians of Vancouver Island believe that the villages of the dead are near their own villages, but invisible; but the most common notion is that of the world of ghosts lying in the distant West beyond a river which must be crossed by canoe. This notion is found on the western plateaus and on the Plains. Visits to that world by people who have been in a trance are one of the common elements of American folklore. They have been reported from almost all over the continent.

Among the Siksika every tent contains an altar—a small excavation in the earth—where sweet gum is burned daily. Prehistoric fire-altars, consisting of blocks of fire-hardened clay or, in rare cases, boxes of stone, form the essential characteristic of many mounds. In religious rites still regularly held by the Pueblo Indians temporary altars are used. A characteristic feature of some of these is the dry-painting traced on sand with powdered minerals or earths of different colors. The construction of the altar, the rites performed before it, and its destruction form interesting features of Hopi ceremonies and date back to ancient times.

An instrument important in many ceremonies in the Southwest was the bullroarer. This was a device for producing rhythmic sound, and consisted of a narrow slat of wood suspended by a cord which was often attached to a wooden handle. The bullroarer, which is often painted with symbolic designs, is whirled rapidly with a uniform motion about the head, and the pulsation of the air against the slat gives a characteristic whizzing or roaring sound. The Hopi, who regard the bullroarer as a prayer-stick of the thunder and its whizzing noise as representing the wind that accompanies thunderstorms, make the tablet portion from a piece of lightning-riven wood and measure the length of the string from the heart to the tips of the fingers of the outstretched right hand. Apache, Hopi, and Zuñi bullroarers bear lightning symbols and in the semi-arid region the implement is used to invoke clouds, lightning, and rain, and to warn the uninitiated that rites are being performed. In the humid area it is used to implore the wind to bring fair weather.

Another important ceremonial instrument was the calumet, sometimes called "peace-pipe" and "war-pipe," found among the tribes of the Plains and the Mississippi Valley. It consisted of either one or two slender, highly symbolic shafts of reed or wood, varying in length from eighteen inches to two feet, the one sometimes representing the male, the other the female shaft. These were usually perforated for a pathway for the breath or spirit, painted with diverse symbolic colors, and adorned with various symbolic objects, and sometimes terminated in a pipe bowl to contain tobacco for making a sacred offering of its benevolent smoke to the gods.

In modern usage, the term "calumet" usually includes the pipe. Its coloring and degree of adornment varied somewhat from tribe to tribe and were largely governed by the occasion for which the calumet was used. From the meager descriptions of the calumet and its uses it would seem that it has a ceremonially symbolic history independent of that of the pipe; and that when the pipe became an altar, by its employment for burning sacrificial tobacco to the gods, convenience and convention united the already highly symbolic calumet shafts and the sacrificial tobacco altar, the pipe-bowl; hence it became one of the most profoundly sacred objects known to the Indians of northern America.

The calumet was employed by ambassadors and travelers as a passport; it was used in ceremonies designed to conciliate foreign and hostile nations and to conclude lasting peace; to ratify the alliance of friendly tribes; to secure favorable weather for journeys; to bring needed rain; and to attest contracts and treaties which could not be violated without incurring the wrath of the gods. The use of the calumet was inculcated by religious precept and example. A chant and a dance have become known as the chant and the dance of the calumet; together they were employed as an invocation to one or more of the gods. By naming in the chant the souls of those against whom war must be waged, such persons were doomed to die at the hands of the person so naming them.

The cross, which in some of its familiar forms is known as the swastika, was in common use all over America in pre-Columbian times. North of the Rio Grande it assumed many forms, some merely ornamental or accidental, but some having deep significance. Primitive man adjusts himself to his environment, real and imaginary, by keeping in mind the cardinal points as he understands them. When the Indian considers the world about him he thinks usually of the four directions, and when he communicates with the mysterious beings and powers with which his imagination peoples it—the rulers of the winds and rains—he turns his face to the four directions in stipulated order and addresses to them his appeals and his offerings. Thus his worship, his ceremonies, his games, and even his more ordinary occupations in many cases are arranged to conform to the cardinal points, and the various symbolic representations associated with them assume the form of the cross. This was and is true of many peoples and is well illustrated in the wonderful altar paintings of the tribes of the arid region. Such crosses, although an essential part of symbolism and religious ceremony, exist only for the purposes of the occasion and are brushed away when the ceremony is

PLATE 14

Cane baskets of the Chetimacha Indians, Louisiana.
In the National Museum

ended, but nevertheless they pass into permanent form as decorations of ceremonial objects—pottery, basketry, and costumes—retaining their significance indefinitely.

In the belief of the Indians, all things are animate and incarnate—men, beasts, lands, waters, rocks, plants, trees, stars, winds, clouds, and night—and all possess volition and immortal life; thus it is that rocks, trees, roots, "stocks and stones," bones, the limbs and parts of the body, in short all natural objects, are verily the living tombs of diverse beings and spirits. Of such is the kingdom of the fetish, for even the least of these may be chosen. Moreover, a fetish is an object which may also represent a vision, a dream, a thought, or an action.

A fetish is acquired by a person, a family, or a people for the purpose of promoting welfare. In return, the fetish requires from its owner worship in the form of prayer, sacrifice, feats, and protection, and from its votaries it receives ill or good treatment in accordance with the character of its behavior toward them. Some fetishes are regarded as more efficacious than others. The fetish or amulet that loses its repute as a promoter of welfare gradually becomes useless and may degenerate into a mere ornament. Then other fetishes are acquired, to be subjected to the same severe test of efficiency in promoting the well-being of their possessors.

Mooney says, in describing the fetish or charm, that it may be "a bone, a feather, a carved or painted stick, a stone arrowhead, a curious fossil or concretion, a tuft of hair, a necklace of red berries, the stuffed skin of a lizard, the dried hand of an enemy, a small bag of pounded charcoal mixed with human blood—anything, in fact, which the owner's medicine dream or imagination might suggest, no matter how uncouth or unaccountable, provided it be easily portable and attachable." The fetish might be the inspiration of a dream or the gift of a medicine-man, or even a trophy taken from a slain enemy, or a bird, animal, or reptile; but however insignificant in itself, it had always, in the owner's mind at least, some symbolic connection with occult power. It might be fastened to the scalp-lock as a pendant, attached to some part of the dress, hung from the bridle bit, concealed between the covers of a shield, or guarded in a special repository in the dwelling. Mothers sometimes tied the fetish to the child's cradle.

Thus in religion, no less than in material culture, the Indians are seen to be in the early formative stages. In no sense masters of their environment, they were like children groping for help from their great mother, Nature. Yet one cannot but be impressed by the important part which the supernatural played in their lives. No occasion was too trivial, no need too pressing, to be referred to the appropriate deity or guardian spirit for sanction. In their simple trust in such protection they put to shame many a professed believer in the tenets of a higher faith.

Thus far we have endeavored to sketch only those aspects of life which were common to many of the aborigines of North America. Fundamentally akin as they were, however, they varied among themselves no less than do the nations of Europe. The Kwakiutl were as different in every respect from the Hopi as the Scandinavians are from the peoples of Rumania or Greece; and both Kwakiutl and Hopi were equally distinct from the Iroquois and the other great families of North America; while the Eskimo have so many unique characteristics that they are by some regarded as a distinct race. Most of these differences were the result of the environing influences of locality and climate rather than of inherent racial traits. This fact has given rise to a classification based on culture rather than on language, it having been found that the tribes tend to resemble in customs and beliefs their neighbors of alien tongues rather than their far-distant kinsmen.

Wissler recognizes nine culture areas north of Mexico, each of which exhibits certain characteristic variations in manners and customs, political organization, and religious beliefs; these are: (1) the Plains Area, (2) the Plateau Area, (3) the California Area; (4) the North Pacific Coast Area, (5) the Eskimo Area, (6) the Mackenzie Area, (7) the Eastern Woodland Area, (8) the Southeastern Area, and (9) the Southwestern Area.

While it will not be possible within the limits of this volume to give an extended account of each of these separate cultures, some of the representative tribes will be described in the following chapters.

REFERENCES

BOAS, FRANZ. Handbook of American Indian languages. Bur. Amer. Ethnol. Bull. 40, Part 1, 1911; Part 2, 1922.

CLARK, W. P. The Indian sign language. Philadelphia, 1885.

GIFFORD, E. W. Pottery-making in the Southwest. Univ. Calif. Pub. Amer. Anthrop. Ethnol. Vol. 23, No. 8, pp. 353–373. Berkeley, 1928.

HANDBOOK OF AMERICAN INDIANS NORTH OF MEXICO. Edited by Frederick Webb Hodge. In two parts. Bur. Amer. Ethnol. Bull. 30, Part 1, 1907; Part 2, 1910.

HOLMES, WILLIAM H. A quarry workshop of the flaked-stone instrument makers in the District of Columbia. Amer. Anthrop. Vol. 3, pp. 1–26, 224–225, 1890.

—— Order of development of primal shaping arts. Proc. Amer. Ass. Adv. Sci. Vol. 42, pp. 289–300, 1894. Reprint. Smithsonian Inst. Ann. Rep. 1901, pp. 501–513. Washington, 1902.

LAFITAU, J. F. Moeurs des sauvages ameriquains comparées aux moeurs des premiers temps. Tomes I–II. Paris, 1724.

MALLERY, GARRICK. Sign language among the North American Indians compared with that among other peoples and deaf-mutes. 1st Ann. Rep. Bur. Ethnol. Washington, 1881.

—— Pictographs of the North American Indians. 4th Ann. Rep. Bur. Ethnol. Washington, 1886.

—— Picture-writing of the American Indians. 10th Ann. Rep. Bur. Ethnol. Washington, 1893.

MASON, OTIS T. Woman's share in primitive culture. New York (Appleton), 1894.

—— Aboriginal American basketry: studies in a textile art without machinery. U. S. Nation. Mus. Ann. Rep. 1902, pp. 171–548 with pls., text figs. In book form, 2 vols. London (Heinemann), 1905.

PLATE 15

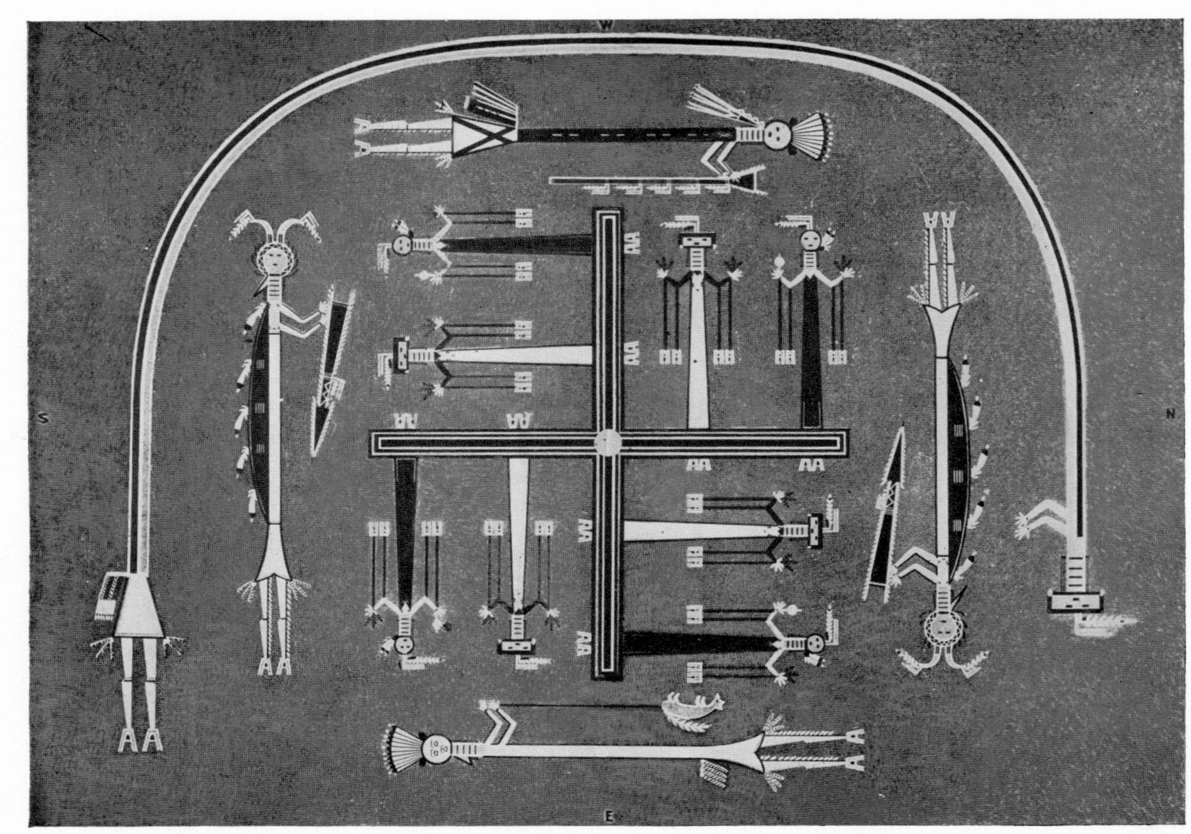

A ceremonial sand painting by Navaho Indians. The drawing is made freehand, the sand running out between the fingers

MICHELSON, TRUMAN. Remarks on American Indian languages: a study in method. J. Washington Acad. Sci. Vol. 7, pp. 222–234, 1917.

POWELL, JOHN W. Introduction to the study of Indian languages. Smithsonian Inst. Bur. Ethnol. Washington, 1880.

—— Indian linguistic families North of Mexico. 7th Ann. Rep. Bur. Amer. Ethnol. Washington, 1891.

WISSLER, CLARK. The American Indian; an introduction to the anthropology of the New World. New York and London (Oxford University Press), 1922.

CHAPTER III

IN ARCTIC SNOWS: THE ESKIMO

Of all the North American tribes none achieved a more perfect adaptation to their environment than the fur-clad brownies of the Arctic who call themselves Inuit, "people," but are known to us by the harsher name Eskimo, "eaters of raw flesh."

Long baffled by the severity of the Arctic climate, only in comparatively recent years have white men succeeded in invading the homeland of the Eskimo so insistently as to persuade him to barter his age-old culture for the incongruous inventions of civilization. Thus, when Dr. Franz Boas visited the Central Eskimo some forty years ago, he found them still pursuing the even tenor of their life, practically untouched by modern innovations.

Fortunately the report of Boas constitutes a most scientific, comprehensive, and detailed description of the life of the primitive Eskimo. Although the researches of later explorers have amplified and modified it to a certain extent, and have contributed additional details concerning the manners and customs of other tribes in other localities, no one is now able to reconstruct for us so perfect a picture of the fast-disappearing Eskimo of the Stone Age.

Mr. Diamond Jenness, of the National Museum of Canada, found much the same conditions as described by Boas existing among the Eskimo even as late as 1918; and Mr. Vilhjalmur Stefansson a few years earlier, in describing an Eskimo tribe hitherto unvisited by any white man, declared that it was exactly as if he had stepped back into the Stone Age. There has been a great change, however, in the short space of little more than a decade. According to Mr. Jenness in a letter of recent date:

> If you drop in now to Cumberland Sound, you will find the Eskimos living not in snow huts, but in twill tents throughout the winter, using European whale boats instead of skin boats, rifles, shot guns, sewing machines, gramophones, etc., writing letters to each other in the Cree syllabary introduced by missionaries, holding regular Sunday services, etc., etc. There are very few caribou on Baffin Island, no hunting of whales, (except the white whale), walrus are occasionally shot with a rifle, and, in summer, seals.

Cumberland Sound and Baffin Island were the chief centers of the extraordinary culture of the Central Eskimo as portrayed by Boas. Therefore we will journey backward a short half century in time in order to restore the picture of these people as they then appeared, turning to the reports of later explorers only when they shed additional light on the ancient customs of this fast vanishing race.[1]

The land of the Eskimo is as different from the everyday world of our common experience as can well be imagined. Theirs is a world where winter reigns the greater part of the year; where for many weeks the sole light of day is a dim uncertain twilight and the long nights are brightened only by the cold light of moon and stars and the fitful streamers of the aurora borealis; a world where land, sea, and sky seem often to meet and mingle in an impenetrable veil of snow and mist.

In this white, frozen universe live the tribes of the Central Eskimo, scattered over the coasts and islands of the Arctic Ocean, often, indeed, building their snow villages on the seven-foot-thick flooring of ice which

[1] To give vividness to the story, the present tense is often retained in what follows, as if the picturesque customs of a brief half-century ago, so appropriate to the Eskimo, still persisted.

covers much of the sea itself. Villages, we call them, these groups of little hillocks, each tiny settlement separated from its nearest neighbor by many miles of trackless snow; half buried in drifts, it seems incredible that such snow mounds can be inhabited by human beings. Yet not only are they so inhabited; these people have made a long journey from their inland summer camp in order to establish themselves here in comfortable winter quarters.

Trudging along by their heavily laden sleds, each with its team of dogs, a little band of Eskimo wanderers has by slow stages reached the shore of a frozen bay or inlet. This, they have decided, will be a suitable spot for their winter settlement, for here they will doubtless find under the ice an abundance of the seals on which their existence largely depends. Having selected the site, they next set about the work of constructing their houses out of the handiest building material available—the fine, dry, compact Arctic snow.

To build a proper snow house—a much more elaborate affair than the small shelters erected as camps on the journey—two men must work together. One cuts from a snow bank huge slabs of snow, each about half as large as himself; the other places these building blocks in position, setting them on edge, end to end in a circle, slanting them and inclining them inward in a gradually ascending narrowing spiral, until the top row is reached. The last blocks must be lifted into position by the first man, from the outside, while the builder, standing inside on a bench or mound of snow, supports the converging slabs with his head until they are finally adjusted and the key block snugly fitted into the last remaining opening at the top. In this way, without scaffolding or cement, a circular dome is constructed from ten to twelve feet high and from twelve to fifteen feet across. This would be a fairly large room, but seems close quarters for a whole family—and more often two families—to say nothing

PLATE 16

Building the snow house. From "The Friendly Arctic." Courtesy of Mr. Vilhjalmur Stefansson

Eskimo waiting at blowhole for the return of the seal

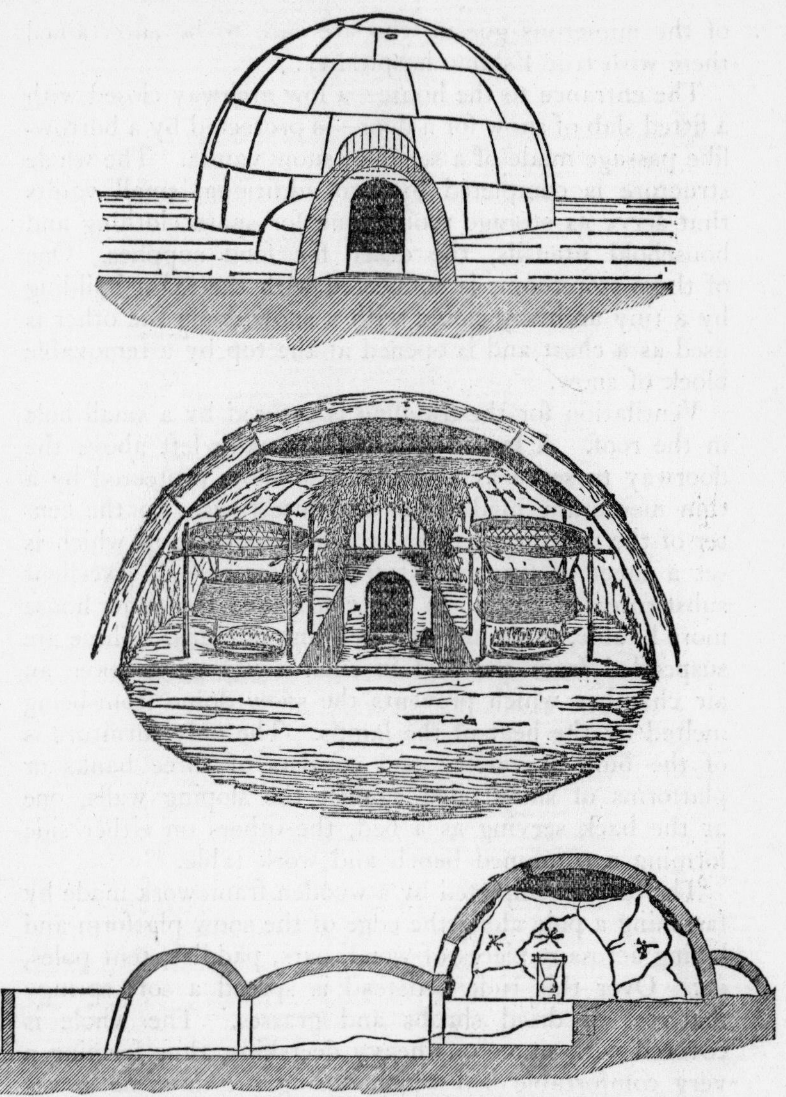

FIG. 1. Top, snow house exterior; middle, cross-section of interior showing stretched sealskin lining, lamps, water containers, and thawing racks; bottom, cross-section of interior and entrance passage

of the numerous guests who are sure to be entertained there with true Eskimo hospitality.

The entrance to the house—a low archway closed with a fitted slab of snow for a door—is protected by a burrow-like passage made of a series of snow vaults. The whole structure is completed by two additional small vaults that serve as storage rooms, one for spare clothing and household utensils, the other for food supplies. One of these storerooms is connected with the main building by a tiny archway closed with a snow door; the other is used as a chest and is opened at the top by a removable block of snow.

Ventilation for the dwelling is secured by a small hole in the roof. A larger opening is usually left above the doorway to serve as a window. This is protected by a thin membrane made from seal intestines. In the center of the membrane there is a lookout hole in which is set a sheet of transparent fresh-water ice—an excellent substitute for glass. In order to make the snow house more livable, it should have a lining of skins. These are suspended from the roof in such a way as to leave an air chamber which prevents the snow dome from being melted by the heat of the lamps. The only furniture is of the built-in variety and consists of three banks or platforms of snow piled against the sloping walls, one at the back serving as a bed, the others on either side forming a combined bench and work table.

The bed is completed by a wooden framework made by fastening a pole along the edge of the snow platform and laying across it pieces of wood, oars, paddles, tent poles, etc. Over this rude bedstead is spread a soft springy mattress of dried shrubs and grasses. The whole is covered with numerous heavy deerskins, thus forming a very comfortable bed which during the daytime serves as a divan for the family and their guests.

On each of the side benches, in front of the bed platform, a fireplace is arranged—probably the smallest fireplace in the world—being simply a stone lamp, over which is placed a framework to support the cooking pots and such articles of clothing as it may be necessary to dry. The house is now ready for its occupants, who have not had to wait for it long, as it takes two competent men only two or three hours to build the entire structure.

Having taken possession of her home, the Eskimo housewife may now light her lamp and begin housekeeping. But to strike a light in the Stone Age was an art in itself, requiring both ingenuity and patience. This toilsome process may be avoided if the household happens to possess the priceless treasure of a box of matches, those magic fire-sticks which may occasionally be obtained from a white trapper or trader if the family is wealthy enough to indulge in such a luxury; or it may be that the man of the house has with him two lumps of iron pyrites which, when struck together give out sparks, as flint on steel—a comparatively easy device for producing fire. In the absence of such conveniences, the housewife must depend on the age-old method of making fire by the friction of wood on wood. The apparatus she must use is of Eskimo invention and consists of a slender rod or drill, the upper end of which is fitted into a bone or ivory socket held between the teeth of the operator, thus leaving the hands free to revolve the shaft by means of a cord and bow or a simple strap. The lower end of the rod is in this way made to revolve on a cross-piece or "hearth" of wood with such speed that the "wood meal" produced by the friction is heated to the glowing point. Some dry tinder, preferably willow catkins, must now be placed upon the tiny glowing embers and blown upon until it bursts into flame. The flame being transferred to a piece of punk or slow match made of soft bark or the matted roots of moss soaked in oil, the wick of the lamp may at last be lighted.

The lamp of the Eskimo is a unique contribution to North American culture, for no other native tribe ever invented any device for producing light and heat except a heap of logs for a fire or a pitch-smeared stick for a torch. An Eskimo lamp is very primitive, being merely a shallow dish made usually of a certain kind of soft soapstone hollowed out, sometimes into a number of separate chambers, and filled with blubber which feeds a wick of dried moss. Without these fragile vessels, however, and their carefully tended flames, the Eskimo as a people must long ago have vanished from the North, where fuel other than the precious blubber of whale, walrus, and seal, or fat of the polar bear and caribou, is practically unobtainable.

FIG. 2. Soapstone lamp, two feet across, weighing thirty pounds. From Point Barrow Eskimo

If two families occupy the same house, each woman has her own fireplace near which she sits on her snow bench, Turkish fashion, while engaged in her traditional duties of cooking and sewing. Since meat for the cooking pot and material for clothing, as well as oil for the lamp, must all be obtained during these winter months from the seal—the little rough seal, not the fur seal of commerce—it is not surprising that the pursuit of this animal should be the chief object of the Eskimo's existence at this time of the year.

As soon as the ice begins to form in the autumn, the seals gnaw or scratch small holes in it to which they come when it is necessary for them to "blow" and to refill their lungs with air. These breathing holes become covered over with snow in winter and are therefore very hard to detect. The Eskimo and their dogs, however, seem to possess a special sense which enables them to track down the seals even through several feet of snow and ice.

PLATE 18

An Eskimo sealing party on Smith Sound. Group in the National Museum

In order to make the most of the short twilight of an Arctic winter day, an Eskimo household must arise long before daybreak. While the woman is busy preparing breakfast, the man fits up his sledge for hunting. The sledge, which has perhaps been made of driftwood with a back formed by deer's antlers still attached to the skull, has runners that are shod with bone or ivory and must be iced in order to make them slide more easily over the snow. This done, the dogs, who during the night have been housed in the covered passageway, are harnessed to the sledge.

Breakfast is ready by this time and is served in two courses. First comes seal meat which has been boiled in the soapstone pot over the lamp. Each person is handed his portion, which he grasps with his left hand. He then takes a mouthful—as large a one as possible—between his teeth, and cuts it off with his knife which he wields in his right hand much as a violinist uses his bow. After the meat has been devoured—the second course is served. This consists of "blood soup," made by mixing blood with the water in which the meat was boiled. The soup is drunk from cups usually made of whalebone or horn. Sometimes one large cup is passed around to each in turn. Having finished his breakfast with a few choice morsels of frozen raw seal meat, the hunter now feels able to face the bitter wind of the Arctic at a temperature of perhaps thirty degrees (F.) below zero.

After loading his sledge with the articles necessary for the day's work, the hunter mounts to his seat in front, takes up his whip, and starts for the hunting grounds. Today he is traveling light and it is easy going. When the sledge has a heavy load the driver must walk beside it, helping to push or pull it over rough places, sometimes lashing his dogs, sometimes encouraging them with such phrases as "Ai! Do you see the seal! Ai! A house! A small house! Now we are going home!" If the sledge stops despite their best endeavors to pull it, the dogs will literally lie down on the job.

Traveling with a light sledge and strong dogs is a very different matter. Now the driver may sit up in front and let his whip trail behind him. If any dog is lazy his name is called out and he is struck with the long curling lash. But let the driver beware lest, calling out the name of one dog, be bring down his whip on the back of an-

FIG. 3. Dog harness of sealskin or deerskin with sealskin tugs. Central Eskimo

other. Instantly the second dog will turn on the one whose name has been called; goaded by an outraged sense of justice, he seeks to be avenged on the culprit. But now the leader intervenes; he has been trained to discipline the others by biting each of the fighting dogs and so bringing both to terms. In harness, however, this often proves disastrous, for the other dogs take up the quarrel and the whole pack soon becomes one howling, biting mass. No amount of lashing or beating will avail to separate them; the only thing to do is to stop the sledge and wait for them to settle their quarrel. Faithful and intelligent as they are, these temperamental creatures require great tact in their management. For instance, if two people are traveling on the same sledge, it is said that they must be careful not to talk to each other, for if the dogs hear them they are apt to stop, sit down, turn around, and listen to the conversation. Indeed so temperamental are the native dogs of the Eskimo that some Arctic explorers prefer to use other varieties when traveling by sledge. In "The Friendly Arctic," Stefansson says:

> Just as with men, the excellence of dogs is largely a matter of temperament. Here, next to his [small] size, lies our grievance against the Eskimo dog. When he is fat and well cared for he works with a great deal of spirit, a sort of boyish exuberance. But as the boy has not the stamina of the man and wants to rest when he gets tired, so the Eskimo dog stops pulling when he feels like it. . . . I have seldom seen an Eskimo dog that will pull well the second day without food, but I have seen half-breed St. Bernards [part Eskimo] who would pull, perhaps not with the same strength, for that would be impossible, but with the same willingness day after day while their strength lasted.

It is of course conceivable that the Eskimo driver, with his encouraging words and familiar voice, can get better results from the native dogs than a white man could. Moreover, he is not reluctant to use the whip, and the dogs are doubtless accustomed to such discipline. A driver of dogs, having no reins with which to control his team, must rely wholly upon his whip and voice.

On reaching the hunting grounds, the driver stops his team and takes his hunting outfit from the sledge, which he turns upside down with the points of the runners and antlers pressed into the snow to keep the dogs from running away. With one of the dogs to guide him, he then sets out to locate the breathing hole of a seal, which may be detected by the tiny mound of snow above it. Having successfully located one of these little mounds, the dog is led back to the sledge, where he is tethered with his companions, and the hunter returns to take up his position at the hole.

After satisfying himself by careful inspection that the hole is still open and has not been abandoned by the seal, the hunter prepares to wait patiently for the animal's return. As a protection against the piercing wind, he builds a semicircular wall of snow, within which he seats himself on a snow mound, his feet on a small piece of fur and his legs bound together by a thong which may be quickly undone and which yet serves to keep him still. At his right hand his knife is stuck into the snow, while to the left his harpoon rests on two pegs, the coil of the line lying in his lap.

Thus, like patience on a monument of snow, the hunter waits, sometimes until after nightfall, for the seal's return to the hole. When he hears its breathing he cautiously releases the thong that binds his legs together and gets to his feet. Holding his harpoon in his right hand and the coil of the line in his left, he strikes through the hole with all his might at the invisible seal below. Generally it is struck on the head and immediately dives, carrying the detachable head of the harpoon with it, like a hook in a fish. And like a fisherman, the Eskimo hunter pays out his line until the seal is exhausted by its struggles or is compelled to come again to the hole to breathe. Then the hunter, who has meantime enlarged the breathing hole by cutting away the snow and ice, is able to haul the seal up and dispatch it with his knife.

Occasionally a hunter will discover that he has brought in a bearded seal, a variety which is greatly prized, being about four times the size of the common seal. In such a case it is his duty to share his prize equally with the other families in the settlement. Such a piece of good fortune is a cause for general rejoicing and the hunter is held in high esteem, both for his prowess and as a public benefactor. This custom of sharing the bearded seal is one of those laws which are peculiarly binding on such a

PLATE 19

Ivory pipestems, with stone and lead bowls, depicting walrus hunt from umiaks and kaiaks, and reindeer scenes. Made by Bering Straits Eskimo

PLATE 20

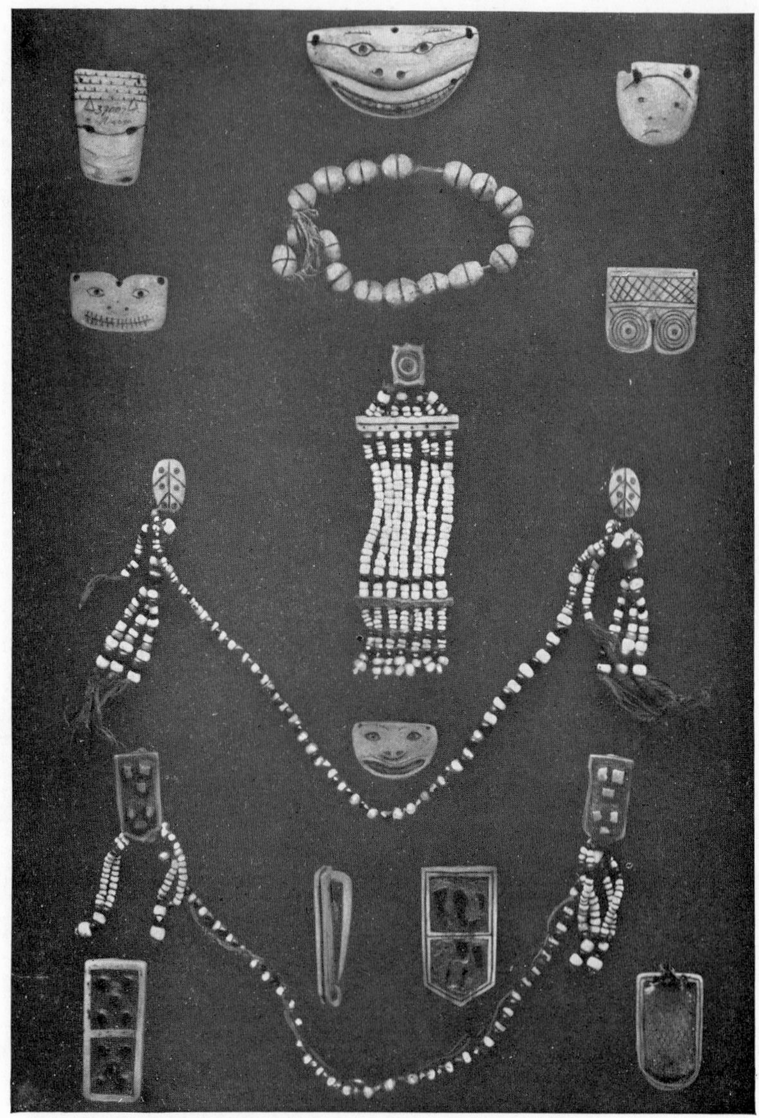

Bead earrings and ivory ornaments of Bering Straits Eskimo

people as the Eskimo, who are under no compulsion to obey any law, except the compelling force of public opinion. Stefansson tells of once meeting an old blind Eskimo man who believed that his blindness had been sent upon him as a punishment for having broken this very law. In his youth he had committed the crime of trying to keep the bearded seal for himself instead of sharing it with his fellows. A year later his sight began to fail and within another year he was totally blind. He was a most miserable man—an "ancient mariner" of the Eskimo—oppressed with a sense of guilt and driven by his conscience to tell his story as a warning to all who would listen to it.

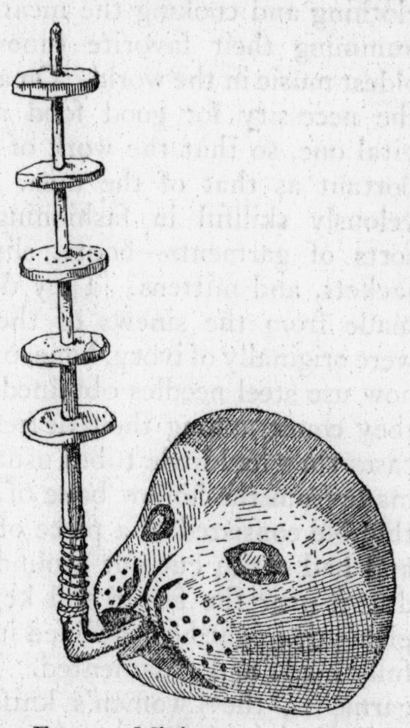

FIG. 4. Miniature mask representing head of small fur seal with air bubbles rising to surface of water. Lower Yukon Eskimo

The size of the seal at this time of the year is of great importance, as it is seldom that a hunter can secure more than one in a day. After being captured, the seal is lashed to the sledge together with the hunting implements, the hunter once more mounts to his seat in front, and the eager dogs start for home, needing neither lash nor voice to urge them on after their long wait in the cold. They may safely be trusted to find their way, even in a blinding snow storm. Doubtless many an Eskimo dog team, like the famous Balto and his comrades, have brought home without guidance a sledge bearing its precious burden of necessary supplies and an exhausted driver.

While the men are away the women busy themselves with various household tasks—making and mending clothing and cooking the meat—all the while incessantly humming their favorite tunes, which are possibly the oldest music in the world. On account of the extreme cold, the necessity for good food and suitable clothing is a vital one, so that the work of the women is quite as important as that of the men. Eskimo women are marvelously skillful in fashioning skins and furs into all sorts of garments—boots, slippers, stockings, trousers, jackets, and mittens. They do their sewing with thread made from the sinews of the deer or whale. Needles were originally of ivory, bone, or copper, though the women now use steel needles obtained from white traders, which they count among their dearest possessions. For needle cases they had little tubes usually of ivory but sometimes made from the hollow bone of a bird's wing. An Eskimo thimble consisted of a piece of the dressed skin of a seal and had a rim cut out around one side by which it was drawn over the finger and kept in place. All these implements might be contained in a fur "housewife," beautifully made and ornamented. For cutting out the various garments, the "women's knife," or *ulo*, was employed. This is shaped like a crescent, with the handle in the middle. Before the introduction of iron and steel by the whites, the blade was of slate or stone; the handle is of wood, bone, or ivory. Such primitive tools, together with skin scrapers and softeners, made up the whole equipment of the Eskimo woman for the important business of sewing, tailoring, and bootmaking.

Outer garments for winter are made of deerskin with the hair outside; inner garments usually of the skins of young deer or seals, with the hair inside. Special attention is paid to the footgear, which consists of deerskin stockings and sometimes two pairs of slippers, the inner ones of bird skin with the feathers inside, the outer ones of sealskin with the hair outside. A pair of carefully made boots, reaching to just below the knee, completes the footgear. It being most important that the feet should be kept dry as well as warm, in order to avoid frostbite, the soles of the boots are usually stuffed with dried grass or moss, which helps to absorb any moisture.

Men, women, and children look much alike in their boots, trousers, and jackets with hoods, the women being distinguished by the long tails to their jackets and by their larger hoods. Everyone, when outdoors, wears enormous fur mittens reaching nearly to the elbow. All these garments are well cut, neatly sewed, and usually trimmed with fur of a contrasting color. The white fur of the baby seal is used for the clothing of very small children, while the dress boots of the men are made of a finely dressed white leather resembling parchment. Ordinary boots are made of deerskin with the hair on and have soles of the tanned skin of the bearded seal; the leather lacings are sometimes finished with tassels made of strips of leather dyed a brilliant red. The jackets, or frocks, are slipped on over the head and are often belted around the waist in the fashion of a Russian blouse. For spring and summer wear the heavy deerskin frocks are replaced by

Fig. 5. Eskimo doll from the Lower Yukon. Head of bone; deerskin costume

others of seal and sometimes of bird skin. Even the heavy winter frocks are often trimmed with bands of white caribou skin, and hoods are sometimes ornamented with a fringe of long white caribou hair around the face. Mittens are also trimmed with bands of white fur. In short, the Eskimo design their clothing with an eye to beauty as well as to utility.

It would seem that in order to outfit a whole family, besides keeping all the garments in repair and preparing the skins of which they are made, the women must work incessantly. Yet they find time during the day to visit

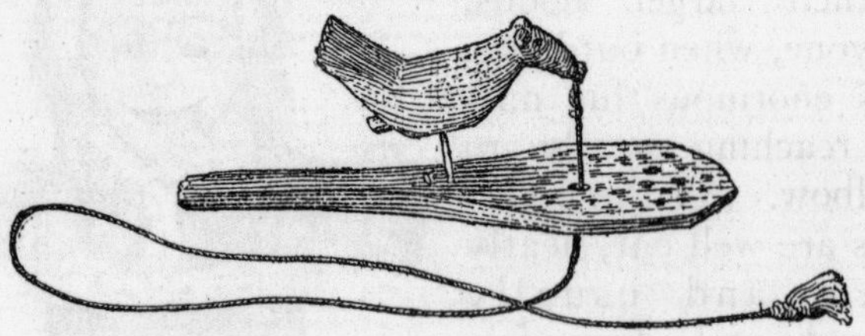

Fig. 6. Toy woodpecker of wood from St. Michael. Bird pecks when child pulls the cord

each other, usually taking a piece of work with them, and to play games and amuse the children. To the women likewise falls the task of rearing the dogs until they are ready to take their places in the team. The broad divan at the back of the house makes a safe romping place for both babies and puppies. About noon the women and children have their dinner, while the men out hunting may lunch on raw liver and meat cut from a newly caught seal. At home, the men's dinner is cooked and ready to be heated up over the lamp as soon as the sledge is heard approaching.

On reaching home, the hunter must first attend to unharnessing the dogs and putting away the traces in the store-room. Having unloaded the sledge, which is then turned upside down and cleared of ice, he is ready to enter the house, dragging in the spoils with the assistance of the women. Indoors, he takes off his outer jacket, which is carefully cleaned of snow and ice and put into the storeroom outside. Dinner is now served to the men and consists of boiled seal or walrus meat and the inevitable "blood soup." The food is not always salted, but sometimes it is cooked in melted sea-water ice which contains a sufficient quantity of salt. Liver is generally eaten raw and is considered a tidbit. The Eskimo drink great quantities of water, obtained by melting snow over the lamp. After the men have eaten their fill, the women take their meal, and then all regale themselves with pieces of frozen raw meat by way of dessert. In this manner an enormous quantity of meat is devoured every night.

After dinner the seals, which have been placed behind the lamp to thaw, are thrown upon the floor and cut up, and the spare meat and skins taken to the storeroom. If, however, there are any needy families in the village, each receives a share of the meat and blubber. This sort of communism is the result of the Eskimo's marvelous adaptation to the severe conditions of his life. It is most important that none should be allowed to go cold or hungry in a climate where existence itself depends on having one's bodily wants liberally supplied. Nor are the hunter's dogs forgotten; they receive some of the blubber and the heads, entrails, bones, and waste pieces of the skins of seals. But nothing satisfies their voracious appetite. They will eat any kind of leather, particularly boots and harnesses, whenever they can get at it. Hence the hunter's care to put such things safely away in the storeroom. When feeding the dogs, it is necessary to keep them off with a whip until the frozen mass of food is broken up, when they all rush at it and in less than half a minute have swallowed their meal.

Having completed their tasks, the men now have leisure to dress for the evening, which means putting on dry stockings and boots in order that those they have been wearing during the day may be dried and mended. These northern people seem to get along quite comfortably without the aid of soap and water. While the women occupy themselves with drying and mending the discarded garments, the men visit one another and spend most of the night in talking, singing, gambling, and telling stories. Some busy themselves in cutting new ivory implements and seal lines, or in carving. Wooden and ivory implements of all sorts are lavishly carved, sometimes in the forms of seals or walrus, sometimes with grotesque designs. Nothing is too small to be carved or

Fig. 7. Ivory instrument for creasing soles of sealskin boots around toe and heel, from Nushagak

etched; belt buckles, buttons, needle cases, fastenings for splicing lines—all receive their share of ornamentation. Even the straight pieces of ivory used in creasing and shaping the soles of boots are etched with minute designs. With some Eskimo tribes such drawings sometimes take the form of picture writing, in which a man will record the number of deer or seals he has captured. The picture writing and etching may have been borrowed from some of the Athapascan tribes to the south, to whose haunts the Eskimo penetrate during the summer camping trips. But for the most part their carvings are original in method and design.

The long winter evenings are made the occasion for much jollity and merrymaking, without the aid of the white man's stimulants which have been forbidden in the Canadian Arctic since about 1890, so that they are practically unknown to the present generation of Eskimo. Forever menaced by the twin terrors of starvation and death by freezing, the Eskimo seem to have developed a sort of Epicurean philosophy which enables them to "eat (meat and blubber), drink (cold water), and be merry" while they may. Without this social temperament, life throughout the long dark winter would be well-nigh insupportable. Everyone is welcome in the snow house and refreshments are supplied in the shape of jars of melted snow which stand near the lamps, and lumps of frozen meat from which all are at liberty to cut portions as they like. The first comers sit on the snow platforms—honored guests on the divan among the warm fur rugs—while those who arrive late must stand or squat in the passage. When anyone addresses the whole assembly, he always turns his face to the wall and avoids facing the listeners. The stories told are well-known legends, and must be repeated in the traditional words familiar to all. Comic songs and dances are much applauded, especially if the fun is directed at someone present.

The women sit by their lamps, in their usual Turkish fashion, working continually either at their sewing, or in drying the wet footgear and mittens and softening the leather by chewing and rubbing. Chewing leather is one of the chief occupations of Eskimo women, begun in early childhood and continued until old age, when the teeth are found worn down to the gums. Yet, strange to say, the Eskimo, since they have come in contact with white traders from whom they may obtain many of the luxuries of civilization, like nothing better than American chewing gum! They are also fond of chewing tobacco whenever they can get it, and Eskimo men are inveterate smokers.

The Eskimo have many games of skill and chance which they play for stakes in the shape of articles contributed by each player for that purpose; for unlike many of the more southern tribes, they use neither shells nor beads as a medium of exchange. Since they pay with the pelts of animals for all articles bought from outsiders, their standard of value is the skin of a seal and the worth of any object is estimated as so many "skins."

If there has been any great success in hunting, such as the capture of a bearded seal or a whale, it is usually celebrated by a big feast in which all the people of the village share. For this purpose the men unite in building a large snow dome called a *qaggi* or "singing house." The qaggi may be as much as fifteen feet high and twenty feet across. It is unfurnished except for a snow pillar in the center, about five feet high, on which the lamps are placed. When the people assemble here for singing and dancing, they are distributed in a very definite manner. The married women stand in a circle nearest the wall, the next row is made up of unmarried women, while the men are seated in the innermost circle. The children stand in two groups, one on each side of the door. All are in gala dress. The women have their hair arranged in enormous pigtails which project horizontally on each side of the face. They wear their finest and newest clothes and are adorned with earrings and other ornaments of ivory. Their faces are usually permanently decorated with tattooing. The favorite ornament of the men of some districts is the labret—a plug of ivory worn in the cheek or lip, which is pierced for that purpose.

The audience being assembled, a performer takes his position in the open space nearest the door. His dancing is a rhythmic stamping and swaying performed practically in one spot. His song, composed extemporaneously, often takes the form of a humorous satire on the foibles of the village people. The Eskimo are clever mimics and enjoy nothing better than an opportunity to make fun of their friends. As an accompaniment to his song and dance the performer beats a drum, or tambourine, called a *kilaut*, the only musical instrument of the Eskimo. It consists of a hoop of whalebone or wood over which the skin of the deer or seal has been stretched and fastened taut by means of a braided cord of sinew passed

PLATE 21

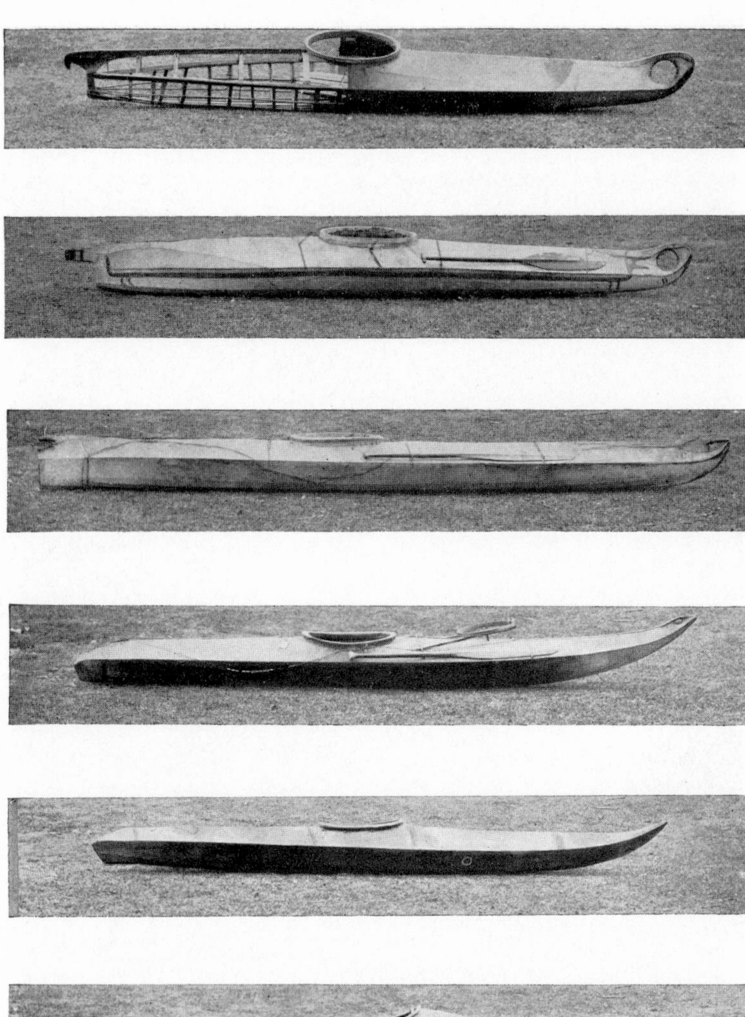

Eskimo kayaks from King's Island, Norton Sound, and Nunivak Island. Made of sealskin stretched over frames of driftwood

PLATE 22

Model of Eskimo umiak from St. Michael. Sealskin or walrus hide is stretched over a framework of driftwood. The sail is of the primitive grass mat type

around a groove on the outside. This instrument the performer holds aloft in one hand and strikes at intervals with a wooden drumstick called a *kentum*, all the while keeping up his grotesque dance and comic song. While engaged in this strenuous vaudeville performance, the dancer wears only his trousers and boots. The women take no part in the dancing, but join in the chorus whenever the singer comes to the refrain, "*amna aya*," which closes every verse of his song.

Later on, the women prepare food in their usual fashion, and there is great feasting and merrymaking throughout the night. On such occasions the never very fast bonds of matrimony are loosened, and there is a general though temporary exchange of wives. Marriage among the Eskimo is a wholly companionate arrangement, to be terminated temporarily or completely at the discretion of either party. A man selects a wife chiefly for her domestic accomplishments, for without her assistance it would be a difficult matter for him to obtain clothing and boiled meat. A woman, on the other hand, desires a husband and a home of her own in order that she may have her own fireside and someone to supply the materials for food, clothing, and fuel. Families are as a rule small, and it is chiefly their affection for the children, aside from practical considerations, which holds husband and wife together. Orphans and unattached grown people are always "adopted" by a family. In times of great plenty a man may even be able to afford more than one wife.

The Eskimo, although so unmoral, are a kindly, peace-loving, carefree people. So improvident are they that even with unlimited facilities for cold storage on every hand they never have much food stored up; consequently if the winter proves unusually stormy, or if for any other reason the hunters fail to bring in their daily seals, it does not take long for the dread specter of famine to make its appearance in the land. Then the lamps are allowed to burn lower and lower till finally they go out and everyone sits in silence within the dark, cold houses. It may even become necessary to kill and eat the faithful dogs; and in times of great distress parents have been known to eat their own children. But the Eskimo are not cannibals at heart, and always refer to such occurrences with the greatest horror.

It is in times of such distress that the people are most apt to turn for help to their holy men, the *angakut*. From them they learn that their chief goddess, whom the Central Eskimo call Sedna, is abroad in the land, with her terrible father, looking for victims to carry off with them to their kingdom of the dead. From the severed joints of Sedna's fingers, according to the myth, sprang all the animals which inhabit the ocean, especially the seal, the walrus, and the whale. It is because Sedna is offended that she keeps the seals imprisoned at the bottom of the sea and will not let them come to their breathing holes and be caught. So Sedna must be propitiated. In order to do this, the *angakoq* goes into a trance during which he visits the dread abode of Sedna and learns her pleasure. Or perhaps the soul of the angakoq may pay a visit to the man in the moon and learn from him what must be done in order to rid the land of famine.

The angakut control also the lesser spirits, called *tornait*, who are often responsible for much mischief. In invoking a *tornaq*, the angakut use a sacred, archaic language not understood by the common people. It is a favorite trick of theirs to have their hands tied together and to be trussed up by a thong passed around their knees and neck. Then the angakoq begins his invocation, and all of a sudden his body lies motionless while his soul flies off to any place he may wish to visit—any part of the earth, or the moon, or the underworld where Sedna reigns. After the soul has returned to the body, the thongs which bound it are found to be untied though they had been fastened by firm knots, and the angakoq, awaking from his trance, is able to relate to devout believers all the wonderful adventures his soul has just passed through.

Many of the angakut undoubtedly believe that they have really had the marvelous experiences they relate on awakening from their trance. Certain it is that to the Eskimo spirits are no less real than are the earthly objects they control and animate. Such spirits are not believed to be in themselves good or evil, but to be used for either good or evil purposes by the angakoq who controls them. The most powerful angakoq is he who has the greatest number of spirits under his control. If he be a bad man, then so much the greater need to conciliate him.

The firm belief of the Copper Eskimo in the magic powers of their angakut is amusingly illustrated in Stefansson's account of their reactions when first shown the wonders of certain modern inventions. When they saw a distant caribou killed by a shot from the gun of the explorer, they said, "Very good, but can you shoot a caribou on the other side of that great mountain, as our magicians can with their magic bows and arrows?" On seeing, through a pair of powerful field glasses, a herd of caribou indistinguishable to the unaided eye, they asked, "Can you show us the caribou that will be here tomorrow, as our magicians can?" And even when told how a modern surgeon can put a man to sleep, cut him open, and then sew him up again so that when he awakes he will know nothing about it except for the stitches in the wound, they had a reply which effectually silenced the boastful white man: Could our surgeons do what one of their medicine men had done? When a certain man had had a terrible backache, this magician had put him to sleep and had then taken out his backbone and put in a new one, *without leaving the tiniest scar!* Could white medicine men do that? Then they were not equal to the Eskimo. And as for the long tubes through which the wise white men examine the moon—that is nothing to the Eskimo, whose magicians can fly to the moon whenever they wish and tell them all about it afterwards.

So if a terrible famine is broken by the heroic efforts of the hunters in braving the storms and the cold and darkness, most of the credit—as well as a large part of the catch—is given to the angakut who have propitiated Sedna so that she has permitted the seals to return to the surface of the sea. A great feast is then held in Sedna's honor, and good fortune again comes to the settlement.[2]

The magic powers of the angakut are also called upon in case of sickness, which may be cured either by the help of the spirits or by inquiring of the sick man what taboos he may have broken. "Did he work when it was forbidden? Did he eat something he was not allowed to eat?" And so on. There are so many of these taboos that no one can possibly know them all, and he is considered the wisest man who knows the greatest number.

The laws prohibiting contact between the meat of deer and that of sea animals are particularly strict. According to the Eskimo, Sedna dislikes the deer and therefore it must not be brought in contact with her favorites; the meat of the whale, seal, or walrus must not be eaten on the same day with venison. Moreover, as Sedna is the special patroness of sea animals, a hunter must make atonement for every one that he kills. When a seal is brought into the house, the women must stop working until it has been cut up. Such taboos of course are well known and strictly observed. Many others, however, that are known to few except the angakut, are equally binding, and ignorance of them is no protection against the evil effects of transgression. Hence the importance of finding out, in the case of any misfortune, whether a

[2] Such were the rites of olden times. Today Christian missionaries are to be found in all parts of the Arctic.

taboo may have been broken in ignorance. This is where the great power of the angakut lies. Theirs is, in fact, the only authority recognized by the Eskimo, who have neither chiefs nor tribal organization. Since the introduction of Christianity among the Eskimo, all these old customs and beliefs are rapidly dying out, and with them the power of the angakut.

Politically, the Eskimo are the freest people on earth, living without the aid of any formal government. There are a certain number of customs and laws handed down from one generation to the next; but no means of enforcing these regulations, except through the power of public opinion. Nor is there any punishment for transgressors except the blood vengeance. A man who is offended by another will sometimes take revenge by killing the offender. It is then the right and duty of the nearest relative of the victim to kill the murderer. This gives rise to a feud which often lasts for a long time and may even be handed down to the next generation. An old custom which still survives in Greenland is a song contest known as the "nith song," from the Norwegian word *nith*, meaning "calumny." The offended person challenges the offender, and they meet before an audience, when they take turns in singing songs, each in ridicule of his enemy. The contest of wit continues until one of the contestants succeeds in getting the last word through the failure of his opponent to reply. The winner is then determined by the votes of the audience.

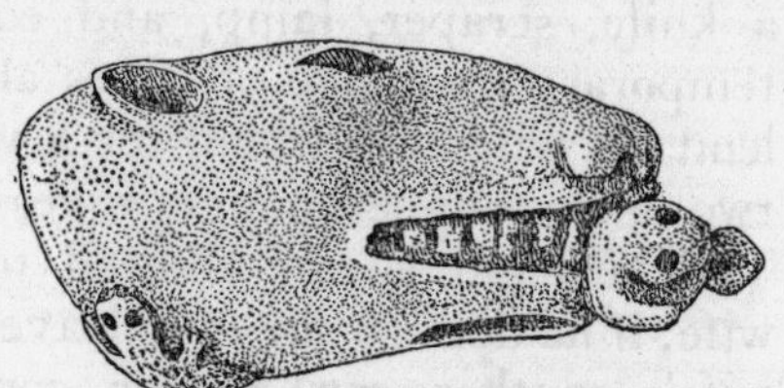

FIG. 8. Cord handle of ivory representing head of polar bear with a small seal in its mouth

The social order of the Eskimo is founded on the family and ties of relationship between families. As has been said, the marriage relation is not particularly binding unless there are children. Marriage between relatives is forbidden, but a man may marry two sisters. While polygamy is allowed, very few men have more than one wife. Before the introduction of various modern "necessities" by the white traders, all that a newly married couple needed in order to set up housekeeping was a hunting outfit for the man, which included a dog team, sledge, harpoon, knife, and spear; and for the woman a knife, scraper, lamp, and cooking pot. Besides the temporary exchange of wives already noted, a man may lend his wife to a friend for a whole season or longer, or two men may exchange wives as a sign of friendship. The husband is not allowed to maltreat or punish his wife; if he does so she may leave him at any time, and the wife's mother can always command a divorce. The slightest pretext is sufficient for a separation, and both may remarry as soon as they like.

Children are treated very kindly and are not whipped or punished. This fact has been noted by all Arctic travelers and explained in various ways. Stefansson attributes it, in the case of the Mackenzie River Eskimo, to their belief that every child is taken under special guardianship by the spirit of some grown person whose death has occurred at about the same time as the birth of the child. Until his own soul is sufficiently strong and wise to guide him, the child is the mouthpiece of this guardian spirit, who must be treated respectfully and conciliated in every way, else it may become offended and abandon the child entirely. So strong is the conviction that the child is for the time the reincarnation of the older person, that parents and relatives do not hesitate to address him as though he were in fact that person. Since the guardian spirit may be of the opposite sex, this frequently leads to strange complications. It is not unusual to hear a boy addressed by his father as "stepmother" and by his mother as "aunt," that having been the relationship existing between the parents and the present guardian spirit of the child.

When the child is about twelve years old, his own soul is considered sufficiently experienced to guide him, so the guardian spirit is withdrawn and his education begins in earnest. The girls are instructed by their mother in the domestic arts, while the father takes the boys out with him on hunting expeditions and teaches them the

FIG. 9. Cord attacher of ivory carved to represent a hair seal with inlaid blue beads for eyes. From Unalaklit

ways of the seal and how it may best be captured; they are also allowed to help with the dog team, and learn how to harness, drive, and care for the dogs.

In spring, when the sun has returned and the snow is beginning to melt, the boys will be taught another way of hunting. At this season the seals break down the snow roofs of their breathing holes, which they enlarge sufficiently to be able to clamber up through them and lie basking and dozing in the warm sunshine for hours at a time. They must now be approached more warily by the hunters, and speared as they sleep, before they have a chance to dive into the water. In order to get near enough to spear a seal, the Eskimo hunter, who in his closely fitting sealskin costume looks not unlike one of the animals himself, creeps up on all fours, stopping at intervals when the seal is awake, and creeping on when it has dropped asleep again. If the animal has seen the hunter, however, it will not do for him to lie perfectly still, for that would arouse its suspicions; he must lift himself up on his elbows and look about him seal-fashion, or roll over and play with his hands and feet as a seal does with its flippers. In this way he "plays seal" until the suspicions of the animal are allayed and it again drops off to sleep, oblivious of danger. If struck by the harpoon head, the line prevents the seal from escaping. In this way an expert hunter may kill from ten to fifteen seals in a day.

The natives are now freed from the fear of famine, but the snow houses in which they have lived so snugly all winter are soon made uninhabitable by the warm rays of the sun, which melt the roofs, causing much discomfort to the occupants. This condition is remedied temporarily by moving into new houses of which the lower half only is built of snow, with a roof of skins. In former days many Eskimo lived in houses of stone, the ruins of which are still found in some places. While the building of such houses seems today to be a lost art, the natives have been known to make use of the old ruins by covering them with roofs which in the winter were made of snow and in the summer of skins.

When the increasing warmth of the sun's rays melts down even the lower half of the snow houses, the Eskimo betake themselves to tents of skin, put up on a framework of poles which are frequently made of many pieces of wood ingeniously lashed together. At this season, when the ice has broken, seals, whales, and walrus were pursued in boats. For this purpose the Eskimo used the *kayak*, a sort of skin-covered canoe decked over in such a way as to leave only a small circular opening, where the hunter sat. By lashing his outer jacket securely around the rim of the cockpit, the boatman could make the kayak practically water-tight. With a double paddle he was able to propel his graceful little boat through the water with great speed. The harpoon used in striking the seal from the kayak was provided with floats made of whole sealskins. These floats, by their bouyancy, prevented the seal from diving, and it was then killed with a spear. The walrus being a more dangerous foe, es-

PLATE 23

Malemut Eskimo family from St. Michael with dog sled made of driftwood

PLATE 24

Eskimo graveyard at Rasbinsky, largest existing village of the Yukon Eskimo. The burial boxes are raised above the ground

pecially if it should turn upon the hunter in his light kayak, was harpooned from a great distance and was never attacked at close quarters until it was exhausted by dragging the float and by loss of blood. Whales were pursued by a number of kayaks together, every boatman endeavoring to drive his harpoon into the animal, which, by loss of blood and the resistance of the floats, was tired out and then killed with lances.

More often whales were pursued in the women's boats, or *umiaks*. These are large, flat-bottomed, skin-covered boats, usually provided with oars and sometimes having a square sail made of seal intestines carefully sewed together. When pursuing a whale the umiak's crew was made up of men, who used paddles instead of oars; a skillful boatman steered the boat and the harpooner stood in the bow watching his opportunity to strike the whale. The harpoon he carried was much larger and heavier than those used for seals and walrus. Not only were larger animals pursued in boats. Geese, ducks, and waterfowl were hunted in the same manner, being killed with specially designed bird spears which were hurled with great speed and force by means of "throwing boards," another ingenious invention of the Eskimo.

When the time came for the southern migration, the umiak was used for traveling by water. During the journey the boat's crew consisted of the women, two of whom usually worked each of the large oars. These long journeys were undertaken for two purposes: to secure wood for making sledges and various household utensils, and to hunt the caribou. On the shores of the Arctic the Eskimo must depend for their supply of wood upon the ocean currents which bring to their coasts such logs as have drifted down the rivers from the forested region in the south. On some shores this wood has been accumulating for centuries, protected from decay by the bacteria-free air of the north. This is especially true of the region bordering on Bering Sea, where the natives build houses of drift-logs, covered with earth and entered by underground passageways.

These tribes of western Alaska, who were in closer touch than were the Eastern and Central Eskimo with other natives of the northwest coast, resembled their more southern neighbors in many customs and beliefs. Here we find large community houses, called *kashims*, occupied by the men and used for holding religious feasts and other celebrations. There was a regular succession of such festivals through the winter, including the Asking Festival, the Festival to the Dead, the Bladder Feast, and the Great Feast to the Dead. The Western Eskimo know the art of weaving grasses into textiles for various purposes, and they share with other Indians a belief in the familiar practices of the medicine men, or shamans, and in the efficacy of the sweat-bath for curing disease as well as for purposes of cleanliness. They differ from the Central Eskimo, too, in the possession of nets of various sizes with which they capture not only the larger kinds of fish, but seals also, as well as all sorts of waterfowl and even small land birds. Nevertheless, they were of old thoroughly Eskimo in their manner of hunting sea animals in boats, especially in their kayaks. To protect themselves from snow and rain they wore over their fur garments waterproofs made of seal intestines. These waterproofs were carefully sewed and not only had drawstrings in the hood and sleeves by which they could be snugly secured around face and wrists, but the edge of the frock also was provided with a similar string by which it might be securely fastened around the rim of the kayak's cockpit, thus making both man and boat impervious to rain and waves.

Truly Eskimo were these people likewise in the roving habit which took them from their houses in the late summer to lead the life of gypsies when great herds of migrating caribou used to roam the land. In these woodland camps, indeed, individuals from almost all the

PLATE 25

Ancient knife sharpener and dagger of nephrite; handle of ivory bound with rawhide to provide a grip; wooden sheath. From Norton Sound Eskimo

Eskimo tribes would meet in a great intratribal community, where they might exchange commodities with one another as well as with the neighboring Indian tribes. Here they would hunt the caribou which formed their principal food at this season. They slept in tents made of the skins of these animals, and cooked their meals, gypsy fashion, over a fire of sticks in the open air. Several families would usually combine in this simple housekeeping, the women taking turns in the preparation of the food. Besides storing up dried venison for the return journey, and deer skins which would later be made into winter garments, the Eskimo busied themselves through the summer in making sledges, snowshovels, bows, spear handles, and other articles of wood.

The Arctic summer, though short, is decidedly hot. Stefansson gives the following vivid picture of his sufferings at this season:

> July was intolerably hot. We had no thermometer, but I feel sure that many a day the temperature must have been over one hundred degrees in the sun, and sometimes for weeks on end there was not a cloud in the sky. At midnight the sun was what we would call an hour high, so that it beat down on us without rest the twenty-four hours through. The hottest period of the day was about eight o'clock in the evening, and the coolest perhaps four or five in the morning. The mosquitoes were so bad that several of our dogs went completely blind for the time, through the swelling closed of their eyes, and all of them were lame from running sores caused by the mosquito stings on the line where the hair meets the pad of the foot. It is true that on our entire expedition we had no experience that more nearly deserved the name of suffering than this of the combined heat and mosquitoes of our Coppermine River summer.

Such is the testimony of one who has lived as an Eskimo among the Eskimo both winter and summer for a number of years. However, there is a fairer side to the picture. Many an Arctic voyager has commented on the singular transformation which even the most northern coasts undergo during the brief but intense summer. Then the great open plains, or tundras, are converted into rich pastures on which the caribou feed. The willows, which here in the Far North are creeping shrubs, are covered first with soft catkins and then with a green mist of tiny leaves. Each sheltered cove has its meadow, where all sorts of flowers seem in haste to bud and blossom. It is said that flowering plants, though stunted, produce blooms quite as large and even more brilliant in color than the corresponding plants farther south. Among Arctic flowers are found the poppy, heather, wild geranium, a white buttercup called the "reindeer flower," the moss campion or cushion pink, and the northern dwarf cornel.

Stefansson, however, has no fault to find with the keen autumn weather in the North. Of this season he says:

> Traveling at this time of year is particularly pleasant, for while the days are still warm, the placid nights are cool and the power of the mosquito has been broken. There are few things in one's experience in the North that are so pleasant to remember as these autumn hunts, when the camp is pitched among a clump of spruce trees at the bottom of some ravine, and when at the end of a day's hunt you can gather around the crakling fire in the enveloping darkness, for the four-months' summer day is just over. The occasional howl of a wolf in the near shadow lends an additional romance, especially if, as not seldom happens, the wolves are so numerous and so near that the dogs become frightened and gather in a close circle around the fire. Few meals can be more satisfying, either, at the end of a hard day's work, than a caribou head that has been rotated continuously before the fire until it is roasted through, even to the base of the tongue and the center of the brain. The dreams of boyhood seldom come true, but I am not sure that there is not sometimes as much romance about the reality of such evenings as there is about the dreams of Crusoe-like adventures on desert islands.

A month later, by the end of September, the mists and fogs have become almost as continuous as the sunshine had been. When the first snow falls, the seal hunters hitch their dogs to the new sleds they have made during the summer, load their provisions upon them, and move north or west toward the coasts where they will again establish their winter quarters.

REFERENCES

Boas, Franz. The Central Eskimo. 6th Ann. Rep. Bur. Ethnol. Washington, 1888.

Brown, R. N. R. The polar regions: a physical and economic geography of the Arctic and Antarctic. London, 1927.

Hoffman, Walter J. The graphic art of the Eskimos, based upon collections in the National Museum. U. S. Nation. Mus. Ann. Rep. 1895, pp. 739–968. Washington, 1897.

Hough, Walter. The lamp of the Eskimo. U. S. Nation. Mus. Ann. Rep. 1896, pp. 1025–1057. Washington, 1898.

Jenness, Diamond. The life of the Copper Eskimos. Rep. Canadian Arctic Exp. 1913–18, Vol. 12, Ottawa, 1922.

—— The people of the twilight. New York (Macmillan), 1928.

Murdoch, John. Ethnological results of the Point Barrow Expedition. 9th Ann. Rep. Bur. Ethnol. Washington, 1892.

Nansen, Fridtjof. Eskimo life. Translated by William Archer. London, 1893.

—— In Northern mists: Arctic explorations in early times. New York (Stokes), 1911.

Nelson, Edward W. The Eskimo about Bering Strait. 18th Ann. Rep. Bur. Amer. Ethnol. Washington, 1900.

Peary, Robert E. Northward over the "Great Ice." Vol. i-ii. New York, 1898.

Rasmussen, Knud. The people of the polar North. Philadelphia (Lippincott), 1908.

Stefansson, Vilhjalmur. My life with the Eskimo. New York (Macmillan), 1913.

—— The friendly Arctic. New York (Macmillan), 1921.

CHAPTER IV

A LEAGUE OF FIVE NATIONS: THE IROQUOIS

THE Athapascan tribes who roamed the great pine forests of Canada formed a connecting link between the Eskimo to the north and the Algonquians to the east and south. The Tinneh, or Dinné, as the most northern branch of this widespread family was called, had adopted many of the practices of their Arctic neighbors, and at the same time displayed traits common to most forest dwellers. In the regions where the birch tree grew they used its bark, as did the other tribes, for their lodges and canoes; while in the looseness of their tribal organization and moral code, and in their dependence on animal food—particularly the caribou—they most resembled the Eskimo. The hunter's existence was indeed forced upon the Tinneh, since the climate of their country was too cold and the soil too poor for agriculture.

Along the shores of the Great Lakes, however, and throughout the fertile valley of the St. Lawrence where lived the Algonkin and the Hurons (the latter an Iroquoian tribe), the first French settlers found great fields of growing corn, for these tribes dwelt in permanent villages and tilled the soil. Among the most interesting of the early chronicles of this region are the *Jesuit Relations*, written by those heroic missionaries who came over from France at the beginning of the seventeenth century, fired by zeal to Christianize the Savages. Joining the colony already established on the banks of the St. Lawrence, they began their labors among the Algonkin and the Hurons, who, already disposed to be friendly toward the French settlers, were soon quite won over by the ministrations of the priests—the "black robes," as the Indians called them.

As the French adventurers pursued their exploration of the new continent, the Jesuit fathers followed close upon their trail, coming down Lake Champlain and penetrating into the wilderness which was later to become the State of New York. It is fascinating to read the *Relations*—reports sent by these priests to the Superior of their order—with their many extraordinary descriptions of the strange country which had been named New France. In the *Relation* for 1657, for instance, we read:

> Besides grapes, plums, and many other fruits,—which it has in common with the fine Province of Europe,—it has a number of others which excel ours in beauty, fragrance, and taste. . . . Stoneless cherries [cranberries] are found there. Fruits grow there which are of the color and size of an apricot [probably the May-apple], whose blossom is like that of the white lily, and which smell and taste like the citron. There are apples as large as a goose's egg [fruits of the pawpaw]. . . . But the most common and the most wonderful plant in these countries is that which we call the universal plant [sassafras?]; because its leaves, when pounded, heal in a short time wounds of all kinds; these leaves, which are as broad as one's hand, have the shape of a lily as depicted in heraldry, and its roots have the smell of the laurel. The most vivid scarlet, the brightest green, the most natural yellow and orange of Europe pale before the various colors that our Savages procure from roots. I say nothing of trees as tall as oaks, whose leaves are as open as cabbages [?]; or of many other plants, peculiar to this country, because as yet we are ignorant of their properties.

Inhabiting this strange land, the Fathers found five warlike Iroquoian tribes—the Mohawk, Oneida, Seneca, Onondaga, and Cayuga—who had formed among themselves a powerful confederation, called by the French the "Iroquois," and later on, by their English friends and allies, the "League of the Five Nations."

These fierce warriors, whose enmity the French had incurred by making unprovoked attacks upon them, were destined to play an important part in the long struggle between the English and the French for dominion over the new continent. The picture of them given in the *Relations* is one of terrible vividness, describing not only the hideous practices of the Iroquois toward their prisoners of war, but also the great heroism of those priests who endured martyrdom at their hands. Most of the details are too horrible to quote here, but the following passage will give some idea of Iroquois methods of warfare:

> These poor Algonquins were in their own country, living in huts in the depths of the great forests, in a place where, in all probability, no Hiroquois had ever been. That is why they thought of nothing but their hunting, and not of defending themselves against those Barbarians. When the latter came upon the tracks of the hunters, they crept upon them stealthily, to massacre them in their first sleep. . . . Those tigers entered their cabin, with arms in their hands, and seized them, some by the hair and others about the body. Some who were awakened by the noise, and who tried to defend themselves, were at once slaughtered. The fight was soon over, and the Hiroquois, finding the poor people already overcome by sleep and fright, bound them with strong cords—men, women, and children; and, in less than an hour, were masters of their lives, of their little wealth, and of their cabins. Seeing themselves victorious, they prepared their supper in the house of the vanquished. Some brought wood and others went for water. Great kettles were placed over the fire. The shambles were not far away. They dismembered those whom they had just slaughtered, cut them in pieces, and threw the feet, legs, arms, and heads into the pot, which they set to boil with joy as great as the sorrow felt by the poor captives who remained alive, when they saw their countrymen serving as the quarry of these Werewolves. The women and children wept bitterly; and those half Demons took pleasure in hearing their doleful chants. When the supper was cooked, these wolves devoured their prey. . . . They ate the flesh of men with as much appetite as, and with more pleasure than, hunters eat that of the Boar or of a Stag.

Terrible as were the Iroquois when on the warpath, in their own homes and among their own kindred they appear in a very different light. They were a semi-agricultural people, living in permanent, fortified villages

PLATE 26

Two types of Chippewa habitations, Minnesota. Left, matting; right, bark

PLATE 27

A birch-bark lodge constructed on their old tribal models by Passamaquoddy Indians of Maine in the depths of the great forests, and changing the location of their homes only when forced to do so through having exhausted the fertility of the soil or the supply of firewood in their immediate vicinity. Their houses, representing one of the highest types of architecture reached by the northern tribes, were long, rectangular communal lodges built of wooden poles and covered with bark. These houses were from fifty to eighty, and sometimes more than one hundred feet long.

The interior of the "long-house" was divided by partitions at intervals of six or eight—in some cases twenty or more—feet, leaving each chamber entirely open, like a stall, upon the passageway, which passed through the center of the house from end to end. At each end was a doorway covered with a curtain of skins or a door of bark. At intervals along the passageway were fire-pits, each shared by four of the apartments, two on a side. An opening in the roof above each fire-pit allowed the smoke to escape. A house with five fires would thus contain twenty apartments, and would accommodate twenty families, unless some apartments were reserved for storage. Raised bunks around the three sides of each apartment served as beds or benches. From the roof-poles were suspended strings of corn in the ear, braided together by the husks; also strings of dried pumpkins and squashes—a word derived from the Algonquian *askutasquash*.

Each long-house in an Iroquois village was the property of the women who inhabited it, while the men, although husbands of the women and fathers of the children, were regarded as belonging to the households of their mothers. As long as a man did his share in providing game for the household and made himself otherwise acceptable, he might lodge with his wife and children and be treated as their honored guest, but if any cause for dissension arose, he would be obliged to leave. It was the women who, for the most part, built the houses and who tilled the soil;

and the corn, tobacco, and vegetables they raised were their common property.

Maize, or Indian corn, was the favorite food of the Iroquois, who hulled the grain by boiling it in ashes and water, and ground it into a coarse flour between stones or by means of a wooden mortar and pestle. After passing the meal through a "sieve basket" of plaited splints or corn husks, the Indian housewife made it up into little loaves or cakes which she boiled in earthenware jars of water into which red-hot stones were dropped. Or the corn meal might be prepared as a gruel mixed with meat and vegetables, a concoction which the Algonquian Indians called *sagamité*. To preserve corn for long periods, it was charred and stored in pits lined with mats of straw.

Another favorite food of the Iroquois was bread made from nuts or sunflower seeds. When the nut paste or sunflower-seed meal was boiled in water, the oil, rising to the top, was skimmed off and preserved in gourds or vessels of bark. The Indians used it, as we use butter, to enrich and flavor food. Lacking salt, the Iroquois naturally preferred dishes of a rather pungent flavor. They relished the dried intestines of animals, which were eaten raw. A special delicacy was the embryo of a bird taken from the egg. The flesh of dogs, their one domestic animal, was held in high esteem. In fact, a lack of squeamishness in regard to food was a matter of pride with the Iroquois braves. Colden says:

> Their Men value themselves, in having all Kind of Food in equal Esteem. A *Mohawk Sachem* told me with a Kind of Pride, that a Man eats every Thing without Distinction, *Bears*, *Cats*, *Dogs*, *Snakes*, *Frogs*, etc., intimating that it is Womanish to have any delicacy in the Choice of Food.

The Iroquois had but one full meal a day. This was a combined breakfast and dinner and was usually eaten before midday. The food was served warm to each person in earthenware or wooden bowls. They had neither tables, nor chairs, nor any room that might serve as a separate dining room or kitchen; each person ate when and where he pleased. The men usually ate first, the women and children afterwards. Toward evening maize, in the form of hominy, was boiled and put aside to be used cold as a lunch in the morning or evening and for the entertainment of visitors; but there was no formal breakfast or supper.

Hospitality was universal among the Iroquois. If a man entered a house, whether he was a villager or a stranger, it was the duty of the women to set food before him. To omit to do this would have been an unpardonable affront. It was contrary to Indian etiquette to ask a visitor to state his business; he must be served with food and tobacco, and his hosts must wait in silence until he should be sufficiently rested and refreshed to speak. This law of hospitality was but one of many communistic practices. It helped to equalize the distribution of food, a most important matter to people living from day to day largely on the uncertain fortune of the chase. Anyone was thus able to secure necessary food so long as there was food in the community.

Not only were the women cooks, farmers, and house builders; they were also skilled in needlework, and spent a great part of their time in fashioning garments out of the skins of animals. In Heriot's "Travels through Canada" is the following description of the garb of the Iroquois:

> The habiliments of the Iroquois consist of several pieces, being a kind of tunic, an apron, a robe calculated to cover the whole, and shoes for the feet. The apron is made of skins well dressed, or of European cloth. . . . The stockings, or leggings, are of skins sewed on the outside, having beyond the seam a double selvage of three inches in breadth, which guards the limbs from being injured by brushing against the underwood and boughs, in passing through the forests. The women wear the same articles of dress, and fix them by garters around the knee; the men attach them by strings to the belt around the waist. These leggings have no feet, but enter into the shoes made of soft

leather, generally of deer skin, and frequently neatly embroidered with the quills of porcupines, stained of different hues. A species of buskin ascending to the calf of the leg is sometimes worn.

The robe is a kind of blanket of about five or six feet square, made of the skins of buffaloes, deer, elk, or of several beaver or marten skins sewed together. All the natives in the neighborhood of Europeans, preserve the fashion of their ancient dress, changing the materials only. For the tunic, linen or cotton shirts are worn, and the remainder of the dress is of woollen stuff. The leather of which the shoes are made is prepared by smoking and thereby rendered impervious to moisture. They adorn the inside of the skins of buffaloes and of deer, by delineating upon them figures of men and animals painted with black and red colours, and also by working them with porcupine quills, stained with variegated tints.

Writing at a still later date, Morgan, in his "League of the Iroquois," has given a description of the full-dress costume the warriors wear in some of their ceremonial dances. He also adds some interesting details with regard to the making and the ornamentation of the various garments.

One of the most prominent articles of apparel was the Kilt, *Gä-kä'-ah*, which was secured around the waist by a belt, and descended to the knee. In ancient times this was made of deerskin. It was fringed and embroidered with porcupine quill-work. . . . In modern times various fabrics have been substituted for the deerskin, although the latter is still used. . . .

Upon the head-dress, *Gus-tó-weh*, the most conspicuous part of the costume, much attention was bestowed. The frame consisted of a band of splint, adjusted around the head, with in some instances a cross-band arching over the top from side to side. A cap of net-work, or other construction, was then made to enclose the frame. Around the splint, in later times, a silver band was fastened, which completed the lower part. From the top a cluster of white feathers depended. Besides this, a single feather of the largest size was set in the crown of the head-dress, inclining backwards from the head. It was secured in a small tube, which was fastened to the cross-splint, and in such a manner as to allow the feather to revolve in the tube. This feather, which was usually the plume of the eagle, is the characteristic of the Iroquois head-dress.

Next was the Leggin, *Gisé-hă*, which was fastened above the knee and descended upon the moccason. It was also originally made of deerskin, and ornamented with quill-work upon the bottom and side, the embroided edge being worn in front. In later times, red broadcloth, embroided with bead-work, has been substituted for the deerskin in most cases. . . .

The Moccason [*Ah-tä-quä*] was also made of deerskin. In the modern moccason the front part is worked with porcupine quills after the ancient fashion, while the part which falls down upon the sides is embroidered with bead-work according to the present taste. . . .

In ancient times the Iroquois used another shoe made of the skin of the elk. They cut the skin above and below the gambrel joint, and then took if off entire. As the hind leg of the elk inclines at the joint nearly at a right angle, it was naturally adapted to the foot. The lower end was sewed firmly with sinew, and the upper part secured above the ankle with deer strings.

As with the Eskimo, and indeed most primitive people, while the women busied themselves at home, the men were usually away on hunting or war expeditions. Until firearms were introduced by the white men, the principal weapon was the bow and arrow. An arrow often had but two feathers, stripped from their quills and fastened to the shaft in such a way as to give them a twist and so make the arrow revolve in its flight. Pointed with a head of flint chipped down to a sharp edge, and propelled from a tautly strung bow, such an arrow could easily bring down the deer, the wildfowl, or an enemy. Sometimes the tips were of horn or bone, which, although not so hard as the flint, could be given longer points and were therefore more dangerous. Arrows were carried in a quiver made of the skin of a small animal taken off entire and dressed with the hair on, or sometimes of unhaired deerskin embroidered with porcupine quills. An ordinary quiver would hold from fifteen to twenty arrows.

Long expeditions were often made by water, in canoes of birch or elm bark. For fashioning a canoe, an Indian usually strips the bark from the tree in a single piece of the required length and width, and after removing the rough outside, proceeds to shape it. The rim he forms of pieces of white ash, or other elastic wood, stitching them around the edges inside and outside by means of bark thread and splints. The ribs are narrow strips of ash set about a foot apart along the bottom of the canoe, turned up along the sides, and secured under the rim. Both ends of an Indian canoe are alike, the two side pieces being brought together to form a sharp and vertical prow. A canoe may be twelve feet long with room for only two men, or forty feet long and able to carry thirty.

Although by no means so inventive as the Eskimo, who in that respect are the cleverest of all the native tribes, the Iroquois were not lacking in ingenuity. Their pump drill for fire-making, for example, if indeed it was native to them and not introduced by Europeans, was a considerable advance on the original primitive method of twirling the end of one stick within a cleft made in another. These drills were weighted at one end by a small disk and were operated with a cord and bow.

The Iroquois were likewise very ingenious in the matter of basket making, particularly in contriving receptacles for special purposes, as the flat sieve basket for sifting corn meal, and the conical basket used in fishing. The fisherman would stand in the rapids of a creek or river, and with a stick would direct the fish into one of these long, closely woven baskets, which, partly submerged, made an effective trap. Such baskets might be woven of corn-husks, of flags, or of splints made from the black ash. The splints were often dyed before they were woven and were moistened to make them more pliable.

One of the most conspicuous articles of Iroquois manufacture was the baby frame, in which the child was securely fastened and thus carried about on the mother's back or suspended from a peg or the limb of a tree. The frame itself consisted of but three pieces of wood, the bottom board, the foot board and the bow at the top on which was spread a covering that protected the baby's head. After the child's arms and legs had been securely pinioned by means of the swaddling bands, it was enveloped in a blanket and lashed upon the frame with belts of bead-work, so that only its face was visible. The frame was often elaborately carved and ornamented, and was suspended from the mother's head by means of one of the burden straps in the weaving of which these Indians showed great skill. These bands were fashioned, by a process of finger weaving, from cords made by twisting filaments of bark together, which formed the warp; while the woof was filled in by passing finer threads of the same material across the cords over and under each alternately from side to side and back again. Morgan says that "in the manufacture of the several species of burden strap, more skill, ingenuity, and patient industry are exhibited, perhaps, than in any other single article fabricated by the Iroquois."

If we accept the following interpretation, from the *Jesuit Relations*, of the Indians' theory of disease, we must admit that they had anticipated Freud by at least three centuries:

> They believe that there are two main sources of disease: one of these is in the mind of the patient himself, which desires something, and will vex the body of the sick man until it possesses the thing required. For they think that there are in every man certain inborn desires, often unknown to themselves, upon which the happiness of individuals depends. For the purpose of ascertaining desires and innate appetites of this character, they summon soothsayers, who, as they think, have a divinely-imparted power to look into the inmost recesses of the mind. . . . They believe that another source of disease is the hidden arts and the charms of sorcerers, which they seek to avert by means of absurd ceremonies.

A third class of diseases, which the Father fails to mention, was recognized by the Iroquois as being due to natural causes and therefore curable by natural remedies.

The treatment of disease was consistent with these theories, as is shown in the two following extracts from the *Relations:*

> They are convinced that they are afflicted with diseases only because the soul is in want of something for which it craves; and that it is only

necessary to give it what it desires, in order to detain it peacefully in the body. . . . A dying man may be seen surrounded by awls, scissors, knives, bells, needles, and a thousand other trifles, from the least of which he expects to obtain health. If at last he happen to die, his death is attributed to the absence of some article that he desired. "He died," they say, "because his soul wished to eat the flesh of a dog, or of a man; because a certain hatchet that he wished for could not be procured; or because a fine pair of leggings that had been taken from him could not be found." If, on the contrary, the sick man recovers his health, he attributes his cure to the gift of the last thing he wished for during his illness, and afterwards he cherishes it forever, preserving it carefully until his death.

The second passage deals with the treatment of a disease supposed to be caused by the magic arts of an enemy:

Towards evening of the ninth of January [1656], we were spectators of the most subtle sorcery of the Country, employed for the cure of a sick woman of our cabin who has long been ailing. The Sorcerer [shaman] entered with a Tortoise-shell [rattle] in his hand, half full of small pebbles,—such are their instruments of magic. He took a seat in the midst of a dozen women who were to assist him in banishing the disease, and the neighbors gathered about to see this superstitious ceremony. All it consists in is, that the Magician strikes the Tortoise-shell against a mat, and intones a song, while the women dance about him, in time with his singing and with the noise of the Tortoise-shell. You see them move their feet, arms, head, and entire body, with such violence that great drops of perspiration soon cover their bodies. At the first trial, the disease was not expelled, or at the second, or at the third; this caused the dance to be prolonged far into the night, while the patient's illness abated not a particle.

Among the Iroquois each family group possessed a tract of land on which the women raised their crops of corn, beans, squash, and other vegetables. The ground was first burned over to clear it of weeds and underbrush. The soil was then loosened with wooden mattocks and the grains of corn deposited in hillocks at a little distance from each other. The success of the Iroquois as farmers is shown by statistics given of the destruction of their stores by American troops at the close of the Revolution. It is said that in Sullivan's expedition in 1779,

PLATE 28

"Their Manner of Fishynge in Virginia." By John White, the first English artist to visit America, in 1585

the Americans destroyed in the villages of the Iroquois 160,000 bushels of grain and in one orchard 1,500 fruit trees, some of them of great age. In this expedition, we are told, no less than forty Indian towns were burnt, of which Genesee, the largest, contained 128 houses.

Another art of the Iroquois, now lost but once carried on extensively by the women, was the making of pottery. Of this industry Morgan says:

> One of the most ancient Indian arts was that of pottery. It was carried to considerable perfection by the Iroquois at an early day, as is shown by the specimens which are still occasionally disentombed from the burial places, where they were deposited beside the dead; but the art itself has been so long disused that it is now entirely lost. Pipes, and earthen pots of various designs and sizes, are the principal objects thus found. Some of these specimens of black pottery, which is the best variety, are of so fine a texture as to admit of a considerable polish, and so firm as to have the appearance of stone. Their common pottery is of a clay color, and is a compound of common clay and pulverized quartz.

It was not, however, skill in the material arts of life that gave the Iroquois their ascendancy over other Indian tribes in the East and compelled the representatives of the most powerful nations in Europe to treat with them as equals. It was an extraordinary genius for social organization, which culminated in a confederation that endured through two centuries and served in some respects as a model for the union of the Colonies. To get a clear idea of the League, one must understand something of the underlying social structure of the Five Nations.

Among the Iroquois it was blood kinship, real or fictitious, that formed the basis of citizenship in a highly complex social fabric. In modern society an individual is identified as belonging to a certain city, township, district, or state, his right to citizenship in his nation depending upon his local habitation rather than upon his name or family connections. Theoretically at least, in the modern state, a man's family—his social status—is entirely distinct from his legal and political rights. "All men," we like to say, "are equal in the eyes of the Law." In short, the individual is the ultimate unit of the modern state, and localized groups of individuals form the larger units.

Among the Indians, on the contrary, and particularly among the Iroquois, the individual was nothing—the family everything. Unless a man belonged to one of the large family groups, either by blood or by adoption, he was regarded as an alien and an enemy. The Iroquois, like many other tribes, traced kinship solely through the mother's line, never through that of the father. The family groups were known as *ohwachira*, or *ohwachia*, for we find, even among these earliest Americans, some—as the Mohawk—who pronounced their *r*'s, and others—as the Onondaga—who discarded that troublesome letter altogether. All the members of an ohwachira being, theoretically at least, descended from the same female ancestor, were regarded as members of the same family, and habitually addressed one another in the terms of such relationship. A woman's immediate household—her husband and children—belonged of course to the same "fireside," but the husband was a member of his mother's ohwachira, never of that of his wife, marriage between members of the same ohwachira being forbidden by law. In a single long-house, however, there would be many firesides, the members of which would belong to the same ohwachira, as would the members of other firesides in other long-houses. The younger members of such related firesides would be regarded as brothers and sisters and would so address each other. The older women would be "sisters" to one another and "mothers" to the younger generation; while the oldest of all would be sisters to those of their own generation and mothers and grandmothers to the others.

When one of the daughters of such a household married, she continued to live at her accustomed fireside until after the birth of her first child. It was then in order for the young family to establish its own fireside, either in the long-house occupied by the wife's family, or in another lodge shared by other members of the wife's ohwachira.

Just as all the women of a child's ohwachira were to him mothers and grandmothers, so the brothers of the women were his uncles and his granduncles. All the kindred of a child's father, even his father's parents, bore to him the relation of uncles and aunts, with the exception of those of his own generation, who were his "cousins."

The headship of an ohwachira was always conferred upon a woman. There was no question of sex equality among the Iroquois—women were supreme.

Among the family groups, or ohwachira, some, of course, would be more closely allied than others. Such allied ohwachira formed a sisterhood or clan, designated by some characteristic name belonging to them exclusively. There were at least three, sometimes more, such clans in the tribes of the Five Nations.

Each ohwachira had originally one Federal male chiefship and one Federal female chiefship. Among the Mohawk, for example, there were nine such ohwachira distributed among three clans as follows:

MOHAWK CLANS

1. Turtle
   a. Turtle of the Rattle Kind
   b. Turtle of the Smooth-Shell Kind
   c. Turtle of the Small Stripe (or convex-back) Kind
2. Wolf
   a. Long-legged, Forest Wolf
   b. Bush Wolf
   c. Cub Wolf
3. Bear
   a. Adult Mother Bear
   b. Weanling Cub
   c. Nursing Cub

No other ohwachira of the Mohawk had a right to a Federal chiefship.

The three clans—Bear, Wolf, and Turtle (or Tortoise)—were common to all of the Five Nations and the only clans of two—the Mohawk and the Oneida. In addition to these, the three other nations, the Cayuga, the Seneca, and the Onondaga, at the time of the founding of the League, had each a number of other clans—the Deer, Eel, Beaver, Snipe, Hawk, and Heron—bringing the number of clans in some tribes up to eight, most of which were common to the three last-named tribes. These additional clans are supposed to have arisen both by natural growth and by the custom of adopting prisoners of war wholesale into a tribe, thereby constituting new clans.

Each nation was governed by a tribal council made up of chiefs of the several clans, who voted, not individually nor by clans, but by *phratries*. The *phratry* was a sisterhood of clans, just as the clan was a sisterhood of ohwachira. This system, while complicated, was necessary for conducting parliamentary business in the Indian fashion, which ignored the principle of rule by majorities, and required absolute unanimity. The chiefs of a clan having agreed upon a course of action, would then consult the wishes of the representatives of their sister clans. These being agreed among themselves could usually come to an agreement with the chiefs of the remaining clan or clans constituting the opposing phratry. At any time, however, a single chief might, by a dissenting voice, obstruct the work of a council.

Each of the Five Nations being governed by this complicated organization, it was but taking one more step to organize a Federal Council, which formed the ruling body of the League. This union was brought about chiefly through the patriotic and farsighted leadership of one man, one of the truly great statesmen of the world—Deganawida.

Deganawida, who lived in the sixteenth century, is described by tradition as a demigod, possibly the very last of the race of demigods to live upon the earth, having a mortal mother and a divine father and being endowed with faculties and abilities far beyond those of common men.

To a poor and humble woman, so the story runs, it had been revealed in a dream that her daughter—a maiden—would bear a child who should be called Deganawida and who should indirectly bring about the ruin of his people. Thinking to thwart this evil destiny, the mother and daughter, as soon as the child was born, carried it to a stream which was frozen over, thrust it into the water through a hole which they cut in the ice, and leaving it to drown, returned to their lodge. But when they awoke the next morning, they found the infant, unharmed, lying asleep between them. Twice again they carried the child to the icy river and endeavored to drown him there. And twice again they awoke in the morning to find him safe asleep between them. So, recognizing that it was the will of the Master of Life that the child should live, they accepted the charge, gave him the name Deganawida, as had been commanded, and thereafter reared him carefully until he grew to manhood.

Deganawida, arrived at man's estate, revealed to his mother and grandmother that he must leave them in order to perform a great work in other lands. The "white canoe"—probably a canoe made of birch bark—in which he is said to have started on his journey, has been confused in later tradition with the ice canoe of the Iroquois Winter God, and by a still further misunderstanding has been described in modern literature as made of flint or stone. Yet the story is but four hundred years old!

Deganawida soon gave proof of his divine origin by the extraordinary *orenda*, or magic power, he displayed in overcoming the obstacles and difficulties of his great task, by his astuteness in his dealings with the tribes, and by his wisdom in establishing the fundamental principles of the League. In short, Deganawida was more than a mere demigod; he was a true prophet, statesman, and lawmaker of the Stone Age of North America. Tradition assigns him to no tribe, but he is by some believed to have been a Huron.

Closely associated with Deganawida in the formation of the League was Hiawatha. Although of great renown, this Iroquois chieftain was an entirely different person from the legendary Chippewa god, Nanabozho, whose exploits have been immortalized by Longfellow under the name of "Hiawatha." The real Hiawatha is the hero of two conflicting traditions, one of which idealizes him as a great and far-seeing statesman, the true originator of the League. The legend which seems to accord more closely with the facts, however, describes him as the disciple and follower of Deganawida.

According to this tradition, Hiawatha was once a cannibal—like the "Demons" of the *Jesuit Relations*—and when first seen by Deganawida was in the act of bringing into his lodge the dead body of a man he had just killed. This body he proceeded to quarter and to cook in a pot of water. Deganawida, unseen by Hiawatha, climbed to the top of the lodge, where, by peering through the smoke-hole in the roof he could watch the cannibal at his gruesome task. While thus looking down, he succeeded by mental suggestion in making Hiawatha realize what a horrible thing he was doing. Mistaking the face of Deganawida, reflected in the boiling water, for his own, Hiawatha was struck by the contrast between its great beauty and the fearful contents of the pot. He exclaimed, "That face and this kind of business do not agree," and then and there resolved never again to eat human flesh. Accordingly he carried the pot some distance from the lodge and emptied it.

Returning, Hiawatha encountered Deganawida, who had descended from the roof and now came forward to meet him. Recognizing the beautiful face which had turned him from his evil ways, Hiawatha became from that moment Deganawida's devoted follower and ally. It is said that he received the name Hiawatha from Deganawida. These two sought to bring about reforms which had for their object the ending of all strife, murder, and war, and the promotion of universal peace and well-being. Closely associated with Deganawida and Hiawatha in this work was Djigonsasen, a renowned woman chief of another Iroquoian tribe, the Neutral Nation.

The most bitter opponent that Deganawida, Hiawatha, and Djigonsasen encountered was a powerful chieftain of the Onondaga, Atotarho or Wathatotarho, a man of great force of character—haughty, crafty, and remorseless—possessing *orenda* of great power. Tradition describes him as a monster, on whose head grew, instead of human hair, great serpents whose horrible folds enveloped his body. By his stratagems Atotarho prevented Hiawatha from addressing the Onondaga council, and by his magic arts he brought about the death of Hiawatha's seven daughters. It was not until after the tribes of the Mohawk, the Oneida, and the Cayuga had joined the confederation that Atotarho and the Onondaga were won over, and then their consent to enter the League was gained only by granting them unusual concessions. It was agreed that the Onondaga should be the leading nation of the confederacy; that their chief town should be the federal capital, where the great councils of the League should be held and where its records should be preserved; and that the nation should be represented in the council by thirteen senators, while no other nation had more than ten.

It was further agreed that no act of the Federal council to which the Onondaga objected should be valid. To enhance the personal dignity of Atotarho, five Federal chiefs were designated as his special aids. In view of all these distinctions, it is not surprising that his successor, who two centuries later retained the same prerogatives, should have been occasionally styled by the English colonists "the Emperor of the Five Nations."

In founding the League, the statesmen of the Iroquois declared that it was established for the promotion of universal peace among all the tribes of men—for the safeguarding of health, happiness, and human life. To that end the Founders advocated as the proper basis of government three great double doctrines or principles—six in all—which were:

1. (a) Health of mind and body.
   (b) Peace among individuals and groups of individuals.
2. (a) Righteousness in conduct; its advocacy in thought and speech.
   (b) Equity in the adjustment of rights and obligations.
3. (a) Physical strength or power; order.
   (b) Orenda, or magic power, of people and institutions.

One of the most important reforms instituted by the League in accordance with these principles was the prohibition of cannibalism as among members of the confederated nations—this did not apply, of course, to enemies in battle—and the substitution of a legal tender in the blood-feud as the price of the life of a man or woman. The price of a man's life was fixed at twenty strings of wampum, ten for the dead man and ten for the forfeited life of his murderer. For the life of a woman, the legal tender was thirty strings of wampum, because the value of a woman's life to the community was regarded as double that of a man's.

With regard to the Federal Council, or governing body of the League, Hewitt says:

The League of the Iroquois had no chief magistrate or so-called head chief. Each tribal council was composed of both Federal and tribal chiefs, one of whom, usually a Federal chief, was the Firekeeper,

PLATE 29

Model of an Iroquois "long-house" sheltering many families

PLATE 30

Chippewa Indians hunting from a birch bark canoe, Minnesota

like a speaker of a modern assembly, among whose duties it was to open and close the sessions of the Council by an appropriate and largely prescribed address. There were in each tribal council chiefs whose office was not hereditary, but who through merit had been installed like other chiefs as chiefs of their tribe. At their death their office ceased. In every tribe there were able men who many times had as much if not more power than any member of the council. Sometimes these men have been called head chiefs of their respective tribes. After attaining this preeminence it was customary to install them as merit chiefs. . . . Another name for this class of chiefs was pine-tree chiefs. . . .

The establishment at Onondaga of the seat of Federal power by the founders of the League of the Iroquois made Onondaga not only one of the most important and widely known towns of the Iroquois tribes, but also of North America north of Mexico. At the zenith of the power of the Iroquois it was the capital of a government whose dominion extended from the Hudson River on the east to the Falls of the Ohio and Lake Michigan on the west, and from the Ottawa River and Lake Simcoe on the north to the Potomac River on the south and the Ohio on the southwest.

Around the Great Council Fire of the League of the Iroquois at Onondaga, with punctilious observance of the parliamentary proprieties recognized in Indian diplomacy and statecraft, and with a decorum that would add grace to many legislative assemblies of the white man, the Federal senators of the Iroquois tribes devised plans, formulated policies, and defined principles of government and political action which not only strengthened their state and promoted their common welfare but also deeply affected the contemporary history of the whites in North America. To this body of half-clad Federal chieftains were repeatedly made overtures of peace and friendship by two of the most powerful kingdoms of Europe, whose statesmen often awaited with apprehension the decision of this senate of North American savages.

John Bartram, in his *Journal*, has given the following account of the proceedings of the council of the League which he attended in 1743 as a representative of the Commonwealth of Pennsylvania, seeking to make a treaty of peace with the Iroquois:

This afternoon the chiefs met in council, and three of them spoke for near a quarter of an hour each. . . .

This the interpreter told me was the opening of the diet, and was in the opinion of these people abundantly sufficient for one day, since there is nothing they contemn as much as precipitation in publick councils; indeed they esteem it at all times a mark of much levity in any one to return an immediate answer to a serious question however obvious, and they consequently spin out a Treaty, where many points are to be moved, to a great length of time. . . .

This council was followed by a feast, after 4 o'clock we all dined together upon 4 great kettles of *Indian* corn soop, which we soon emptied, and then every chief returned to his home. . . .

About noon the council sat a 2d time, and our interpreter had his audience, being charged by the governor with the conduct of the treaty. *Conrad Weiser* (the interpreter) had engaged the *Indian* speaker to open the affair to the chiefs assembled in council; he made a speech near half an hour, and delivered 3 broad belts and 5 strings of *Wampum* to the council, on the proper occasions. There was a pole laid a cross from one chamber to another over the passage, on this their belts and strings were hung, that all the council might see them and here have the matters in remembrance: The conference held till 3, after which we dined, this repast consisted of 3 great kettles of *Indian* corn soop, or thin hominy, with dry'd eels and other fish boiled in it, and one kettle full of young squashes and their flowers boiled in water, and a little meal mixed; this dish was but a weak food, last of all was served a great bowl full of *Indian* dumplings, made of new soft corn, cut or scraped off the ear, then with the addition of some boiled beans, lapped well up in *Indian* corn leaves, this is good hearty provision.

After dinner, we had a favourable answer, corroborated by several belts of *Wampum*, with a short speech to each, these we carried away as our tokens of peace and friendship. The harangue concluded with a charge to sit still as yet, for tho' they had dispatched our business first, it was not because they were weary of us, but to make us easy. This compliment preceded other business, which lasted till near sun set, when we regaled on a great bowl of boiled cakes, 6 or 7 inches diameter, and about 2 thick, with another of boiled squash, soon after, the chiefs in a friendly manner took their leave of us, and departed every one to his lodging: this night we treated two of the chiefs that lived in the council hall, which as I mentioned, was our quarters: they drank chearfully, wishing a long continuance of uninterrupted amity between the *Indians* and the *English*.

Colden, in his "History of the Five Indian Nations" has this to say concerning Indian oratory:

The People of the *Five Nations* are much given to *Speech-making*, ever the natural Consequence of a perfect Republican Government: Where no single Person has a Power to compel, the Arts of Persuasion alone must prevail. As their best Speakers distinguish themselves in their publick Councils and Treaties with other Nations, and thereby gain the Esteem and Applause of their Countrymen, (the only Superiority which any one of them has over the others) it is probable they apply themselves to this Art, by some Kind of Study and Exercise, in a great Measure. It is impossible for me to judge how far they excel, as I am ignorant of their Language; but the Speakers whom I have heard, had all a great Fluency of Words, and much more Grace in their Manner, than any Man could expect, among a People entirely ignorant of all the liberal Arts and Sciences. . . .

They have no Labeals in their Language, nor can they pronounce perfectly any Word wherein there is a Labeal; and when one endeavours to teach them to pronounce these Words, they tell one, they think it ridiculous that they must shut their Lips to speak. Their Language abounds with Gutterals and strong Aspirations, these make it very sonorous and bold; and their Speeches abound with Metaphors, after the manner of the Eastern Nations, as will best appear by the Speeches that I have copied.

Among the speeches thus preserved for us is one made by a Mohawk sachem to the English on the occasion of the sacking of the town of Schenectady by the French in 1690. Colden's account is in part as follows:

The *Mohawk Sachems* came to *Albany* to condole, according to their Custom, with their Friends, when any Misfortune befals them. I shall give their Speech on this Occasion, as it will be of Use to the Reader, in order to his forming a true Notion of the *Indian Genius*. They spoke the twenty-fifth of *March* as follows:

"Brethren, the Murder of our Brethren at *Schenectady* by the *French* grieves us as much as if it had been done to ourselves, for we are in the same Chain. . . . Be not therefore discouraged. We give this belt [of wampum] *to wipe away your tears*. . . .

"Our Chain is a strong Chain, it is a Silver Chain, it can neither rust nor be broken. We, as to our Parts, are resolute to continue the War.

"We will never desist, so long as a Man of us remains. Take Heart, do not pack up and go away, this will give Heart to a dastardly Enemy; We are of the Race of the Bear, and a Bear you know never yields, while one Drop of Blood is left. *We must all be Bears;* giving a sixth Belt.

"Brethren, be patient, this Disaster is an Affliction which has fallen from Heaven upon us. The Sun, which hath been cloudy, and sent this Disaster, will shine again with its pleasant Beams. Take Courage, said he, Courage, repeating the word several Times as they gave a seventh Belt."

Great virtue resided, according to Indian belief, in the belts and strings of wampum which, among the Iroquois, were the indispensable accompaniment of every ceremonial occasion whether political or religious. The primitive wampum of the Iroquois is said to have consisted of strings of a small fresh-water spiral shell, which was replaced at a later day by manufactured beads made from the shell of the common clam or quahog and probably introduced among the Indians by the Dutch. These beads were of two colors, purple and white, and were perforated lengthwise and strung on sinew or bark thread. Whether in the form of strings or when woven into belts, the wampum beads served as a permanent token of the speeches "talked into" them, and were used to record treaty stipulations, to convey messages, and for many religious and social purposes. Morgan gives the following description of a wampum belt:

> Wampum belts were made by covering one side of a deerskin belt with these beads, arranged after various devices, and with most laborious skill. As a belt four or five feet long by four inches wide would require several thousands of these beads, they were estimated at a great price. . . . Sometimes they are all of one color, in others variegated, and in still others woven with the figures of men to symbolize, by their attitudes, the objects or events they were designed to commemorate.

Tokens of all public acts, preserved in the belts of wampum, were in the care of the Onondaga chief who bore the title of "Keeper of the Wampum."

As originally constituted the Federal Council comprised forty-seven chiefs. Upon Skanawati, a powerful chief of the Onondaga, of the Turtle clan, were conferred the double powers of Firekeeper and Chief Warrior of the Federal Council. As bearer of two distinct titles it was said of him that his body was divided in twain. These offices Skanawati continued to hold until after the admission to the League of two important groups of the Seneca, each of which was controlled by a powerful chief.

In order to induce these two leaders to join the League, they were given the offices of a modern secretary of state, and secretary of war respectively, so that Skanawati was no longer Chief Warrior (Secretary of War). The Federal Council then numbered forty-nine, and this number was never changed, although when the Tuscarora and other tribes were later admitted to the League, their tribal chiefs were permitted to represent them in the Federal Council.

Of Skanawati as a representative Iroquois chieftain, Hewitt says:

> The character of some of the chief men and statesmen of the Onondaga appears in the following incident: Early in 1648 the Hurons resolved to send another embassy to Onondaga. This embassy consisted of six men, accompanied by one of the three Onondaga ambassadors then officially in their country, the other two, including Skanawati, the head of the Onondaga embassy, and the firekeeper of the Federal council, remaining as hostages. The new Huron embassy was unfortunate, for its members were captured and killed by a force of more than 100 Mohawk and Seneca who had lurked about the borders of the Huron country. The Onondaga accompanying this embassy was spared, and two Hurons succeeded in escaping. When this distressing information reached the ears of Skanawati early in April, this proud Onondaga ambassador, who had remained with the Hurons as a hostage, suddenly disappeared. Naturally the Hurons suspected that he had stealthily fled away, but a few days after his disappearance his corpse was discovered in the forest lying on a bed of fir branches, where he had, from chagrin, taken his own life by cutting his throat. In order to exonerate themselves the Hurons notified his companion, who explained that the cause of Skanawati's despair was the shame he felt at the contempt for the sacredness of his person shown by the Seneca and the Mohawk in going to the Huron country and slaughtering the Huron people while his own life was in pledge for the keeping of the faith of his people. Of such men was the great Federal Council of the Iroquois composed.

Horatio Hale, who edited the Iroquois "Book of Rites," says:

> By the ordinances of their League, it was required that the number of their federal senate should be maintained undiminished. On the death of one of its members, it was the duty of the nation to which he

belonged to notify the other nations of the event, and of the time and place at which he would be lamented and his successor installed. The notice was given in the usual manner, by official messengers, who bore for credentials certain [designated] strings of wampum, appropriate to the occasion. The place of meeting was commonly the chief town of the nation which had suffered the loss. . . .

It was customary for the chiefs of the mourning nation, on receiving word of the near approach of their guests, to go forth to a designated spot where a fire was kindled, and there await the arrival of the others. The visiting chiefs, having assembled at the customary meeting place "at the edge of the woods," moved forward in solemn procession, chanting the names of the founders of the League in the prescribed words that had been handed down from generation to generation. After each of the revered names, an invocation was uttered, sometimes:

Do ye continue to listen,
Ye rulers!

sometimes:

That was the roll of you,
You who were joined in the work,
You who completed the work,
The Great League.

Thus solemnly chanting, the chiefs arrive at the symbolic fireside, where they are welcomed according to a prescribed ritual by a chief of the mourning nation and escorted to the tribal council house, to the accompaniment of the same processional, taking up the long list of the forty-nine names where it had been left off. There was little chance of one of the sacred names being missed, for they had been perpetuated in the Federal Council since its founding. The departed chief for whom the nations mourned had borne one of the great names, and his successor would continue to bear it.

The solemn rite of condolence for the loss of the dead and of the installation of his successor forms the subject matter of the "Book of Rites," which gives both the Indian text and an English translation. One of the essential parts of this rite, the "Requickening Address," has also been translated by Hewitt, who gives the following interpretation of the ceremony:

The tribes of the League or Confederation are organized in two basic organic units—in two sisterhoods of tribes—each of which is constituted of two or more tribes which are correlated one with another as sisters, this being the descriptive term indicative of their kinship relations; the tribes of one of these sisterhoods of tribes address the tribes of the other sisterhoods as "our cousins."

The sisterhood of clans or the sisterhood of tribes, representing symbolically the male sex, is addressed as "my father's clansmen" or "our father's clansmen" because the side of the male sex is the father's side or father clan-group, or father tribe-group. Again the sisterhood of clans, or the sisterhood of tribes representing symbolically the female sex, is addressed as "my offspring" or "our offspring," because, in the fireside family, the children belong to the "mother," and as this is the mother group or side—the mother clan-group—it is also the "offspring" group or side; but this group or side may also be addressed as "woman," as may be seen in the words of the so-called "six songs." Thus, it is seen that the fundamental dualism consists of the concepts—male sex or principle, the father, the fatherhood, in nature, on the one hand, and the female sex or principle, the mother, the motherhood, in nature, on the other. . . .

The federal or league dualism consisted, on the father side, of the Mohawk, the Onondaga, and the Seneca tribes, and on the mother side, of the Oneida and the Cayuga tribes, the three tribes forming a sisterhood of tribes, and the two tribes forming another sisterhood of tribes. These sisterhoods have also been called phratries of tribes in the literature relating to these Iroquoian tribes and their League or Confederation.

In every place of public assembly there is, or at least there is assumed to be, a hearth or fire-altar, some distance from either end of the song-bench which occupies the central part of the room or space, and which serves as a divisional line between the father and the mother sides or tribal groups of the League, for the father group of tribes occupies one side of the fire, and the mother group of tribes the other, in both civil and religious public assemblies.

It is one of the rules or laws of the federal organization that in the case of the death of one or more chiefs in either tribal sisterhood the tribes of this sisterhood become mourners for a year or until the vacant chiefship or chiefships shall have been filled in accordance with strict rules of ritualistic procedure, which govern a large part of the proceedings of the so-called Council of Condolence and Installation of Chiefs. It is then the official duty of the other sisterhood of tribes to perform the rights and ceremonies of this council for the rehabilitation of its cousin sisterhood of tribes; for during the period of its mourning it should not transact any public business. . . .

The Requickening Address in the ritual of the Condoling and Installation Council of the League or Confederation of the Iroquois derives its name from its designed or purposed power and function to restore to life—to requicken the dead chief and lawgiver in the person of a legally chosen cotribesman, and, to heal and to soothe the wounded and bereaved mind of a cousin sisterhood of tribes—a cotribesman who shall live in the official name of the dead lawgiver. In Iroquoian polity the office never dies, only its bearer can die. . . . The polity of the Iroquois as expressed in the ordinances of the League requires that the number of chiefs constituting their federal council should be maintained undiminished in number. . . . So potent—and so terrible—so full of orenda or magic power—are the matters comprised in the ritual of this great council that it is regarded as imperative to hold this Council of Condolence and Installation only in the autumn and winter. It is so deeply concerned with the dead and with the powers that requicken and preserve the living from the power of the Destroyer, and so it was thought to be deadly and destructive to growing seeds and plants and fruits were it held during the spring or summer—the period of growth and rebirth. Its purpose in part is to nullify and overcome the power of Death and to restore to its normal condition the orenda, or magic power, of the stricken sisterhood of tribes, whether of the father or mother side. It was taught that the death of even one person weakened the orenda or magic power of the people, and so the death of a ruler was a greater blow; and to restore the life of the people the various institutions of the Condoling and Installation Council were devised to thwart the assaults of death and to repair any injury done by it to the power of the people to live in health and peace. . . .

The Requickening Address sets out in detail the evils and wounds which befall a stricken people—the calamitous effects of death's power, and it asserts that it counteracts these evils and restores to life the dying people in the person of their newly installed chief. . . .

This address is accompanied by fourteen strings of wampum. The orator delivers one of these wampum strings to the mourning side at the conclusion of every material statement. Hence his address is also called the Fourteen Matters, and also *Ne Adondak'sah*, *i.e.*, The Wampum Strings of Requickening.

PLATE 31

Thayendanegea, or Joseph Brant, Mohawk chief and colonel in the British Army during the Revolution. Artist unknown. Courtesy of Mr. David I. Bushnell, Junior

In his account of the Condoling Council in the "Book of Rites," Hale says:

> The chant and the Book end abruptly with the mournful exclamation "Now we [two] are dejected in mind." . . . As the council is held, nominally at least, for the purpose of condolence, and as it necessarily revives the memory of the departed worthies of their republic, it is natural that the ceremonies throughout should be of a melancholy cast. . . In fact, when we consider that the founders of the League, with remarkable skill and judgment, managed to compress into a single day the protracted and wasteful obsequies customary among other tribes of the same race, we shall not be surprised to find that they sought to make the ceremonies of the day as solemn and impressive as possible.

The other ceremonies of the Iroquois were not of this solemn character. Morgan enumerates six regular festivals, or thanksgivings, which were observed by them. These were the Maple, Planting, Strawberry, Green Corn, Harvest, and New Year's or White Dog festivals. The Maple festival, usually called the Maple Dance, was the first festival of the spring and was observed as a local feast in all the villages of the League. The other feasts followed in regular succession, and culminated in the great New Year's or White Dog Festival, which was held in mid-winter, and was the most elaborate and important feast of all.

All these feasts were of a religious character, and were celebrated by symbolic rites and dances, chief among which were the Feather dance, the Fish dance, and the Trotting dance. The Feast of the White Dog lasted seven days, the mornings being devoted to observances marked by song and sacrifice, and the evenings to dancing and feasting. The white dog offered as a messenger to bear the prayers of the people to the Life God was strangled and then burned. In strangling the dog, which was done on the second day of the festival, they were careful not to shed its blood or break its bones. It was then spotted with red paint and decorated with feathers, and a string of white wampum was hung around its neck. Voluntary offerings, in the shape of ornaments of various kinds, were placed upon the body. The dog was then suspended by the neck about eight feet from the ground, on the branching prong of a pole. There it hung until the morning of the fifth day, when it was taken down to be burned.

The burning of the dog was marked by great ceremony in which the impersonator of the Master of Life played an important part. A procession was formed around the burning altar on which the body of the dog was finally laid with great solemnity during the intoning of the final address. The people then returned to the council house, where the Feather dance was performed, and the rest of the day was given up to feasting and merrymaking, as a token to the Master of Life that his children were happy and grateful for all his blessings. After two more days of such observances, the ceremony was brought to an end with the Peach-stone or (Plum-stone) game. This was a ceremonial game in which six peach- or plum-stones, burned on one side to blacken them, were rolled about like dice in a bowl, the count depending upon the number which came up of one color, and the stakes being represented by beans. In this contest, the people were represented by players who played two at a time under the supervision of managers and watched by a delighted throng of spectators. The playing of the Peach-stone game was the concluding exercise not only of the New Year's, but also of the Green Corn and the Harvest festivals.

The Peach-stone game derived its significance from its connection with an incident in the legendary history of the Iroquois Master of Life, De‘haĕ^n‘hiyawă’’kho^n’, who, as the personification of the life force, was the creator of all living things upon the earth. His beneficent activities are thus recounted by Hewitt:

> De‘haĕ$^{n‘}$hiyawă’’kho^n’ then toiled at his tasks, forming the various kinds of animals and birds and making various varieties of useful trees, shrubs, and plants. In all this work his grandmother and his

twin brother [O‘hā’ä′, the personification of winter] sought to thwart him by all manner of devices, but by the timely counsel of his father [of the race of The Great Turtle] he was able to defeat their efforts. De‘haĕ^n‘hiyawă′’kho^n’ labored to prepare the earth for man, the human being, whom later he was to create. . . . Finally the grandmother, who had exhausted all her methods of opposition, challenged her grandson to a game of the bowl and plum pits, the prize of the winner to be the rulership of the phenomena, processes, and the flora and fauna of the earth. The grandson willingly accepted the challenge.

In accordance with custom, ten days were allowed the contestants to prepare for the struggle of their powerful orendas. At the end of this time the grandmother came to the lodge of her grandson, bringing her bowl and plum pits. He said he would use her bowl, but not her plum pits, as these were something alive and under the control of the mind of the grandmother, or the user. The plum pits in this game serve as dice. The dice of De‘haĕ^n‘hiyawă′’kho^n’ were the tops of the heads of chickadees, who had responded to his call for aid. He took six of the tops of the heads, and they remained magically alive. When he and his grandmother were ready De‘haĕ^n‘hiyawă′’kho^n’ called in a loud voice, "All you whose bodies I have formed, do you now put forth to the uttermost your orenda, in order that we may conquer in this struggle, so that you may live!" Then, when it came his turn to shake the bowl, he exclaimed, "Now, verily, shall appear the good or ill fortune of all the things that I have done or made!" But the grandmother failed to score, while De‘haĕ^n‘hiyawă′’kho^n’ made the highest score possible at one shake of the bowl, and so won the government and rulership of all living things.

Finally this great bet between De‘haĕ^n‘hiyawă′’kho^n’ and his redoubtable grandmother is dramatized and played at the annual New Year festival and also at the annual harvest festival or ingathering of crops.

Beset on all sides by enemies, it was but natural that the Iroquois should be almost continually at war. War might be declared either by the federal council or by an individual nation. Having enlisted volunteers, a war chief would go through his village dressed in full costume, singing songs, and dancing the war-dance. He would soon be joined by other singing, dancing warriors, dressed in full regalia. By the time the band had assembled, the women would have a quantity of charred corn prepared with which they filled the deerskin pouches of the warriors as provision for the journey. With but a small supply of this concentrated food it was possible for the Indians to make long expeditions. By mixing the ground corn with water a nourishing meal could be quickly prepared without the necessity of making a fire and thus running the risk of betraying their location to the enemy.

A band would take the warpath in single file, moving through the forest silently and rapidly. On their return, as soon as they reached the outskirts of their village, they sent a messenger to announce their approach by a long-drawn, wailing cry, "*Ku'we! Ku'we!*" repeated to indicate the number of prisoners or scalps they had taken. They then entered the village in a dancing procession, bringing their captives and trophies with them. After being received by a spokesman with a speech of welcome and congratulation, a reply was made by one of the band, who described their adventures. This ceremony was concluded by another war-dance.

The women of the tribe usually decided the fate of the captives, which might be either adoption or death by torture, although exchange of prisoners between enemies was sometimes practiced by the Indians. All prisoners were subjected to the ordeal of the *gantlet*, which meant that each unfortunate was forced to run between two rows of women and children who were provided with whips, clubs, knives, etc., with which to strike the prisoner as he ran. Those who fell from exhaustion were killed outright as unworthy to be saved, but those who reached the goal in safety might be adopted into an ohwachira and given the names of the dead Iroquois whose places they were to take. A captive offered for adoption to a family who had lost one of its number through accident or disease would probably be spared if he succeeded in "running the gauntlet." But if he were offered as a substitute for one who had been killed or taken prisoner by an enemy, he was consigned to torture and death. It is recorded that one warrior whose brother had been killed

PLATE 32

Wampum belts in the National Museum. Described by Beauchamp in Bull. N. Y. State Mus. No. 41, Vol. 8, 1901. Fig. 1. Belt said to have belonged to Tecumseh. White figures of men and houses. Two joining hands, with flag, indicate an alliance. Fig. 2. Belt probably not Indian work. Letters I. G. S. may be initials of John Graves Simcoe, Governor-General of Upper Canada, 1791-94. Fig. 3. Small belt, supposed to have belonged to the Mohawk, of white and purple beads, with thongs of twisted buckskin

PLATE 32

Wampum belts in the National Museum. Described by Beauchamp in Bull. N. Y. State Mus. No. 41, Vol. 8, 1901. Fig. 1. Belt said to have belonged to Tecumseh. White figures of men and houses. Two joining hands, with flag, indicate an alliance. Fig. 2. Belt probably not Indian work. Letters I. G. S. may be initials of John Graves Simcoe, Governor-General of Upper Canada, 1791-94. Fig. 3. Small belt, supposed to have belonged to the Mohawk, of white and purple beads, with thongs of twisted buckskin

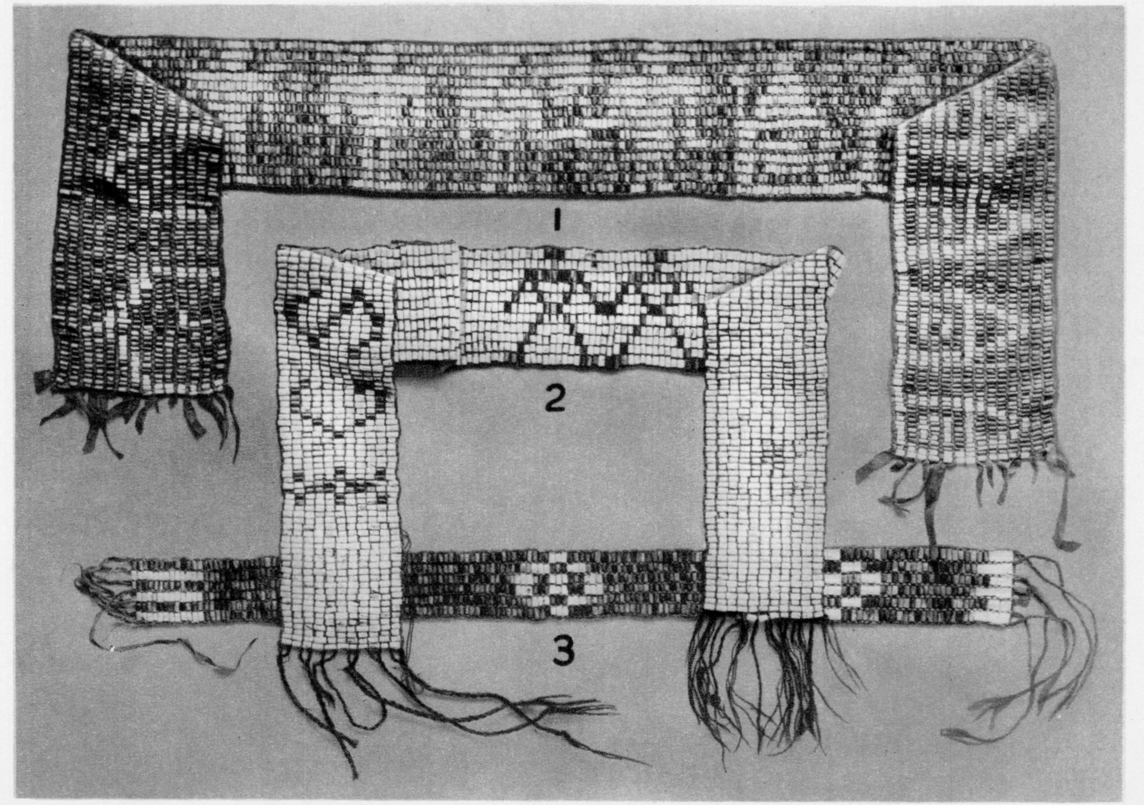
1
2
3

put to death no less than forty prisoners. The horrible custom of cannibalism in war, still practiced by the Iroquois at the time of the discovery, was in part at least due to their belief that by partaking of the flesh of a man who had died bravely under torture the participants in the act would imbibe something of the dead man's courage.

Another barbarous custom of the Iroquois and of some of the other Eastern tribes, but not originally so widespread as has been supposed, was that of scalping a fallen foe. This was accomplished by a deft circular incision of the knife, and a tug at the scalp-lock, usually allowed to grow longer for that purpose, by which the entire scalp, or a part of it, was removed. As a rule scalps were taken as trophies from those already dead, but the process, while painful, was not necessarily fatal, and was often practiced on a victim as a means of torture and occasionally served as a punishment and a warning to the scalped man's tribe, to which he might be returned. Usually, however, the entire head of a foe slain in battle was taken as a trophy of the slayer's valor.

The Iroquois were relentless enemies, and did not scruple to destroy their foes by any means in their power. Although not strong in numbers, their methods of warfare, particularly after they had been supplied by the Dutch with fire-arms, terrorized and intimidated the surrounding tribes so effectually that their mastery was acknowledged as far south as the Tennessee River. Many hostile tribes were practically exterminated, and the remnants adopted, helping thereby to swell the numbers and increase the prestige of the Iroquois. When the Tuscarora, a related people, were driven from their homeland by the white settlers of North Carolina, they took refuge with the Iroquois, who were thereafter known as the Six Nations.

In their domestic life the Iroquois were on a remarkably high plane. They held women in great honor and were kind and indulgent parents, seldom punishing their children, who, while enjoying the utmost liberty, were, as a rule, docile and obedient. Marriages were arranged by the parents of the young people and were solemnized by an exchange of gifts. Husband and wife were, of course, always of different clans, marriage between members of the same clan, and between those of the same phratry, being formerly forbidden.

With regard to the character of the Iroquois, Hale says:

> The Indians must be judged, like every other people, not by the traits which they display in the fury of a desperate warfare, but by their ordinary demeanor in time of peace, and especially by the character of their social and domestic life. . . . At home the Indians are the most kindly and generous of men. Constant good humor, unfailing courtesy, ready sympathy with distress, and a truly lavish liberality mark their intercourse with one another. . . .
>
> The Iroquois, who had seemed little better than demons to the missionaries while they knew them only as enemies to the French or their Huron allies, astonished them, on a nearer acquaintance, by the development of similar traits of natural goodness. . . .
>
> We become conscious of the fact that the aspect in which these Indians have presented themselves to the outside world has been in a large measure deceptive and factitious. The ferocity, craft and cruelty, which have been deemed their leading traits, have been merely the natural accompaniments of wars of self-preservation, and no more indicated their genuine character than the war-paint, plume and tomahawk of the warrior displayed the customary guise in which he appeared among his own people. The cruelties of war, when war is a struggle for national existence, are common to all races. The persistent desire for peace, pursued for centuries in federal unions, and in alliances and treaties with other nations, has been manifested by few as steadily as by the countrymen of Hiawatha [and Deganawida].

Such were the Iroquois, who were destined to match their prowess and their wit against the strong arm and trained intelligence of the white invaders of their land. Had the whites delayed their coming for another century, they might have found a truly formidable empire arrayed against them. And if the Iroquois had been left until the present day to work out their destiny, it is not at all improbable that they might have developed their wampum hieroglyphics into a genuine written language and have been by this time well on the way to a civilization of their own. What the character of that civilization would have been can only be conjectured; but, if Hale's estimate of them be not too greatly idealized, it is possible that these Indians might have succeeded in establishing an enduring State based on the six foundation stones of the League—health, happiness, righteousness, justice, power, and strength of character.

REFERENCES

BARTRAM, JOHN. Observations on the inhabitants, climate, soil, rivers, productions, animals, and other matters worthy of notice made by Mr. John Bartram in his travels from Pensilvania to Onondaga, Oswego, and the Lake Ontario in Canada. London, 1751.

CARTIER, JACQUES. Brief récit, et succinte narration, de la nauigation faicte es ysles de Canada. Paris, 1545.

CHAMPLAIN, SAMUEL DE. Voyages: ou journals ès découvertes de la Nouvelle France. Tomes I–II. Paris, 1830.

COLDEN, CADWALLADER. The history of the Five Indian Nations of Canada, which are dependent on the province of New York in America. London, 1747.

CUSICK, DAVIS. Sketches of ancient history of the Six Nations. 2d ed. Tuscarora, N. Y., 1828.

HALE, HORATIO. Hiawatha and the Iroquois Confederation: a study in anthropology. Salem, Mass., 1881.

——, editor. The Iroquois book of rites. (Brinton's library of aboriginal literature, No. 2.) Philadelphia, 1883.

HERIOT, GEORGE. Travels through the Canadas. London, 1807.

HEWITT, J. N. B. Iroquoian Cosmology. First part. 21st Ann. Rep. Bur. Amer. Ethnol. Washington, 1904.

—— The requickening address of the League of the Iroquois. *In:* Holmes anniversary volume, pp. 163–179. Washington, 1916.

—— Some esoteric aspects of the League of the Iroquois. Proc. 19th Int. Cong. Americanists, 1915, pp. 322–326. Washington, 1917.

—— A constitutional league of peace in the stone age of America: the League of the Iroquois and its constitution. Smithsonian Inst. Ann. Rep. 1918, pp. 527–545. Washington, 1920.

HEWITT, J. N. B. Iroquoian Cosmology. Second part, with introduction and notes. 43rd Ann. Rep. Bur. Amer. Ethnol. [In press.]

KENTON, EDNA, editor. The Indians of North America, from "The Jesuit relations and allied documents: travels and explorations of the Jesuit missionaries in New France, 1610–1791," edited by Reuben Gold Thwaites. Vols. I–II. New York (Harcourt, Brace & Co.), [1927].

LESCARBOT, MARC. Histoire de la Novvelle-France. Paris, 1612.

MORGAN, LEWIS H. League of the Ho-dé-no-sau-nee or Iroquois. Rochester, New York, and Boston, 1851.

—— Houses and house-life of the American Aborigines. Cont. N. Amer. Ethnol. Vol. 4. Washington, 1881.

SAGARD THEODAT, GABRIEL. Histoire de Canada. Tomes I–IV. Paris, 1636.

—— Le grand voyage du pays des Hurons. Tomes I–II. Paris, 1865.

SMITH, ERMINNIE A. Myths of the Iroquois. 2d Ann. Rep. Bur. Ethnol. Washington, 1883.

CHAPTER V

CLIFF DWELLERS AND THEIR DESCENDANTS: THE PUEBLOS

WHILE the French and English were struggling for dominion in the East, other adventurers of a quite different type had already set about the conquest of the more alluring empire of the Southwest. The invaders of the northeastern coast were, for the most part, permanent colonists bent upon establishing homes in a rude and savage land. The native inhabitants of that land seemed to these determined pioneers merely so many obstacles to be cleared away like the forests in order to make room for the fields and homesteads of the new Americans.

The Spaniards, in the South and West, had another purpose. Though obliged to relinquish the hope of finding the eastern coast of India on the farther side of the Atlantic, they still dreamed of boundless treasures hidden away somewhere on the vast new continent. Their aim, therefore, was to explore and possess the country rather than to settle it. Led by the dream of conquest, they had sailed westward through the Gulf of Mexico to the land of the Aztecs, only to find there a barbarous people, more advanced than their eastern neighbors in many ways, but far from possessing the riches which the Spaniards sought.

The disappointed conquerors were the more ready, therefore, to heed rumors which began to reach them from time to time of a greater and richer kingdom to the north. These reports told of a fabulous Province of Cibola where were seven wonderful cities, filled with treasures of gold and silver and turquoise, to be reached only by a long journey through trackless desert lands.

Undaunted by the difficulties and thinking only of the vast riches in prospect, a force of 400 Spaniards and 20,000 friendly Indians (according to Castañeda, the chronicler of the expedition) was got together under the command of Nuño de Guzman. The difficulties of travel proved so great, however, that the army got no farther than the borderland of New Spain, where Guzman, in 1530, established the town of Culiacan to mark the northern outpost of the Spanish possessions in the province called New Galicia, and hastened back again to Mexico City.

Three years earlier an expedition of 300 men under Pámfilo de Narvaez, likewise in search of fabulous treasures, had been sent out from Spain to explore the peninsula of Florida. Of this luckless band only four, including their leader, Cabeza de Vaca, and a negro called Stephen or Estevan, survived and, after eight years of incredible suffering, succeeded in making their way westward to the Spanish province of New Galicia. There they related their adventures, embellishing them with marvelous stories of the riches which, they had heard, were to be found in the still unexplored country.

Spurred on by renewed visions of great cities and boundless wealth in the region to the north, the Spaniards nevertheless wisely determined first to test the truth of these new reports. Accordingly the Governor of New Galicia, Francisco Vasquez de Coronado, dispatched a small scouting party, under the leadership of the Franciscan, Fray Marcos de Nizza, and with the negro Estevan as guide, to explore the country. In a short time Fray Marcos returned, reporting that Estevan had reached Cibola but had been killed there by the natives; and that he himself, following after, had seen one of the Seven Cities from a distance, and was satisfied, from its appearance and from the reports which had been sent back to him from time to time by Estevan, that it was a rich and populous land.

Soon afterwards Coronado's famous expedition, with Fray Marcos as guide, set out to find the Seven Cities. The friar faithfully conducted the leader, and his mail-clad mounted troops and foot-soldiers armed with cross-bows and firearms, to the province of Cibola and its Seven Cities, which proved to be the country occupied by the seven ancient pueblos of the Zuñi Indians. The account of Castañeda reflects the bitter disappointment of the Spaniards. He relates that when the soldiers got their first glimpse of the "city" which the Spaniards called Cibola and which has been identified as the ancient Zuñi pueblo of Hawik'uh, "such were the curses that were hurled at Friar Marcos that I pray God may protect him from them." He continues:

> It is a little, unattractive village looking as if it had been crumpled all up together. There are mansions in New Spain which make a better appearance at a distance. It is a village of about 200 warriors, is three and four stories high, with the houses small and having only a few rooms, and without a courtyard. One yard serves for each section. The people of the whole district had collected here, for there are seven villages in the province, and some of the others are even larger and stronger than Cibola. These folks waited for the army drawn up by divisions in front of the village. When they refused to have peace on the terms the interpreters extended to them, but appeared defiant, the Santiago [the Spanish war-cry, used in battle with the "Infidels"] was given, and they were at once put to flight. The Spaniards then attacked the village, which was taken with not a little difficulty, since they held the narrow and crooked entrance [defending themselves by hurling great stones from their terraces upon the Spaniards]. . . . But the first fury of the Spaniards could not be resisted, and in less than an hour they entered the village and captured it. They discovered food there, which was the thing they were most in need of. After this the whole province was at peace.

After the subjugation of the Zuñi, the Spaniards visited and seized most of the other Indian pueblos. Castañeda lists some sixty-six villages and estimates their population at about 20,000. From these towns, in spite of their

PLATE 33

Casa Blanca, Canyon de Chelly, Arizona. Ruined cliff dwelling and pueblo, deserted before the white man's advent

PLATE 34

Ancient cave dwellings of the Rio Grande, New Mexico

poverty, Coronado replenished his supplies of food and clothing, and leaving part of his force to hold the new possessions, pressed on with the rest of the army to follow another rainbow. This new object of the Spaniards' quest was called Quivira, and their chief informant and guide, who had told of great riches to be found there, was a certain treacherous Indian, an adopted captive of the Pueblos, whom his white dupes called "the Turk." Reaching Quivira after many hardships and finding that it was merely the tent-village of a wandering Indian tribe, the disappointed adventurers promptly garroted "the Turk," who confessed that he had led them out on the plains at the instigation of the Pueblos in the hope that they might lose their way and be slaughtered by some hostile Indian tribe. After long wandering on the trackless prairie, Coronado and his little army at last succeeded in finding their way back to their companions in the Pueblo country.

Two years of fruitless exploration and barren conquests finally convinced Coronado that the quest was vain; baffled, disheartened, and ill, he led his soldiers back to New Spain, leaving behind him a number of Franciscan friars to establish missions and convert to Christianity the 20,000 (or perhaps only 10,000) new subjects of the King of Spain. Thus nearly four hundred years ago the "blessings of civilization and the Christian religion" were brought to the Pueblo Indians. Yet when first visited by Americans, some three hundred years later, these Indians were found to be still living in their ancient way, for the most part, and still practicing the rites of their own religion. Finding them difficult to subdue and too poor to exploit, the Spaniards, after nominally subjugating them, had allowed them to remain in undisturbed possession of their homes.

The Pueblo Indians, although speaking four distinct languages, of which there are several separate dialects, and occupying detached towns that are entirely independent and self-governing, must nevertheless be regarded as a single group because of the similarity of their traditions, customs, and religious practices, a similarity strengthened by frequent intermarriage.

Their country comprises the high plateaus or mesas of New Mexico and Arizona. These are literally tablelands—flat-topped, precipitous heights rising in terraces to the foot-hills of the Rocky Mountains. This is an arid land, parched by a blazing sun in summer and in winter swept by wind-driven snows. It is the country of the canyons, which have been cut by the rushing mountain torrents to a depth of thousands of feet through the soft sandstone formation of the mesas. Many streams have seemingly exhausted themselves in this gigantic task, for they are today no more than rivulets almost lost in the depths of the gorges, sometimes, indeed, quite smothered in their sandy beds before they have found an outlet into some larger stream. In summer, however, when the mountain snows melt, and brief but terrific thunderstorms are frequent, the rivers are often turned into raging torrents that overspread their banks and dash themselves against the walls of their deep prisons.

Ages ago the ancestors of the Pueblo Indians found in the sheer walls of these river gorges a safe retreat from the fiercer tribes around them. Here they hid, building their stone houses in the deeper recesses of the cliffs and scooping out cavelike dwellings in the softer strata of the precipices. The ruins of these ancient homes, abandoned long before the coming of the Spaniards, are found as far north as Colorado and Utah. In the course of centuries, because of overcrowding or for other reasons, the cliff dwellers moved farther and farther south along the river courses, still building or burrowing in the canyon walls and still cultivating the arable land along the river banks. Even when they began to construct their houses on the mesas above the river gorges, they long retained the old home sites as convenient places in summer for overlooking and guarding the growing crops.

In his novel "The Delight Makers," Bandelier has pictured such a cliff-dwelling community and has peopled with the life of bygone ages a certain site actually discovered and described by him. This is the canyon of the Tyuoni, or the Rito de los Frijoles, a small tributary of the Rio Grande in New Mexico, nearly opposite the town of Santa Fé. It is supposed to have been the ancient home of the tribe of Queres (Keres, or Keresan Indians) who now occupy the pueblo of Cochiti. In "The Delight Makers" Bandelier describes them as they must have lived long before the Spaniards broke the quiet of ancient Cochiti with the trampling of horses and the barking of guns. Hundreds of years before that event the Rito was already deserted. Today nothing remains but the ruins of the former homes and the traditions of the modern Queres. The young hero of Bandelier's story is typical of the Pueblos as they must have appeared to the Spaniards, and is thus described:

> His costume was very plain. A garment of unbleached cotton, coarsely woven, covered the body as low as the knee. The garment, sleeveless and soiled by wear, was tied over the right shoulder. A reddish-brown scarf or belt of the same material fastened it around the waist. Feet, arms, and the left shoulder were bare. Primitive as was the costume, there was, nevertheless, an attempt here and there at decoration. The belt was ornamented with black and white stitches; from each ear hung a turquoise suspended by a cotton thread, and a necklace of coloured pebbles strung on yucca fibre encircled the neck.

Where the width of the canyon permitted, the cliff dwellers often built pueblos in every essential similar to those of today. In their ruins are found traces of the curious structures called *kivas* or (by the Spaniards) *estufas*. Of these semisubterranean buildings, Bandelier says:

> A circular structure thirty feet in diameter rose a few feet only above the soil, like the upper part of a sunken cylinder. Its top was

flat, and large flags of stone formed a rough staircase leading to its roof. In the center, a square opening appeared, out of which a tall beam, notched at regular intervals like a primitive ladder, protruded, and down which also the beam disappeared as if it extended into the bowels of the earth. This edifice, half underground, half above the soil, was what today is called in New Mexico an estufa. . . .

The estufas were more numerous in a single pueblo formerly than they are now. Nor are they always sunken. At the Rito there were at least ten, five of which were circular chambers in the rock of the cliffs. These chambers or halls were, in the times we speak of, gathering places for men exclusively. No woman was permitted to enter, unless for the purpose of carrying food to the inmates. Each clan had its own estufa, and the young men slept in it under the surveillance of one or more of the aged principals, until they married and frequently even afterward.

There the young men became acquainted with the affairs of their individual connections, and little by little also with the business of the tribe. There, during the long evenings of winter, old men taught them the songs and prayers embodying traditions and myths, first of their own clan, then of their tribe. The estufa was school, club-house, nay, armory to a certain extent. It was more. Many of the prominent religious exercises took place in it. The estufa on special occasions became transformed into a temple for the clan who had reared it.

It will be noticed that the estufas, or kivas, of the Pueblo Indians fulfilled many of the same purposes as the kashims of the Western Eskimo. They were built wholly by the men; the dwelling houses, chiefly by the women, although the men brought the timber used in the ceilings, which often had to be transported for long distances, and put it in place, also assisting with the heavier stone construction. The Pueblos used stone and clay (or *adobe*, as the Spaniards call it) in building their houses, not so much for the sake of durability or safety as for the same reason that the Eskimo used snow and the Iroquois bark—because they were the materials that happened to be at hand. For this reason, largely, the ancient buildings in the canyons were of stone construction, made from the bowlders along the streams or the sandstone of the cliffs, merely cemented together by mud—not true adobe, which is a sort of plastic clay. Later pueblos, erected on

PLATE 35

The foot trail to the pueblo of Acoma, New Mexico. Oldest inhabited settlement in the United States

PLATE 36

The horse trail to Acoma Pueblo, New Mexico. This and the foot trail are the only means of approach

the mesas farther south, were built almost wholly of the sun-dried adobe bricks on a foundation of stone, the whole covered with a smooth layer of the adobe. This was put on by hand, and in such ancient walls as are now standing, the marks of small palms and fingers still remain, showing that then as now the women and children were the plasterers. Substantial as these dwellings were, they were by no means permanent abiding places for their builders, who moved on from one site to another, usually in a southerly direction, leaving their former homes as storehouses in which men of our own time find many strange treasures of the past.

The same story of sites abandoned, of massive buildings, which must have required the work of generations to erect, deserted for new ones built at a like cost of time and labor, has been repeated over and over again; until, as Bandelier says, not a single pueblo inhabited at the present day occupies the same site as in Coronado's time, with the exception of Acoma, built by a tribe of Keresan Indians, which is the oldest occupied settlement in the United States.

Acoma stands on the top of a mesa which Lummis describes as "one rock—a dizzy air-island above the plain—three hundred and fifty-seven feet high [and seven thousand feet above sea level], seventy acres in area upon its irregular but practically level top—a stone table upheld by ineffable precipices which are not merely perpendicular but in great part actually overhanging. The contour of those cliffs is an endless enchantment. . . . It is the noblest specimen of fantastic erosion on the continent." Upon this Gibraltar of the Southwest, stands the "sky-built city," the pueblo of Acoma, three stories high, forming a solid wall at the back, but terraced in front, each story opening on the roof of the story beneath, "like a flight of three gigantic steps." As a rule the only entrance to the rooms of the first story is through hatchways in the roof, which are reached by ladders on the outside and provided with other ladders for descent inside. Very small doorways open out on the roofs of the first and second stories, and both of the upper roofs are reached by steps on the division walls which separate the houses from each other. The rooms from front to back are communicating, and each floor (sometimes two or three floors) is occupied by one family. The whole building houses about 500 people. Although the oldest of the occupied pueblos, Acoma has nevertheless suffered some changes of Spanish origin; the corner firepits are now provided with adobe flues, topped by curious chimneys made of a series of unbottomed earthen jars; the hatchways and the doorways, once covered only with skins or cotton blankets, are now securely fastened with doors of wood; while the window openings are often inclosed with sheets of gypsum, and sometimes with American glass.

Before the coming of the Spaniards these Pueblo Indians had no four-footed friend or servant to do their bidding or to bear their burdens. Of the building of Acoma, Lummis says:

> No other town in the world is reached only by such vertiginous trails, or rather by such ladders of the rock; and yet up these awful rocks the patient Quéres have brought upon their backs every timber, every stone, every bit of adobe mud to build that strange city and its marvellous church. There are timbers fourteen inches square and forty feet long, brought by human muscle alone from the mountains twenty miles away. The church walls are sixty feet high and ten feet through; and the building covers more ground than any modern cathedral in the United States. The graveyard in front, nearly two hundred feet square, took forty years in the building; for first the gentle toilers had to frame a giant box with stone walls, a box forty feet deep at the outer edge, and then fill it backful by backful with earth from the far plain. In the weird stone "ladders" by which the top of the cliff is reached, the patient moccasined feet of forgotten centuries have sunk their imprint six inches deep in the rock. Antiquity and mystery haunt every nook. The very air is hazy with romance. How have they lived and loved and suffered here in their skyward home, these quiet Hano Oshatch—the Children of the Sun.

Ancient as Acoma is—and it was an ancient city when the Spaniards first saw it—there are legends of a still older Acoma, which suffered a tragic fate in the dim distant past. The pueblo then stood on the great rock now known as the Mesa Encantada, or the Enchanted Mesa, three miles north of its present site, and twice as high. On a day when the people were down in the plain beneath, tending their crops, an earthquake split the mesa and overthrew the steep ladder-rock which was the only means of ascent. The people in the plain were thus made homeless "and three doomed women, left at home, were shut aloft to perish upon the accursed cliff."

Even today the people must descend from the heights to do their farming on the plateau, where their crops have been greatly increased both in kind and quantity since the Spaniards added wheat to the original staple, corn, and many vegetables to the ancient beans, squashes, and melons, besides planting orchards of peach trees. Where once turkeys were the only creatures shepherded—kept for their feathers chiefly, as were also captive eagles—flocks of sheep and goats, and herds of horses and cattle are now pastured, while patient burros carry burdens even to the top of the mesa up a specially constructed trail. The ancient way of farming is today being rapidly replaced by more modern and profitable methods. In order to be near their flocks and crops, the Queres have built in their well-watered valley a summer pueblo called appropriately Acomita. And practically every farmer is the owner of at least one horse.

Greatly changed as are their outdoor occupations, life at the pueblo itself—as in most Indian pueblos—goes on much as it did when the Queres lived in the Rito, so many centuries ago. The women still grind their corn at the grinding stones which are found in every household today and in every ruined pueblo and cliff dwelling of the past. These stones, called *metates*, are flat slabs set slantingly in small compartments made of adobe walls about two feet high. There are usually three metates that are used successively in grinding the corn, the first being the roughest and the last the smoothest stone. The grinding is invariably done by women, one of whom kneels beside each metate, armed with a stone shaped somewhat like a flat rolling pin. The first scatters on the rough slab in front of her unbroken kernels of corn which she then proceeds to crush with her stone pin, using an up-and-down motion like that of a woman scrubbing clothes on a washboard. When a sufficient quantity of the corn has been crushed, it is passed to the next worker who in like manner grinds it on her smoother stone, whence it passes to the third woman who completes the process by means of her still smoother metate. In this way the corn is reduced to a fairly smooth meal. This is the ancient method of the Pueblos as is shown by the remains of metates found in even the oldest cliff dwellings. The Pueblos today grind their wheat into flour by the same tedious process.

The meal is made into a thin batter and baked on flat stones in the open fireplace today just as it was when the Queres lived in the Rito. Except for some few American innovations the pueblos are as bare of furniture now as they were before the white men found them. It seems strange that with their comparatively permanent dwellings, the Indians should not have constructed some sort of tables and chairs. But they were content with rude benches—usually of adobe or stone—built around the walls of the room. The earthen or flagged floors—always scrupulously clean—serve as a commodious couch on which at night are spread skins and blankets that by day are rolled up and placed on the benches. During the day much time is spent on the sunny terraces outdoors.

One of the tasks of the women of Acoma is bringing water to the pueblo. This strenuous but picturesque custom is thus described by Lummis:

Modern water jars from the pueblo of Acoma, New Mexico. In the National Museum

There are no dwellings on the southern mesa; but thither leads—down the side of the crag-hyphen and up again—a trail, deep worn in the rock, to the great reservoir, chief of the many hollows which serve Acoma for water-works. . . . In the high, dry air of this altitude these natural stone reservoirs keep the rain-water cool and fresh the whole year around; and the supply almost never fails. When it does, there are fine springs in the plain whereupon to draw. Every drop of water in the house is brought by the women in three to five gallon *tinajas* upon their heads—an exercise which may be largely responsible for the superb necks and chests and the confident poise of head notable among all Pueblo women. There is no more picturesque sight than the long file of these comely maids and matrons marching homeward in the sunset glow with their careless head-burdens.

At the time of Coronado's invasion the people of Acoma fared better than did the Zuñi, since they did not resist the Spanish conquerors, but received them kindly, believing them to be gods. Half a century later, in 1598, when another Spanish soldier, Juan de Oñate, visited them, the Acomas voluntarily submitted, intending to entrap the Spaniards later. Oñate and his immediate followers, unsuspicious of the danger, escaped it by pushing on toward Tusayan, the name the Spaniards gave to the country of the Hopi. But Oñate's lieutenant, Juan de Zaldivar, arriving later on his way to join the commander, was enticed, with his few followers, by the Acomas up to their city, where all but five were put to death with the clubs and clumsy flint knives of their treacherous hosts. These five succeeded in breaking away from their assailants, and —since there was no other way of escape—hurled themselves from the top of the cliff, wounded as they were. Miraculously, one only jumped to his death. The rest escaped to join Oñate's army in Tusayan and to there find avengers for their murdered comrades. A month later the citadel of Acoma was stormed by a determined band of seventy men led by Zaldivar, who after three days of hand-to-hand fighting finally forced the people of Acoma to submit to the power of Spain.

Thirty years afterward, in 1629, the Acomas were converted to Christianity (outwardly, at least) by Fray Juan Ramirez, one of the heroic band of Franciscan friars who followed in the wake of Spain's conquests as the Jesuit priests did for France. Although the Acomas tried at first to transfix him with their arrows before he could ascend to their high city, the heroic friar withstood their wrath and finally succeeded in winning them to his faith. He lived alone among the people of Acoma for twenty years, teaching them not only religion but their letters also, and inspiring them to build their first church.

In 1680 the Acomas joined with the other Pueblos in a general massacre of all the Spaniards, in the course of which the solitary friar, Lucas Maldonado, then in Acoma, was set upon and killed, and the church built for Fray Juan Ramirez was torn down. For only twelve years did the Pueblos keep their independence. Then, in 1692, Diego de Vargas reconquered the country, and Acoma surrendered peaceably to the Spanish arms. After once more rebelling in 1696, the Acomas again yielded, and about 1700 the Mission was reestablished and the church rebuilt. Since then there has been peace in Acoma, but for a generation or more there has been no resident priest to minister to the people, who seem more and more inclined to revert to the pagan religion of their forefathers.

The history of Acoma in the three hundred and fifty years of the Spanish occupation has been repeated with varying details in most of the other pueblos. As has been said, the Zuñi were the most intractable, rebelling again and again, and even deserting their homes for others which they built on a high tableland called Thunder (or Corn) Mountain. There they lived for twelve years after the great rebellion of 1680, until de Vargas came and succeeded in coaxing them down once more to the valley of the Zuñi River. They, too, were outwardly good Catholics, while still practicing, at first secretly and today openly, the rites of their ancient faith.

CLIFF DWELLERS AND THEIR DESCENDANTS

As Bandelier studied the ways of the Queres, so Frank H. Cushing devoted his life to solving the intricacies of Zuñi psychology and mythology, even living among them for years as a Zuñi in order to win their confidence, for no Spaniard nor other foreigner had ever before been admitted to their religious ceremonies.

Buried in half-forgotten numbers of the *Century Magazine* is Cushing's vivid account of his first visit to the Zuñi and of his adoption by them. How he received his marching orders and his first impression of Zuñiland he recounts as follows:

One hot summer day in 1879, as I was sitting in my office in the ivy-mantled old South Tower of the Smithsonian Institution, a messenger boy tapped at my door and said:

"Professor Baird wishes to see you, sir."

The professor, picking up his umbrella and papers, came toward the door as I entered.

"Have n't I heard you say you would like to go to New Mexico to study the cliff-houses and Pueblo Indians?"

"Yes, sir."

"Would you still like to go?"

"Yes, sir."

"Very well, then, be ready to accompany Colonel Stevenson's collecting party, as ethnologist, within four days. I want you to find out all you can about some typical tribe of Pueblo Indians. Make your own choice of field, and use your own methods; only get the information. You will probably be gone three months. Write me frequently. I'm in a hurry this evening. Look to Major Powell, of the Bureau of Ethnology, if you want further directions. Good-day."

Thus it happened that, on a sultry afternoon in late September, by no means firmly seated in the first saddle I had ever bestridden, I was belaboring a lazy Government mule just at the entrance of a pass between two great banded red-and-gray sandstone mesas, in the midst of a waterless wilderness. . . . Beyond the pass I followed the winding road up a series of cedar-clad sand-hills to where they abruptly terminated in a black lava descent of nearly two hundred feet. . . .

Descending, I chanced to meet, over toward the river, an Indian. He was bare-headed, his hair banged even with his eyebrows in front, and done up in a neat knot behind, with long locks hanging down either side. He wore a red shirt and white cotton pantalets, slitted at the sides from the knees down so as to expose his bare legs, and rawhide soled moccasins. Strings of shell-beads around his neck, and a leather belt around his waist, into which were stuck a boomerang or two, completed his costume. Knitting-work in hand, he left his band of dirty white and black sheep and snuffling goats in charge of a wise-looking, grizzled-faced, bob-tailed mongrel cur, and came, with a sort of shuffling dog-trot, toward the road, calling out, "Hai! hai!" and extending his hand, with a most good-natured smile.

I shook the proffered hand warmly, and said, "Zuñi?"

"E!" exclaimed the Indian, as he reverentially breathed on my hand and from his own. . . .

I hastened on with all the speed I could scourge out of my obstinate, kicking mule, down the road to where the rivulet crossed it, and up again, nearer and nearer to the strange structures.

Imagine numberless long, box-shaped adobe ranches, connected with one another in extended rows and squares, with others, less and less numerous, piled up on them lengthwise and crosswise, in two, three, even six stories, each receding from the one below it like the steps of a broken stairflight,—as it were, a gigantic pyramidal mud honeycomb with far outstretching base,—and you can gain a fair conception of the architecture of Zuñi.

Everywhere this structure bristled with ladder-poles, chimneys, and rafters. The ladders were heavy and long, with carved slab cross-pieces at the tops, and leaned at all angles against the roofs. The chimneys looked more like huge bamboo-joints than anything else I can compare them with, for they were made up of bottomless earthen pots, set one upon the other and cemented together with mud, so that they stood up, like many-lobed, oriental spires, from every roof-top. Wonderfully like the holes in an ant-hill seemed the little windows and door-ways which everywhere pierced the walls of this giant habitation, and like ant-hills themselves seemed the curious little round-topped ovens which stood here and there along these walls or on the terrace edges. . . .

Not an Indian was anywhere to be seen, save on the topmost terraces of this strange city. There hundreds of them were congregated gazing so intently down into one of the plazas beyond that none of them observed my approach, until I had hastily dismounted, tied my mule to a corral post, climbed the refuse-strewn hill and two or three ladders leading up to the house-tops. The regular *thud*, *thud* of rattles and drums, the cadence of rude music which sounded more like the soughing of a storm wind amid the forests of a mountain than the accompaniment of a dance, urged me forward, until I was suddenly confronted by forty or fifty of the men, who came rushing toward me with excited discussion and gesticulation. One of them approached and spoke something in Spanish, motioning me away, but I did not understand him, so I grasped his hand and breathed on it as I had

PLATE 38

Pueblo of Zuñi, New Mexico. Largest of the pueblos which are still occupied

PLATE 39

Ceremony of the Sword Swallowers, pueblo of Zuñi, New Mexico seen the herder do. Lucky thought! The old man was pleased, smiled, breathed in turn on my hand, and then hastily addressed the others, who, after watching me with approving curiosity, gathered around to shake hands and exchange breaths. . . .

At last, gaining my wished-for position on the edge of the terrace, I came face to face with nearly the whole population of Zuñi. The music had ceased and the dancers had temporarily retired, but all over the upper terraces were young men in groups and pairs, jauntily mantled in red, green, blue, black, and figured blankets, only the upper portions of their painted faces and occasional patches of their silver-bedecked persons being exposed. Here and there an elaborately plumed straw hat surmounted one of these enveloped statues, aside from which not an article of civilized apparel appeared. Opposite, women and girls, attired in clean, blue-black, embroidered blanket dresses, neat, softly draped head-shawls, and huge-legged, white buckskin moccasins, were standing and sitting on the lower terraces, or in one side of the court below. . . . Old, gray-haired men, muffled in heavy, striped serapes, sat or squatted around, or leaned on their crooked sticks. Innumerable children, some naked, others half clad in tattered cotton shirts and short trousers, were chasing one another about the terraces, wrestling, screeching, or pelting any stray dog that came around, while a few imitated the older people by sitting in silent expectation.

After a brief interval, a priest, with plumed head and trailing white buckskin mantle, gravely stepped in through a tunnel under the houses, scattering on the ground, as he came, sacred meal from a vessel which he held in one hand, while with the other he waved a beautiful wand of macaw plumes. He was followed by some twenty dancers elaborately costumed from head to foot. Close-fitting plumed wigs covered their heads, and black, long-bearded, yellow-eyed masks, with huge rows of teeth from ear to ear, red tongues lolling out between them, gave frightful grinning expressions to their faces. Their half-nude bodies were painted black and yellow, while badges of buckskin were crossed over their shoulders, and skirts of the same material, secured at the waists with elaborately embroidered and fringed sashes, depended to the ankles. Their feet were incased in green and red buskins, and to the legs were bound clanging rattles of tortoise-shell and deer-hoofs. Their necks were decorated with heavy necklaces of shell beads and coral, shining disks of *haliotis* [shell] hanging from them in front and behind; while the arms were bedecked with green bands, fluttering turkey plumes, silver bangles and wrist-guards of the same material. Each carried in his right hand a painted gourd rattle, in his left, bow, arrows and long wands of yucca.

As the leader sounded his rattle they all fell into a semicircular line across the plaza, and began stepping rapidly up and down, swaying from side to side, facing first one way, then the other, in perfect unison, and in exact time to their rattles and strange measures of wild music.

Sprawling about the ground in front of and behind the row of dancers, in attitudes grotesque yet graceful, I observed for the first time ten most ludicrous characters, nude save for their skirts and neck-cloths of black tattered blanketing, their heads entirely covered with flexible, round, warty masks. Both masks and persons were smeared over with pink mud, giving the appearance of reptiles in human form that had ascended from the bottom of some muddy pool and dried so nearly the color of the ground and the surrounding houses that at first it had been difficult to distinguish them.

One of them seated himself a little way off and began pounding, with a short, knotty war-club, a buffalo-skin bale, which he held between his knees, while the others, motionless save for their heads, which they were continually twisting and screwing about, or nodding in time to the drummer's strokes, kept up a series of comments and banterings which sometimes convulsed the whole throng of spectators with laughter.

In a footnote Cushing explains that "these were the *Keó-ye-mo-shi*, or 'Guardians of the "Sacred Dance,"' whose business it is to entertain the spectators during the intervals of the dance, by rude buffoonery and jokes, in which comic speeches and puns play an important part. The office is sacred, and elective annually from among the priesthood of the nation." These so-called clown priests are found in all the Pueblo tribes, usually forming a distinct order of the priesthood. Among the Queres they are called the *Koshare*, the "Delight Makers" of Bandelier's novel.

Thus auspiciously was the adventurous young scientist initiated into his life work. But his purpose of winning the confidence and friendship of the Zuñi people was not accomplished until he had succeeded in overcoming their first suspicions and instinctive hostility and had faced with tact and courage more than one situation involving personal risk and danger.

All went well until the Indians observed their young

guest, on one occasion, busily sketching in colors the dancers in the courtyard preparing for one of their sacred dances. This time, however, their suspicions gave way to admiration. "They were wonder-struck," says Cushing, "and would pass their fingers over the figures as though they expected to feel them. Failing in this, they would look at the back of the leaves, as children look behind mirrors to see what has become of the images."

On another occasion, the young scientist had sketched the portrait of a pretty little girl. The child's grandmother, looking over the sketches, recognized the portrait. "She shook her head, frowned, and covering her face with her hands, began to cry and howl most dolefully. . . . At intervals during the remainder of the day, I could hear her talking, scolding, and sobbing over what she regarded as a great misfortune to her family."

It was then that Cushing, in order to overcome the unreasonable opposition of the Zuñi to his sketching, decided to live among them and share their life. He was given a room in the house of the Zuñi governor, an old chief who had been disposed to favor the bold investigator from the beginning.

Here, after the departure of the rest of his party for another field of investigation, Cushing was further initiated into the Zuñi way of living, although his writing and sketching were still frowned upon and he himself was kept under close surveillance. The governor seemed especially anxious to persuade the young man to forswear civilization and become altogether Zuñi.

Neither persuasion, warning, nor threats, however, availed to induce the scientist to give up the objectionable practice of carrying his notebook about with him wherever he went and making notes and sketches of all that he saw. The governor advised him against it; council of chiefs was held; and they even attempted forcibly to prevent him from indulging in the unpopular habit.

A second council was called [this time in secret]. . . . It discussed various plans for either disposing of me, or compelling me to desist. Among others was the proposal that I be thrown off the great mesa [Thunder Mountain] . . . but it was urged that should this be done, "*Wa-sin-to-na*" [the usual Pueblo name for the United States Government] might visit my death on the whole nation. . . .

At last a plan was hit upon which the simple natives thought would free them from all their perplexities. Surely, no objection could be offered to the "death of a Navajo" [by which was meant a sacrifice of life, either animal or human, at the Great Knife Dance,—the ancient war *Ká-ka* of the Zuñi]. Forthwith the Knife Dance was ordered, as it was thought possible that the appearance of this dance would be sufficient to intimidate me, without recourse to the additional violence. . . .

When the great dance appeared . . . the dancers filed in through the covered way, preceded by a priest, and arranged themselves in a line across the court. Their costumes were not unlike those of the first dance I had witnessed, save that the masks were flatter and smeared with blood, and the beards and hair were long and streaming. In their right hands the performers carried huge, leaf-shaped, blood-stained knives of stone, which, during the movements of the dance, they brandished wildly in the air, in time and accompaniment to their wild songs and regular steps, often pointing them toward me.

As the day advanced, spectators began to throng the terraces and court, few, however, approaching to where I was sitting [on one of the terraces of the dance court]; and the masked clowns made their appearance.

I had been busy with memoranda and had succeeded in sketching three or four of the costumes, when there dashed into the court two remarkable characters. Their bodies, nude save for short breech-clouts, were painted with ashes. Skull-caps, tufted with split corn-husks, and heavy streaks of black under their eyes and over their mouths, gave them a most ghastly and ferocious appearance. Each wore around his neck a short, twisted rope of black fibre, and each was armed with a war-club or ladder-round.

These terrifying apparitions, shouting "Kill him! Kill him!" began to climb a ladder to the roof at the point where Cushing was sitting, and where a number of Indians had already collected around him, cutting off all chance of escape. The young scientist, finding himself thus at the mercy of an infuriated band of savage fanatics, displayed

PLATE 40

A Zuñi matron carrying water jar. Unmarried women wear their hair coiled over the ears

PLATE 41

Ceremonial dance of the Corn Maidens, pueblo of Zuñi, New Mexico

a coolness and resourcefulness worthy of a soldier facing like fearful odds on the field of battle:

I forced a laugh, quickly drew my hunting knife from the bottom of the pouch, waved it two or three times in the air so that it flashed in the sunlight, and laid it conspicuously in front of me. Still smiling, I carefully placed my book—open—by the side of the pouch and laid a stone on it to show that I intended to resume the sketching. Then I half rose, clinging to the ladder-pole with one hand, and holding the other in readiness to clutch the knife. The one below [on the ladder] suddenly grabbed the skirt of the other and shouted, "Hold on, he is a *ki-he!* a *ki-he!* [by which he meant a friend sent by the gods]. We have been mistaken. This is no Navajo."

In order to appease the gods, however—and the spectators—a dog was immediately procured and sacrificed with hideous barbarity.

Whether the Indians had really designed to murder me, or merely to intimidate me, my coolness, as well as my waving of the knife toward the sun, both largely accidental, had made a great impression on them. For never afterward was I molested to any serious extent in attempting to make notes and sketches.

That night, the old chief was profuse in his congratulations and words of praise. I had completed in him, that day, the winning of the truest of friends; and by so doing had decided the fate of my mission among the Zuñi Indians.

Soon afterwards the old governor prevailed upon Cushing to adopt the Zuñi style of dress, and gave him a separate little house to live in, where he was required by his new guardian to sleep in the cold on a hard bed made by spreading sheepskins on the floor, with only two blankets as covers, in order, as the old chief expressed it, to "harden his meat." To all these discomforts the young man cheerfully submitted, for he was now permitted to attend even the most sacred assemblies to which no outsider had, in modern times, ever been admitted. Thus did this young soldier on the outposts of scientific knowledge obey the orders of his superior office. "Use your own methods," Secretary Baird had said, "only, *get the information.*"

But it was surely something more than the scientist's

zeal which led Cushing later on to take the final step of being received into the tribe as the foster son of the old chief who had shown him so much kindness. His foster father himself performed the ceremony of piercing the young man's ears and of bestowing upon him the Indian name, *Té-na-tsa-li*:

> When all was over, my father took me to the window, and looking down with a smile on his face, explained that I was "named after a magical plant which grew on a single mountain in the west, the flowers of which were the most beautiful in the world, and of many colors, and the roots and juices of which were a panacea for all injuries to the flesh of man. That by this name,—which only one man in a generation could bear,—would I be known as long as the sun rose and set, and smiled on the Coru people of the earth, as a *Shí-wi* (Zuñi)."

So it came about that for four years, instead of the three months originally allotted to him, Frank H. Cushing, or Medicine Flower, as the Indians called him, remained among the Zuñi, sharing their daily life, attending their councils and witnessing their most sacred and ancient rites. With the result that, aside from the comprehensiveness and accuracy of the knowledge thus obtained, Cushing was able to interpret the Zuñi psychology with a sympathetic understanding rarely attained by the scientific student, especially in the case of a white man coming into contact with a primitive people. Thus through the eyes of this sensitive observer we gain an insight into Zuñi philosophy and Zuñi tradition, which might otherwise have remained a sealed book for all time.

Like other Pueblos, the Zuñi believe that they originally emerged from their underground birthplace, or *Sipapu*, led by the Hero Twins, children of the Sun and Moon who in their turn were brother and sister, children of the Sky Father and the Earth Mother. Fire and the sun are the principal objects of Zuñi worship, together with many lesser gods personifying various objects and forces of nature.

Although today a homogeneous nation, occupying one pueblo and speaking one language, which represents a distinct linguistic stock and is intelligible to no other Indian tribe, the Zuñi, according to Cushing, are descended from two parental stocks, one from the north, the other from the southwest, who came together after the former had already settled in the Zuñi valley. These were later augmented by individuals from other tribes and stocks.

In the Zuñi valley they multiplied and spread, until, when Coronado came upon them, there were seven independent fortress-like pueblos, compactly built of stone and adobe, each turning toward the river front its many-terraced castle and presenting to the approach of friend and foe alike a high, blank wall, pierced only here and there by passageways leading through the building to the court beyond. The cities of Cibola were of the mystic number of seven, and today Zuñi may be divided roughly into seven quarters, each dedicated to one of the seven quarters of the universe—north, west, south, east, the upper, the under world, and the middle from which the others proceed and in which they come together again. These "world quarters" in turn are typified by the seven cardinal points of the Zuñi compass and by seven colors or combinations of colors. For example, North is symbolized by yellow, the color of winter sunlight and the aurora; blue, signifying the twilight and the Pacific, typifies the West; red, for summer and for fire, is the South; white, dawn-light, is the color of the East; the Zenith is many-colored, like sunlight on clouds; black, the color of deep caves and springs, stands for the Lower Regions; while the Midmost or Middle is of all colors.

At one time not long ago the Zuñi comprised nineteen clans divided into seven phratries representing the seven world quarters. The midmost phratry includes but one clan, the *Píchi-kwe* or Parrot-Macaw people, regarded as the mother clan of the entire tribe. Each of the other phratries originally consisted of three clans, some of which are now extinct. In the various ceremonials throughout the year, the phratry, or group of clans, most nearly related to the season or the purpose of the ceremony is given precedence.

The social organization of the Zuñi is further complicated by many societies or priesthoods, each of which has its special function appropriate to one or another of the religious ceremonials. To these orders belong the hideously painted priests and merrymakers described by Cushing in the story of his first adventures in Zuñi. They, too, are divided roughly into seven groups with reference to the seven world quarters, from the Ice-wand people, for the north, to the Rattle-snake people, for the lower region, the seventh or middle region being assigned to the ancient order of the *Kâ'kâ* or *A'kâkâ-kwe*, the Mystic Dance Drama people.

In the office of the *K'yäk'lu*, or keeper of the rituals of creation, the Zuñi have, moreover, succeeded in preserving their myths and traditions in what Cushing terms "a series of sacred epics, a sort of inchoate Bible." In this way they preserved the solidarity of the tribe even when it was divided among the "Seven Cities," making their outlying pueblos subsidiary to the central one representing the "middle region."

It is a matter for much wonderment, when one reads the details of Zuñi history during the 350 years of Spanish domination, that their native social and religious organization should have been preserved down to the present day. Again and again, after fleeing from their beleaguered towns to their stronghold on the high mesa or "Thunder Mountain," they returned and made submission to their Spanish masters. The Franciscan friars established missions among them, many were baptized, churches were built. Still the Zuñi, in hidden kivas, like the ancient Christians in the Catacombs of

PLATE 42

Family group of the Hopi Indians in the National Museum. Women grinding and parching corn, baking, basket weaving; men returning from the hunt

Rome, practiced in secret the religion of their fathers, and in secret the priests and elders instructed the younger members of the tribe in the myths and the sacred rites of their people.

All would go well so long as the Zuñi were permitted to be loyal pagans as well as good Christians. Unfortunately, the zeal of the Fathers and the efficiency of the civil police seldom permitted this compromise to continue long. Then the Zuñi, driven to rebellion, would again massacre the soldiers and the priests, again plunder and burn the churches, and again take refuge in their citadel on Thunder Mountain.

In 1680 came the general uprising of all the Pueblo tribes under the leadership of the prophet-patriot, Pope. The Zuñi, joining in the rebellion, killed one of their priests, and successfully overthrew the Spanish power.

Later, when the Spaniards had again gained the ascendancy, and had for the last time persuaded the Zuñi to descend from their stronghold, the Indians built massive kivas in hidden nooks, where they might practice their religious rites in secret, undisturbed by Spanish intervention. Between 1775 and 1780 the Spaniards, still apparently hoping to Christianize these invincible pagans, built the old Church of Our Lady of Guadalupe now in ruins in the grand plaza of Zuñi, the decorations of which were partly gifts from the King of Spain and partly the work of resident monks. But under the crumbling plaster now falling from the ruined walls are revealed paintings evidently executed by Zuñi artists who mingled pagan symbols of their gods with the designs supplied by the friars. It is supposed that it was the discovery of this sacrilege which caused the priests to cover with plaster the offending images.

The mission flourished for a while, but when the priests again tried to suppress the native rites, the people grew disaffected. Unless they were allowed to remain pagan at heart, they were not willing to conform to even the outward observances of Christianity. So the old church had to be abandoned, "never again," says Cushing, "to be reoccupied save on occasions of the parochial visits of priests resident in far-away Mexican towns or in other Indian pueblos." Henceforth the Zuñi were left undisturbed in the practice of their ancient faith.

Northwest of Zuñi, in the province that the Spaniards called Tusayan, Coronado found another tribe of Pueblo Indians, speaking neither the languages of the Queres nor that of the Zuñi, but belonging to a quite distinct linguistic stock—the Shoshonean. These people called themselves the Hópitu, or "peaceful people," a name which has been shortened to Hopi, and which is used now in preference to the older name, Moqui, by which they were first known. The term Moqui is peculiarly objectionable to the Hopi, since it was first given them by hostile Pueblo tribes and means, in the Hopi language, "the dead."

The Shoshonean stock is a large and important family, including, besides the Hopi, their near relatives, the Ute and Comanche, as well as other tribes, widely separated from these, in California. Moreover, the Shoshonean, as well as the Piman group of languages, has been found by linguists to be related to the Nahautl group of Mexico, which includes the Aztec. Of all the Shoshonean family, however, the Hopi are the only ones who have adapted themselves to the Pueblo way of life. In traditions and in customs, with but a few minor local differences, they are of a piece with the other Pueblo Indians.

Like the Zuñi, the Hopi changed the location of their pueblos after the coming of the Spaniards. They forsook the lower range of plains, and rebuilt their cities on the higher mesas. But, unlike the Zuñi, they have preferred the comparative safety of their present elevated position to the convenience of life at the lower level. The Spaniards found them living in seven pueblos, and today there are seven cities on the high flat mountain tops. Only six of these, however, are occupied by the Hopi. The seventh,

Tewa or Hano, is the home of an alien tribe, who took refuge there when driven from their home by the Spaniards in the seventeenth century. The Tewas are of Tanoan stock the fourth great family of Pueblo Indians, whose villages in New Mexico include Taos, the largest of all the pueblos.

The first American to visit the Hopi pueblos was Lieutenant Joseph C. Ives in command of the Colorado Exploring Expedition in 1858. His account of the pueblo of Mishongnovi, quoted by Morgan in "Houses and House Life," reminds one of descriptions of Acoma and Zuñi:

> The town is nearly square and surrounded by stone walls 15 feet high, the top of which forms a landing extending around the whole. . . .
>
> Each pueblo is built around a rectangular court. . . . The exterior walls, which are of stone, have no openings, and would have to be scaled or battered down before access could be gained to the interior. The successive stories are set back, one behind the other. The lower rooms are reached by trap-doors from the first landing. The houses are three rooms deep, and open upon the interior court. The arrangement is as strong and compact as could well be devised, but as the court is common, and the landings are separated by no partitions, it involves a certain community of residence. . . .
>
> The faces of the bluffs have been ingeniously converted into terraces. These were faced with neat masonry, and contained gardens, each surrounded with a raised edge so as to retain water upon the surface. Pipes from the reservoir permitted them at any time to be irrigated. [Colorado Exploring Expedition, pp. 120, 121.]

One of the most interesting of the occupied pueblos of the Hopi is Walpi, situated at the extreme end of what is known as the "First Mesa," upon which are found also the pueblos of Sichumnovi and Tewa or Hano. The largest of all the Hopi pueblos is Oraibi, which Donaldson says "contains almost as many inhabitants as all the rest combined, *viz.* 900." He gives its altitude as 6,730 feet.

Perhaps the best description of the site of the pueblo of Walpi is to be found in Victor Mindeleff's "Study of Pueblo Architecture":

> The Walpi promonotory is so abrupt and difficult of access that there is no trail by which horses can be brought to the village without

passing through Hano and Sichimovi, traversing the whole length of the mesa tongue and crossing a break or depression in the mesa summit close to the village. Several foot trails give access to the village, partly over the nearly perpendicular faces of the rock. . . . All the water used in these villages except such as is caught during showers in the basin-like water pockets of the mesa top, is laboriously brought up these trails in large earthenware canteens slung over the backs of the women.

Supplies of every kind, provisions, harvested crops, fuel, etc., are brought up these steep trails, and often from a distance of several miles, yet these conservative people tenaciously cling to the inconvenient situation selected by their fathers long after the necessity for so doing has passed away.

On this steep and nearly inaccessible promontory the people of Walpi built their city, house by house, it is said, beginning with a few small clusters, which were added to from time to time as the inhabitants of the lower site moved up and joined the pioneers on the summit. This gradual building resulted in a much more rambling and irregular plan than that of the typical pueblo. Throughout Tusayan at the present day the single room seems to be regarded as the pueblo unit and is considered a complete house. By the addition of many of these units, in course of time, the pueblo attains the distinction of a complete village. Doubtless the manner of building is today much the same as it was when the first house of the present Walpi was constructed. Mindeleff describes the process as follows:

A suitable site having been selected, the builder considers what the dimensions of the house should be, and these he measures by paces, placing a stone or other mark at each corner. He then goes to the woods and cuts a sufficient number of timbers for the roof of a length corresponding to the width of his house. Stones are also gathered and roughly dressed, and in all these operations he is assisted by his friends, usually of his own gens [or clan]. These assistants receive no compensation except their food, but that of itself entails considerable expense on the builder, and causes him to build his house with as few helpers as possible.

The material having been accumulated, the builder goes to the village chief, who prepares for him four small eagle feathers. The

PLATE 43

Pueblo of Walpi, Arizona, showing terraced sheep corrals. Seven hundred feet above the plain

PLATE 44

A court in the pueblo of Oraibi, Arizona, largest of the Hopi villages

chief ties a short cotton string to the stem of each, sprinkles them with votive meal, and breathes upon them his prayers for the welfare of the proposed home and its occupants. These feathers are called *Nakwa kwoci*, a term meaning "a breathed prayer," and the prayers are addressed to Masauwu, the Sun, and to other deities concerned in house-life. These feathers are placed in the four corners of the house and a large stone is laid over each of them. The builder then decides where the door is to be located, and marks the place by setting some food on each side of it; he then passes around the site from right to left, sprinkling piki ["paper bread"] crumbs and other particles of food, mixed with native tobacco, along the lines to be occupied by the walls. As he sprinkles this offering he sings to the Sun his *Kitdauwi*, house song: "*Si-ai, a-hai, si-ai, a-hai.*" The meaning of these words the people have now forgotten.

According to Mindeleff, the Hopi women are the builders as well as the plasterers of the houses. He witnessed the building of a house in Oraibi of which he says:

There was but one man present at this house-building, whose grudgingly performed duty consisted of lifting the larger roof beams and lintels into place and of giving occasional assistance in the heavier work. The ground about this house was strewn with quantities of broken stone for masonry, which seemed to be all prepared and brought to the spot before building began; but often the various divisions of the work are carried on by both men and women simultaneously. While the men were dressing the stones, the women brought earth and water and mixed a mud plaster. Then the walls were laid in irregular courses, using the mortar very sparingly.

The house [or room] is always built in the form of a parallelogram, the walls being from 7 to 8 feet high and of irregular thickness, sometimes varying from 15 to 22 inches in different parts of the same wall. . . .

The making of the roof is the work of the women. When it is finished, the women proceed to spread a thick coating of mud for a floor. After this follows the application of plaster to the walls. Formerly a custom prevailed of leaving a small space on the wall unplastered, a belief then existing that a certain Katchina (or minor deity) came and finished it, and although the space remained bare, it was considered to be covered with an invisible plaster. . . .

A hole is left in one corner of the roof, and under this the woman builds a fireplace and chimney. The former is usually but a small cavity about a foot square in the corner of the floor. Over this a chimney hood is constructed, its lower rim being about 3 feet from the floor. . . .

All the natives, as far as could be ascertained, regard this single-roomed house as being complete in itself, but they also consider it the nucleus of the larger structure. When more space is desired, as when the daughters of the house marry and require room for themselves, another house is built in front of and adjoining the first one, and a second story is often added to the original house. The same ceremony is observed in building the ground story in front, but there is no ceremony for the second and additional stories.

The kivas, or ceremonial chambers, of the Hopi differ from those of the other pueblos in being in the shape of parallelograms instead of circular and entirely subterranean instead of only partially so. They are usually constructed in the face of the mesa cliff, by excavating it to the required depth and height, and then building up the outer wall with masonry.

The ceremonies conducted within these chambers, as well as the more public rites, or "dances," have been witnessed and recorded by Dr. J. Walter Fewkes. These include the so-called Katcina mysteries, the rituals of the sun and fire worship, and the celebrated Snake Dance. While many of the details of these ceremonies are bizarre and barbaric, they have certain hidden, symbolic meanings which, when understood, illuminate much that would otherwise seem merely fantastic or even horrible. The ruling passion of the Indian—his intense conservatism and reverence for the past—either underrated or altogether ignored by the zealous Spanish missionaries, was the chief reason for the failure of the priests genuinely to Christianize the Pueblos, even after three hundred years of close contact. This conservatism, which finds expression in a sort of ancestor worship, is especially embodied in the Katcina ceremonies.

The Katcinas, impersonated by masked men or by effigies, are deified spirits of the dead. The rites dedicated to them are, like most other Pueblo ceremonials, partly dramatizations of old myths and legends, and partly incantations, designed to influence these lesser gods and through them the greater divinities in such a way that the Sky Father and Earth Mother shall bestow the blessings of sunshine, rain, and a bountiful harvest upon their children, the Hopitu. The Katcina ceremonies are celebrated during the winter months within the kivas. Special altars are erected, and many prayer-plumes and piñon needles offered to the gods. And upon a background of fine white sand spread upon the floor are traced in various colored minerals the curious "dry paintings," whose patterns are handed down through the priesthood from generation to generation. After being produced with infinite pains, these pictures are obliterated at the end of the ceremonies.

There are two principal ceremonies connected with the sun worship of the Hopi; one in mid-winter, on the shortest day of the year, the purpose of which is to induce the Sun to return and warm the land; and the other in midsummer, on the longest day, to compel the Sky God to water the fields and make the corn grow and ripen. These results are not brought about by prayer, but by the compelling power of the ancient magic rites. The most striking objects connected with these rites are the extraordinary altars and the two chief *dramatis personae*, the Sky God, represented by effigies of the Horned Serpent manipulated by hidden priests, and the Sun, impersonated by a man masked and decorated to represent a bird.

The ceremonies dedicated to the Fire God are scarcely less elaborate and important than those through which homage is paid to the Sun. There are two "new fire" ceremonies, one in November, the other in midsummer, the former being the more elaborate. Masawu, the Fire God, is the chief personage impersonated in this rite. Before he makes his entry into the pueblo, the trails have been symbolically closed to all mortals by prayer meal scattered across them, all fires have been extinguished in the houses, and the streets are deserted. Masawu stalks through the dark and silent pueblo until he reaches the kiva where the priests are already assembled.

Within the kiva amid chants and the ringing of bells and noise of rattles, the appointed priests twirl their drills in the depressions of the long fireboard or firestone, which is the ancient and sacred way in which the new fire must be produced. In a minute or two smoke arises, in another minute or two sparks begin to fly, and, falling through slots in the fireboard, ignite the corn pollen and cedar bark laid beneath the board as tinder. With this flame the fuel heaped in readiness in the central firepit of the kiva is lighted.

Masawu, the Fire God, now steps forward and lays on the sacred flame his offering of a prayer plume and piñon needle, followed by the priests who make each in turn a similar offering. Messengers now light torches at the new fire and bear them through the town to start the household fires. At the close of the ceremonies the new fire is extinguished and the ashes carried to the rim of the mesa and thrown over the cliff with pinches of prayer meal.

Snakes being representatives of the Sky God are held in especial veneration by the Hopi and figure largely in the so-called Snake Dance, the ceremony celebrated every two years in Walpi, and every year in some one of the Hopi villages, at midsummer, in order to bring about the necessary rainfall. This weird rite has been observed and described many times. Its chief features are the large snakes—often deadly rattlesnakes—which the dancers handle fearlessly and usually with no serious consequences. This has been attributed to the gentleness with which the snakes are treated and to the fact that, in the case of the rattlesnakes, they are handled in such a way that they have no opportunity for coiling—a necessary preliminary to striking.

But if it is unfair to judge a people by their practices

PLATE 45

The Snake Dance, an episode in the Hopi prayer for rain. Group in the National Museum

in war, it is no less unjust to estimate their character by actions born of age-old superstition and religious frenzy. The picture of a painted savage holding between his teeth the slippery, writhing body of a venomous snake is far less agreeable than that of a peaceful, industrious, law-abiding citizen of the United States. And of the two, we must regard the latter as by far the truer portrait of the average Hopi man.

The Hopi are given the following high rating in the "Handbook":

> In mental traits the Hopi are the equal of any Indian tribe. They posses a high artistic sense, exhibited by their pottery, basketry, and weaving. They are industrious, imitative, keen in bargaining, have some inventive genius, and are quick of perception. . . . They are tractable, docile, hospitable, and frugal, and have always sought to be peaceable. . . .
>
> The Hopi are monogamists, and as a rule are faithful in their marital relations. Murder is unknown, theft is rare, and lying is universally condemned. Children are respectful and obedient to their elders and are never flogged except when ceremonially initiated as kachinas. From their earliest years they are taught industry and the necessity of leading upright lives.

For every Indian pueblo occupied today there are dozens of ruins scattered far and wide over the plateau region. These are the remains of houses occupied during the long-continued, straggling migrations of the Pueblo tribes and their remote ancestors, the cliff dwellers. Most of the cliff dwellings are found in the northern canyons and some of the most interesting and best preserved specimens are now included in the National Park of the Mesa Verde. Long detailed descriptions have been written of these curious structures, built within inaccessible caverns in the face of the sandstone bluffs of the canyons, overlooking the farmlands on the river bottom, which was the only place where crops might be raised with any degree of success. "Cliff-Palace," "Spruce-Tree House," and other ruins, have been made the subjects of special monographs by Doctor Fewkes.

In places where the river lands are widened, by the spreading apart of the canyon walls, into pleasant, fertile valleys, stone pueblos were erected of a plan and construction superior to any of those inhabited today. Such were the great pueblos on the Chaco River, of which the Pueblo Bonito is said to be the finest specimen; in these and other ruins have been found specimens of pottery more symmetrical and artistic than any made by the Pueblos of today. Such buildings were evidently erected in the Golden Age of the Pueblo Indians. But eventually they, too, were abandoned for some unknown reason, and the people built themselves new homes on high, defensive sites like that of Acoma.

Another type of dwelling, the ruins of which may now be seen in many of the canyons of New Mexico, is known as the "cavate lodge," which is an artificial cave, sometimes three or four rooms deep, hollowed out of the softer strata of the sandstone cliffs. These dwellings are so primitive that it is thought they were intended chiefly for lookouts, refuges, or storehouses. Sometimes one or more of the rooms was walled up as a tomb for the dead.

A modification of the cavate lodge is often found where a natural cave has been transformed into a dwelling by the simple process of walling up the entrance with stone masonry, leaving openings for the door and windows. In such structures may be seen the crude beginnings of the complex architecture of the pueblos.

The stone and adobe dwellings, the fine pottery, basketry, and weaving, the irrigation canals and the agricultural pursuits of the Pueblos unite to make them appear a people far more civilized than other North American Indians. But all these characteristics were the result of their sedentary way of life. Although today they are skilled silversmiths, at the time of the discovery they knew no more of metal work than did their kindred in other parts of the country, nor were they any nearer a written language than were the other tribes. They present a striking illustration of the influence of environment on the development of civilization. Some of the earliest beginnings of their distinctive culture are found in the ruins of ancient Pecos in New Mexico. With reference to the evolution of this culture, Kidder has pointed out that agriculture in the New World must have originated in the highlands of Mexico and Central America, for in that region is found a heavy seeded grass which was probably the wild ancestor of corn.

Corn-growing once established in the Southwest brought about the gradual transformation of a nomadic people into a race of farmers. They now had leisure to perfect their arts, which the most ancient ruins show included basketry but not pottery. The early forerunners of the Pueblo Indians are known as the Basket Makers. Their gradual progress toward a higher stage of culture known as the post-Basket Maker period, is thus described by Kidder:

> In the course of time the Basket Makers, becoming more and more dependent upon their crops and correspondingly more sedentary in habit, either discovered for themselves, or more probably, learned from tribes to the south, that vessels fashioned from clay, dried in the sun, and finally fired, were easier to make, and more suitable for holding water and for cooking, than the baskets that had hitherto served these purposes. At about the same time they began to enlarge their storage cists into dwellings, to wall them higher with slabs, and to provide them with pole-and-brush roofs.

The next stage found by archeologists in excavating the ancient ruins, and called by them the pre-Pueblo period, presents several distinct characteristics, these being: the presence of bows and arrows; the use of cotton; and particularly the practice of skull deformities which Kidder interprets as indicating the arrival in the Southwest of a new race which eventually became the preponderating one. With regard to the evolution of the pre-Pueblo period into the classic culture of the Pueblo Indians, Kidder says:

> At the present time we have enough data as to pre-Pueblo ruins to enable us to characterize them fairly accurately. We also have

abundant data as to the developed Pueblo culture. But the small pueblo-like ruins that presumably were built during the transition period between the two are, as Morris observes, practically unknown. I use the term "transition" advisedly, for it is evident that there was no sharp break, either in culture or in race between pre-Pueblo and Pueblo. It is most important then, that these small ruins be sought out and excavated, because in them we should find the germs of all the traits that were later developed and combined to form the classic Pueblo culture.

In connection with this still unsolved problem it is interesting to find in Bandelier's "Final Report," written in 1889 (p. 28), the following passage: "We notice remains of more permanent habitations—vestiges of household pottery—along the Canadian River in the steppes, far away from those sections where the 'Pueblos' have dwelt and dwell today." In a footnote he adds:

Ruins are found both east and west of Wagon Mound. I have not been able to visit them, and cannot therefore speak of their character. Those east lie on Canadian River, and twenty-five miles east from the railroad. The pottery, of which I have seen specimens, appears to be similar to that made by the Pueblos. One specimen had the bright glossy ornaments, apparently covered with a very coarse glaze, peculiar to some of the older Pueblo pottery.

These Canadian River ruins have in recent years been investigated by Moorehead, who says, concerning the type of culture he found there:

It is not Mississippi valley form; it is not Pueblo; it probably marks the transition. . . . So far as the writer can observe, we have a tribe originally living in the buffalo country and of "Plains Culture" status which changed as it spread westward up the Canadian. . . . As they moved farther away from the buffalo country they continued to change and develop until they established themselves in permanent villages—were no longer nomads—and finally became the Pueblo-Cliff Dweller people.

Kidder thus sums up the achievements of the Pueblo Indians:

Few races have gone as far toward civilization as did the Pueblos while still retaining the essential democracy of primitive life. Most other peoples, as they advanced from savagery, have first set up for

Casa Grande, Arizona. Ceremonial house of prehistoric village; built of adobe, originally three stories in height

themselves, and later fallen under the domination of rulers temporal or religious; aristocracies or theocracies have sprung up, and the gap between the masses and the classes has become wider and wider. But among the Pueblos no such tendency ever made headway; there were neither very rich nor very poor, every family lived in the same sort of quarters, and ate the same sort of foods, as every other family. Pre-eminence in social or religious life was to be gained solely by individual ability and was the reward of services rendered to the community.

In the 16th century the Pueblos had fallen from many of their old ranges, were reduced in numbers, and had lost something of their former skill in material accomplishments. But their customs had not changed, and they still held out undismayed among their savage enemies. There can be little doubt that had they been allowed to work out their own salvation, they would eventually have overcome their difficulties, and might well have built up a civilization of a sort not yet attempted by any group of men. It is the tragedy of native American history that so much human effort has come to naught, and that so many hopeful experiments in life and in living were cut short by the devastating blight of the white man's arrival.

REFERENCES

Bandelier, Adolf F. The Delight Makers. [New edition.] New York (Dodd, Mead & Co.), [1916].

—— Final report of investigations among the Indians of the Southwestern United States. Parts 1 and 2. Papers Archaeol. Inst. Amer. (Amer. Ser.) Vols. 3 and 4, 1890; 1892.

—— The Gilded Man (El Dorado) and other pictures of the Spanish occupancy of America. New York (Appleton), 1893.

Chapin, Frederick H. The land of the Cliff-Dwellers. Boston (Appalachian Mountain Club), 1892.

Cushing, Frank H. My adventures in Zuñi. Century Magazine, Dec., 1882; Feb., May, 1883.

—— Outlines of Zuñi creation myths. 13th Ann. Rep. Bur. Ethnol. Washington, 1896.

—— Zuñi folk tales. New York (Putnam), 1901.

Donaldson, Thomas. Moqui Pueblo Indians of Arizona and Pueblo Indians of New Mexico. Extra Census Bull. 11th Census U. S. Washington, 1898.

Fewkes, J. W. The Snake ceremonial at Walpi. J. Amer. Ethnol. Archaeol. Vol. 4, 1894.

—— Tusayan Katcinas. 15th Ann. Rep. Bur. Ethnol. Washington, 1897.

—— Antiquities of the Mesa Verde National Park: Spruce-Tree House. Bur. Amer. Ethnol. Bull. 41. Washington, 1911.

—— Antiquities of the Mesa Verde National Park: Cliff-Palace. Bur. Amer. Ethnol. Bull. 51. Washington, 1911.

—— A prehistoric Mesa Verde pueblo and its people. Smithsonian Inst. Ann. Rep. 1916, pp. 461–488. Washington, 1917.

—— Sun worship of the Hopi Indians. Smithsonian Inst. Ann. Rep. 1918, pp. 493–526. Washington, 1920.

FEWKES, J. W. Fire worship of the Hopi Indians. Smithsonian Inst. Ann. Rep. 1920, pp. 589–610. Washington, 1922.

HOUGH, WALTER. Culture of the ancient pueblos of the upper Gila River Region, New Mexico and Arizona. U. S. Nation. Mus. Bull. 87. Washington, 1914.

—— The Hopi Indians. Cedar Rapids, Iowa (Iowa Press), 1915.

KIDDER, A. V. An introduction to the study of Southwestern archaeology with a preliminary account of the excavations at Pecos. New Haven (Yale University Press), 1924.

LUMMIS, CHARLES F. The Land of Poco Tiempo. New York (Scribner's), 1925.

MINDELEFF, V. A study of Pueblo architecture: Tusayan and Cibola. 8th Ann. Rep. Bur. Ethnol. Washington, 1891.

MOOREHEAD, W. K. Recent explorations in northwestern Texas. Amer. Anthrop. (N. S.). Vol. 23, pp. 1–11, 1921.

NORDENSKIÖLD, G. The Cliff Dwellers of the Mesa Verde, Southwestern Colorado, their pottery and implements. Stockholm, [1893].

STEVENSON, MATILDA COXE. The Zuñi Indians, their mythology, esoteric fraternities, and ceremonies. 23rd Ann. Rep. Bur. Amer. Ethnol. Washington, 1904.

WINSHIP, GEORGE P. The Coronado expedition, 1540–1542. 14th Ann. Rep. Bur. Ethnol. Washington, 1896.

CHAPTER VI

INDIANS OF THE PLAINS

In striking contrast to the industrious and peaceable Pueblos were their near neighbors and arch enemies, the Navaho and Apache. The Navaho were of Athapascan stock and had migrated from their ancient northern home, doubtless in pursuit of the buffalo, which ranged freely over the North American plateau from the southern shores of Hudson Bay to the northern borders of the Gulf of Mexico. These hunters from the north finally settled in eastern Arizona, where the Navaho Reservation is now located. There they dwelt in their characteristic "hogans"—cabins constructed of the trunks of small trees set upright, filled in with boughs, and covered with mud—and practiced irrigation for their growing crops. Still they did not altogether forego their marauding habits, but would often swoop down on their nearest neighbors, the Hopi and other Pueblo tribes, plundering crops and carrying off women into captivity. Indeed it may have been these captive Pueblo women who first taught the Navaho the art of weaving the beautiful blankets for which they are now so famous, although among both the Hopi and the Navaho today this work is usually done by the men.

The Apache, on the other hand, though related to the Navaho, never settled in a permanent community, but clung to their old nomadic existence, living on the buffalo and other animals and on what plunder they could wrest from the more prosperous village Indians. Coveting the horses of the Spanish settlers, they possessed themselves of these and of their wild descendants, with which the plains were soon overrun, and were then able to terrorize the whole of the Southwest. None were immune from their sudden and deadly raids, and many communities were practically wiped out of existence. It was because of such raids by the Apache and other marauding tribes that the Pima Indians were driven from the Casas Grandes, which are supposed to have been their ancient dwellings, and eventually settled on the banks of the Gila and Salt rivers in Arizona, where they no longer built stone and adobe houses but lived in small dome-shaped huts made of pliable poles and covered with thatch and mud.

In "The Land of Poco Tiempo," Lummis gives the following vivid picture of the Apache and his ways:

> A white man would have starved to death without his commissary; but the Apache had an elastic adaptability which enabled him to eat more, or live on less, as circumstances might require, than anyone else. To him the desert afforded a *menu* when he had time to stop for it. . . . With imperative cudgel he punches, belabors, and scatters [a tangle of leaves and twigs] and presently extracts a score of fat prairie-mice—a feast indeed. Or, with a long and supple switch he trudges among the sand hillocks with intermittent lashings of the ground, and returns with a toothsome string of gracile lizards. Hapless the rattlesnake who shall erect himself on burring coil to make mouths at an Apache when the belt hangs loose! Evicted from that lozenged hide, his delicate gray meat shall make a dainty *entrée*. . . . When his hardy broncho at last succumbs . . . his services are not yet ended. The tenderest portions of him . . . are hastily hacked off to dangle in sun-cured strips across the back of his successor. His long intestine, mayhap, is cleaned—after Chihuicahui [*i.e.*, Apache] notions of cleaning—and becomes a water-keg of great capacity and matchless portability. If transportation is adequate, twenty feet or so of this unique canteen is wound around a led-horse; if horses be scarce, four or five feet of it is slung, life-preserver fashion, about the neck of some athletic brave, and gives a family water for a week.

Besides mice, lizards, and snakes, the desert supplied the Apache with a variety of vegetable foods. Chief among these were the mesquite bean, which was reduced to meal and made into cakes; the fruit of the "Spanish bayonet," which is not unlike dates when dried; the mountain acorn; and above all, the mescal plant, the varied uses of which Lummis enumerates as follows:

> This bristling benefactor gives the aborigine a quasi-bread which is at once nutritious and lasting; two athletic intoxicants; thread and even clothing, and countless minor staples. It grows throughout the whole vast realm the Apache ranged, an ever-present base of supplies.

On the vast grassy plains east of the desert home of the Apache dwelt many powerful and warlike Indian tribes, chiefly of the great Siouan family, numbering among them the Sioux or Dakota, the Omaha, the Mandan, and many other distinct and often mutually hostile nations.

The Sioux, from whom the Siouan family takes its name, are typical of the Plains tribes in general, and correspond perhaps most nearly to the popular ideal of the American Indian. Among them we find the customs and the costumes everywhere associated with our usual ideas of the Indians. They wore the deerskin shirt and leggings, fringed and ornamented with quills or beadwork, the moccasins, likewise embroidered with colored quills or beads, and the great feather headdress, often reaching to the ground, all of which are imitated today in the dress of children "playing Indian." Another characteristic garment of the Plains Indian was the robe of buffalo skin, tanned to a wonderful softness and beautifully white, on which was sometimes painted the record of the warrior's deeds. In later years, these robes were replaced by blankets.

The Plains Indians used for their tents the same sort of tanned and whitened skins that their robes were made of, and ornamented them in a similar way with paintings.

Before the coming of the Spaniards the only domesticated animal on the prairies was the dog, but the Siouan tribes, like the Apache, very soon learned to tame and train the wild horses; and by the time these Indians were first encountered by Americans, they had become skilled and accomplished horsemen. The acquisition of horses helped the Indians greatly in hunting the buffalo. How important that animal was in their economy may be seen in Castañeda's description, which is the earliest account that we have of the Plains tribes:

They came to a country level as the sea, and in these plains there was such a multitude of cows that they are numberless. These cows are like those of Castile, and somewhat larger, as they have a little hump on the withers, and they are more reddish, approaching black; their hair, more than a span long, hangs down around their horns and ears and chin, and along the neck and shoulders like manes, and down from the knees; all the rest is a very fine wool, like merino; they have very good, tender meat, and much fat. Having proceeded many days through these plains, they came to a settlement of about 200 inhabited houses. The houses were made of the skins of cows, tanned white, like pavilions or army tents. The maintenance or sustenance of these Indians comes entirely from the cows, because they neither sow nor reap corn. With the skins they make their houses, with the skins they clothe and shoe themselves; of the skins they make rope, and also of the wool; from the sinews they make thread, with which they sew their clothes and also their houses; from the bones they make awls; the dung serves them for wood [fuel], because there is nothing else in that country; the stomachs serve them for pitchers and vessels from which they drink; they live on the flesh; they sometimes eat it half roasted and warmed over the dung, at other times raw; seizing it with their fingers, they pull it out with one hand and with a flint knife in the other they cut off mouthfuls, and thus swallow it half chewed; they eat the fat raw, without warming it; they drink the blood just as it leaves the cows, and at other times after it has run out, cold and raw; they have no other means of livelihood. These people have dogs like those in this country, except that they are somewhat larger, and they load these dogs like beasts of burden, and make saddles for them like our pack saddles; and they fasten them with their leather thongs, and these make their backs sore on the withers like pack animals. When they go hunting, they load these with their necessities, and when they move—for these Indians are not settled in one place, since they travel wherever the cows move, to support themselves—these dogs carry their houses and they have the sticks of their houses [tent-poles] dragging along tied on to the pack-saddles besides the load which they carry on top, and the load may be, according to the dog, from thirty-five to fifty pounds.

While the picture of uncouth savages given by Castañeda may have been true of the special tribe that he described, later observers have testified to the dignity, decorum, and ceremoniousness of the Siouan Indians. In this connection McGee says:

The warriors, habituated to expressing and recognizing tribal affiliation and status in dress and deportment, were notably observant of social minutiae, and this habit extended into every activity of their lives. They were ceremonious among themselves and crafty toward enemies, tactful diplomatists as well as brave soldiers, shrewd strategists as well as fierce fighters; ever they were skillful readers of human nature, even when ruthless takers of human life. . . . Their stoicism was displayed largely in war—as when the captured warrior went exultingly to the torture, taunting and tempting his captors to multiply their atrocities even until his tongue was torn from its roots, in order that his fortitude might be proved.

In "The Oregon Trail" Parkman gives a vivid account of the breaking up of a Sioux encampment—a village of the Oglala tribe—and the ensuing buffalo hunt:

At daybreak, however, as I was coming up from the river after my morning's ablutions, I saw that a movement was contemplated. Some of the lodges were reduced to nothing but bare skeletons of poles; the leather covering of others was flapping in the wind as the squaws pulled it off. One or two chiefs of note had resolved, it seemed, on moving; and so having set their squaws at work, the example was followed by the rest of the village. One by one the lodges were sinking down in rapid succession, and where the great circle of the village had been only a few moments before, nothing now remained but a ring of horses and Indians, crowded in confusion together. The ruins of the lodges were spread over the ground, together with kettles, stone mallets, great ladles of horn, buffalo-robes and cases of painted hide, filled with dried meat. Squaws bustled about in busy preparation, the old hags screaming to one another at the stretch of their leathern lungs. The shaggy horses were patiently standing while the lodge-poles were lashed to their sides, and the baggage piled upon their backs. The dogs, with tongues lolling out, lay lazily panting and waiting for the time of departure. Each warrior sat on the ground by the decaying embers of his fire, unmoved amid the confusion, holding in his hand the long trailing rope of his horse.

As their preparations were completed, each family moved off the ground. The crowd was rapidly melting away. I could see them

PLATE 47

Navaho hogan (earth lodge) and blanket loom. Arizona

PLATE 48

Navaho family spinning and weaving the famous Navaho blankets out-of-doors. Arizona

crossing the river, and passing in quick succession along the profile of the hill on the farther side. When all were gone, I mounted and set out after them, followed by Raymond, and, as we gained the summit the whole village came in view at once, straggling away for a mile or more over the barren plains before us. Everywhere glittered the iron points of lances. The sun never shone upon a more strange array. Here were the heavy-laden pack-horses, some wretched old women leading them, and two or three children clinging to their backs. Here were mules or ponies covered from head to tail with gaudy trappings, and mounted by some gay young squaw, grinning bashfulness and pleasure as the Meneaska looked at her. Boys with miniature bows and arrows wandered over the plains, little naked children ran along on foot, and numberless dogs scampered among the feet of the horses. The young braves, gaudy with paint and feathers, rode in groups among the crowd, often galloping, two or three at once along the line, to try the speed of their horses. Here and there you might see a rank of sturdy pedestrians stalking along in their white buffalo-robes. These were the dignitaries of the village, the old men and warriors, to whose age and experience that wandering democracy yielded a silent deference. With the rough prairie and the broken hills for its background, the restless scene was striking and picturesque beyond description. Days and weeks made me familiar with it, but never impaired its effect upon my fancy.

As we moved, on, the broken column grew yet more scattered and disorderly, until, as we approached the foot of a hill, I saw the old men before mentioned seating themselves in a line upon the grounds, in advance of the whole. They lighted a pipe and sat smoking, laughing, and telling stories, while the people, stopping as they successively came up were soon gathered in a crowd behind them. Then the old men rose, drew their buffalo robes over their shoulders, and strode on as before. Gaining the top of a hill, we found a steep declivity before us. There was not a minute's pause. The whole descended in a mass, amid dust and confusion. The horses braced their feet as they slid down, women and children screamed, dogs yelped as they were trodden upon, while stones and earth went rolling to the bottom. In a few moments I could see the village from the summit, spreading again far and wide over the plain below. . . .

Our encampment that afternoon was not far from a spur of the Black Hills, whose ridges, bristling with fir trees, rose from the plains a mile or two on our right. That they might move more rapidly towards their proposed hunting-grounds, the Indians determined to leave at this place their stock of dried meat and other superfluous articles. Some left even their lodges, and contented themselves with carrying a few hides to make a shelter from the sun and rain. Half the inhabitants set out in the afternoon, with loaded pack-horses, towards the mountains. Here they suspended the dried meat upon trees, where the wolves and grizzly bears could not get at it. All returned at evening. . . .

As we galloped across a plain thickly set with sage bushes, the foremost riders vanished suddenly from sight, as if diving into the earth. The arid soil was cracked into a deep ravine. Down we all went in succession and galloped in a line along the bottom, until we found a point where, one by one, the horses could scramble out. Soon after, we came upon a wide shallow stream, and as we rode swiftly over the hard sand-beds and through the thin sheets of rippling water, many of the savage horsemen threw themselves to the ground, knelt on the sand, snatched a hasty draught, and leaping back again to their seats, galloped on as before.

Meanwhile scouts kept in advance of the party; and now we began to see them on the ridges of the hills, waving their robes in token that buffalo were visible. These however, proved to be nothing more than old straggling bulls, feeding upon the neighboring plains, who would stare for a moment at the hostile array and then gallop clumsily off. At length we could discern several of these scouts making their signals to us at once; no longer waving their robes boldly from the top of the hill, but standing lower down, so that they could not be seen from the plains beyond. Game worth pursuing had evidently been discovered. The excited Indians now urged forward their tired horses even more rapidly than before. . . . The Indians, still about a hundred in number, galloped in a dense body at some distance in advance, a cloud of dust flying in the wind behind them. I could not overtake them until they had stopped on the side of the hill where the scouts were standing. Here each hunter sprang in haste from the tired animal he had ridden, and leaped upon the fresh horse he had brought with him. There was not a saddle or bridle in the whole party. A piece of buffalo-robe, girthed over the horse's back, served in the place of the one, and a cord of twisted hair, lashed round his lower jaw, answered for the other. Eagle feathers dangled from every mane and tail, as marks of courage and speed. As for the rider, he wore no other clothing than a light cincture at his waist, and a pair of moccasins. He had a heavy whip, with a handle of solid elk-horn, and a lash of knotted bull-hide, fastened to his wrist by a band. His bow was in his hand, and his quiver of otter or panther skin hung at his shoulder. Thus equipped, some thirty of the hunters galloped away towards the left, in order to make a circuit under cover of the hills, that the buffalo might be assailed on both sides at once. The rest impatiently waited until time enough had elapsed for their companions to reach the required position. Then riding upward in a body, we gained the ridge of the hill, and for the first time came in sight of the buffalo on the plain beyond.

They were a band of cows, four or five hundred in number, crowded together near the bank of a wide stream that was soaking across the sand-beds of the valley. This valley was a large circular basin, sun-scorched and broken, scantily covered with herbage, and surrounded with high barren hills, from an opening in which we could see our allies galloping out upon the plain. The wind blew from that direction. The buffalo, aware of their approach, had begun to move, though very slowly and in a compact mass. I have no farther recollection of seeing the game until we were in the midst of them, for as we rode down the hill other objects engrossed my attention. Numerous old bulls were scattered over the plain, and ungallantly deserting their charge at our approach began to wade and plunge through the quicksands of the stream, and gallop away towards the hills. One old veteran was straggling behind the rest, with one of his fore-legs, which had been broken by some accident, dangling about uselessly. His appearance as he went shambling along on three legs, was so ludicrous that I could not help pausing for a moment to look at him. As I came near, he would try to rush upon me, nearly throwing himself down at every awkward attempt. Looking up, I saw the whole body of Indians full an hundred yards in advance. I lashed Pauline in pursuit and reached them just in time; for at that moment, each hunter, as if by a common impulse, violently struck his horse, each horse sprang forward, and, scattering in the charge in order to assail the entire herd at once, we all rushed headlong upon the buffalo. We were among them in an instant. Amid the trampling and the yells I could see their dark figures running hither and thither through clouds of dust, and the horsemen darting in pursuit. While we were charging on one side, our companions attacked the bewildered and panic-stricken herd on the other. The uproar and confusion lasted but a moment. The dust cleared away, and the buffalo could be seen scattering as from a common centre flying over the plains singly, or in long files and small compact bodies, while behind them followed the Indians, riding at furious speed, and yelling as they launched arrow after arrow into their sides. The carcasses were strewn thickly over the ground. Here and there stood wounded buffalo, their bleeding sides feathered with arrows; and as I rode by them their eyes would glare, they would bristle like gigantic cats, and feebly attempt to rush up and gore my horse. . . .

The hunters began to return. The boys, who had held the horses, behind the hill, made their appearance, and the work of flaying and cutting up began in earnest all over the field. I noticed my host Kongra-Tonga beyond the stream, just alighting by the side of a cow which he had killed. Riding up to him, I found him in the act of drawing out an arrow, which, with the exception of the notch at the end, had entirely disappeared in the animal. I asked him to give it to me, and I still retain it as a proof, though by no means the most striking one that could be offered of the force and dexterity with which the Indians discharge their arrows.

The hides and meat were piled upon the horses, and the hunters began to leave the ground. . . .

And now the hunters, two or three at a time, came rapidly in, and each consigning his horses to the squaws, entered his lodge with the air of a man whose day's work was done. The squaws flung down the load from the burdened horses, and vast piles of meat and hides were soon gathered before every lodge. By this time it was darkening fast, and the whole village was illumined by the glare of fires. All the squaws and children were gathered about the piles of meat, exploring them in search of the daintiest portions. Some of these they roasted on sticks before the fires, but often they dispensed with this superfluous operation. Late into the night the fires were still glowing upon the groups of feasters engaged in this savage banquet around them. . . .

We remained encamped on this spot five days, during three of which the hunters were at work incessantly, and immense quantities of meat and hides were brought in. . . .

Hour after hour the squaws would pass and repass with their vessels of water between the stream and the lodges. . . . In all quarters the meat, hung on cords of hide, was drying in the sun, and around the lodges, the squaws, young and old, were laboring on the fresh hides stretched upon the ground, scraping the hair from one side and the still adhering flesh from the other, and rubbing into them the brains of the buffalo, in order to render them soft and pliant.

It should not be thought that the Plains Indians had no means of livelihood but hunting the buffalo, and that they lived exclusively in skin tents, or tipis. While hunting was their chief occupation, and while their movements were largely regulated by the wanderings of the buffalo, nevertheless there were seasons, while the herds grazed on their favorite pasture lands, when most of the hunters were able to establish fairly permanent villages and to practice agriculture to a limited extent. At such times they raised considerable quantities of the principal Indian staples, maize, squash, and beans.

PLATE 49

Family group of the Sioux Indians in the National Museum. Women making pemmican, tanning skin; children doing beadwork

Some of the Plains tribes, as the Osage, who were originally woodland dwellers, once lived in bark houses similar to those of the Eastern Indians, but these were replaced by the skin tipis or by the earth lodges used by some of these Indians at the time that they were first encountered by white men. The construction of both tipi and lodge is described in detail by Miss Fletcher and Doctor La Flesche in their monograph on "The Omaha Tribe":

The tipi was a conical tent. Formerly the cover was made of 9 to 12 buffalo skins tanned on both sides. To cut and sew this cover so that it would fit well and be shapely when stretched over the circular framework of poles required skilful workmanship. . . . The tent poles were 14 to 16 feet long. Straight young cedar poles were preferred. The bark was removed and the poles were rubbed smooth. The setting up of a tent was always a woman's task. She first took four poles, laid them together on the ground, and then tied them firmly with a thong about 3 feet from one end. She then raised the poles and spread their free ends apart and thrust them firmly into the ground. These four tied poles formed the true framework of the tent. Other poles—10 to 20 in number, according to the size of the tent—were arranged in a circle, one end pressed well into the ground, the other laid in the forks made by the tied ends of the four poles. The last pole to be placed in position was one to which the semicircular skin cover had been tied, which was then stretched around the whole framework, the two edges being securely pinned or tied together, leaving an oval opening which formed the doorway and over which a skin was hung.

The earth lodge was a circular dwelling, having walls about 8 feet high and a dome-shaped roof, with a central opening for the escape of smoke and the admission of light. The task of building an earth lodge was shared by men and women. The marking out of the site and the cutting of the heavy logs was done by the men. When the location was chosen, a stick was thrust into the spot where the fireplace was to be, one end of a rawhide rope was fastened to a stick and a circle 20 to 60 feet in diameter was drawn on the earth to mark where the wall was to be erected. The sod within the circle was removed, the ground excavated about a foot in depth, and the earth thrown around the circle like an embankment. . . . Split posts were set close together, having one end braced against the bottom of the bank and the other end leaning against beams [supported by an inner row of small crotched posts], thus forming a wall of timber. The opening generally, though not always, faced the east. Midway between the central fireplace and the wall were planted 4 to 8 large crotched posts about 10 feet in height on which heavy beams rested, these serving to support the roof. This was made of long, slender, tapering trees stripped of their bark. . . . The slender ends were cut so as to form the circular opening for the smoke. . . . Outside the woodwork of the walls and roof, branches of willow were laid crosswise and bound tight to each slab and pole. Over the willows a heavy thatch of coarse grass was arranged so as to shed water. On the grass was placed a thick coating of sod. . . The entrance way, 6 to 10 feet long, projected from the door and was built in the same manner as the lodge and formed part of it. A curtain of skin hung at the inner and one at the outer door of this entrance way. . . . Couches were arranged around the wall in the spaces between the posts of the framework. These were provided with skins and pillows and served as seats by day and as beds by night.

There were some poetic and charming customs relating to child life among the Omaha, the first of these being the introduction of the child to the universe, when the priest intoned the following beautiful prayer:

Ho! Ye Sun, Moon, Stars, all ye that move in the heavens,
I bid you hear me!
Into your midst has come a new life.
Consent ye, I implore!
Make its path smooth, that it may reach the brow of the first hill!
Ho! Ye Winds, Clouds, Rain, Mist, all ye that move in the air,
I bid you hear me!
Into your midst has come a new life.
Consent ye, I implore!
Make its path smooth, that it may reach the brow of the second hill!
Ho! Ye Hills, Valleys, Rivers, Lakes, Trees, Grasses, all ye of earth,
I bid you hear me!
Into your midst has come a new life.
Consent ye, I implore!
Make its path smooth, that it may reach the brow of the third hill!
Ho! Ye Birds, great and small, that fly in the air,
Ho! Ye Animals, great and small, that dwell in the forest,
Ho! Ye Insects that creep among the grasses and burrow in the ground,
I bid you hear me!
Into you midst has come a new life.
Consent ye, I implore!
Make its path smooth, that it may reach the brow of the fourth hill!

Ho! All ye of the heavens, all ye of the air, all ye of the earth:
I bid you all to hear me!
Into your midst has come a new life.
Consent ye, consent ye all, I implore!
Make its path smooth, that it shall travel beyond the four hills!

The next ceremony in the life of the child was that by which he was introduced to the tribe. It was known as "turning the child." Through this ceremony he took his place as a member of the tribe and his baby name was discarded. A significant feature of the ceremony consisted in supplying the child with new moccasins to take the place of those it had worn as an infant. Baby moccasins were made with a small hole in the sole of one, to signify, to a spirit messenger from the other world, that the child was not ready to go on a journey, its moccasins were worn out—a pretty conceit for cheating Death. When the new moccasins were put on the child at the close of the "turning" ceremony, it was to signify that the child was ready for his life journey.

The culminating point of the ceremony was reached when the officiating priest ceremonially "turned" the child, that is, presented him in succession to the east, south, west, and north, each time turning him completely around, from left to right, and intoning the following song:

Turned by the winds goes the one I send yonder;
Yonder he goes who is whirled by the winds;
Goes, where the four hills of life and the four winds are standing;
There, in the midst of the winds do I send him,
Into the midst of the winds, standing there.
(The Thunder rolls.)

In the case of a boy, another ceremony was added, called Wébashna meaning "to cut the hair," by which the boy was said to be consecrated to the Thunder, the power controlling the life and death of the warrior.

The hair of a person was popularly believed to have a vital connection with the life of the body, so that anyone becoming possessed of a lock of hair might work his will on the individual from whom it came. . . . It is to be noted that later, when the hair was suffered to grow on the boy's head, a lock on the crown of the head was parted in a circle from the rest of the hair and kept constantly distinct and neatly braided. Upon this lock the war honors of the warrior were worn, and it was this lock that was cut from the head of a slain enemy and formed the central object in the triumph ceremonies, for the reason that it preeminently represented the life of the man who had been slain in battle.

On the return of the boy to his home at the conclusion of the ceremonies, the father cut his son's hair in the symbolical manner of his gens; as, for instance, in the case of the Wathi'gishe, whose tabu was the tongue and head of the buffalo, all the hair was cut from the child's head except a tuft over the forehead, one on each side of the crown, and a short lock at the nape of the neck, representing the head, horns, and tail of the buffalo. Another curious pattern was that of a gens who were forbidden to touch any sort of insect, and consisted of a number of little locks left around the base of the skull from which all the rest of the hair had been cut, which were said to represent the many legs of insects. Whatever the pattern, the boy's hair was worn thus until he had cut all of his second set of teeth. It was then allowed to grow, the scalp lock being parted off and kept braided, no matter how unkempt the rest of the hair might be.

Later on, the youth, as an initiation into manhood, was required to keep a severe and protracted fast, during which time the animal, bird, or other object which was to become his personal fetish through life, was revealed to him in a vision. This object the boy was to seek and possess through life as his "personal totem"—the *oyaron* of the Iroquois.

The tribal subdivisions of the Omaha are spoken of as *gentes* instead of *clans* because descent was traced through the father instead of through the mother as in the case of many other Indian tribes. The tribe as a whole was governed by a Council of Seven Chiefs. During their deliberations, which were made with much solemnity

PLATE 50

"The Buffalo Hunt." Painting by Stanley in the National Museum

and ceremony, the most essential rite was the smoking of the two Sacred Pipes by the two principal chiefs.

The ancient tribal organization and the old customs are now things of the past, to be learned only from the old men of the tribe. Fortunately most of this fast vanishing lore has been carefully preserved in the memoir on the Omaha from which the foregoing facts have been gleaned.

The Mandan Indians, a division of the Siouan family, who formerly lived on the banks of the upper Missouri, were first visited and described by white men in 1738. After several accounts of less importance had appeared, George Catlin, the artist, who visited the Mandan in the spring of 1833, gave an extended description of the tribe in his book on the North American Indians, which appeared in 1841.

Two years after Catlin's account, Prince Maximilian of Wied published his "Voyage en l'Amérique du Nord" in which he gave a detailed and accurate description of the Mandan villages as they appeared during his visit there in the winter of 1833–4. At the time of Prince Maximilian's visit, the Mandan, because of the ravages of the smallpox and the attacks of hostile tribes, had been so reduced that they had been forced to abandon their original villages, nine or ten in number, and had moved farther up the river where they built two villages in the neighborhood of the Arikara, a Caddoan tribe, with whom they made an alliance against the dreaded Sioux.

The status of the Mandan women, according to Maximilian, was not a very enviable one. Although conceding that they were as a rule well treated, he says that they were expected to do all the really laborious work, such as fetching fuel, carrying water, cooking, tanning skins, making clothing, cultivating the fields, and building the lodges with some assistance from the men. Polygamy was allowed, although few men had more than four wives and the majority only one. Among the Mandan the husband was regarded as the head of the household, and usually shared his lodge with the families of his married sons. Sometimes women were treated with such harshness and brutality that they committed suicide by hanging. "The women," Maximilian says, "have nothing to indemnify them for their incessant and laborious work, not even good clothing, for this right of the fair sex in Europe is claimed among the Indians by the men. It is singular," he adds, "that these women who are condemned constantly to work like slaves, refuse to do any work whatever if they marry a white man, and, the Whites being entirely in the power of the Indians and the relations of their wives, they are obliged to submit to this."

One of the occupations of the Mandan women was the manufacture of pottery. They made their pots and vessels from a dark, slate-colored clay burnt to a yellowish-red and mixed with flint or granite which was reduced to powder by the action of fire. The Mandan vessels were shaped and smoothed by means of a round stone. After being completed, the pot was filled and surrounded with dry shavings and then burnt, but never glazed.

The men manufactured their own weapons and the curious boats, called bull-boats, in which they navigated the river. These boats were circular, and consisted of a light framework of wood covered with buffalo skin. They were propelled by means of a paddle, and looked very much like giant wash-tubs. For transporting their belongings over the plains, the Indians employed the "travois," a sort of sledge, drawn by a single dog or horse, which was sometimes improvised from the family tent by using the poles as the shafts and the skin cover as the body of the litter.

Catlin, who spent some time among the Mandan shortly before Prince Maximilian's visit, not only made many paintings of their dwellings and costumes, but also described them in detail in his "Letters and Notes," which he illustrated with line drawings copied from his own

paintings. Among these delicate yet spirited drawings we find pictures of the river banks and bluffs, of the mountains and the prairies, with antelopes, prairie dogs, and buffalo in their native haunts and characteristic attitudes. Through these scenes we are led finally to the site of the Mandan villages of which there is the following description:

Their village has a most novel appearance to the eye of a stranger; their lodges are closely grouped together, leaving but just room enough for walking and riding between them; and appear from without, to be built entirely of dirt; but one is surprised when he enters them, to see the neatness, comfort, and spacious dimensions of the earth-covered dwellings. They all have a circular form, and are from forty to sixty feet in diameter. . . . On top of, and over the poles forming the roof, is placed a complete mat of willow-boughs, of half a foot or more in thickness, which protects the timbers from the dampness of the earth, with which the lodge is covered from bottom to top, to the depth of two or three feet; and then with a hard or tough clay, which is impervious to water, and which with long use becomes quite hard, and a lounging place for the whole family in pleasant weather—for sage—for wooing lovers—for dogs and all. . . .

On the roofs of the lodges, besides the groups of living, are buffaloes' skulls, skin canoes [bull boats], pots and pottery; sleds and sledges—and suspended on poles, erected some twenty feet above the doors of their wigwams, are displayed in a pleasant day, the scalps of warriors, preserved as trophies; and thus proudly exposed as evidence of their warlike deeds. In other parts are raised on poles the warriors' pure and whitened shields and quivers, with medicine-bags attached; and here and there a sacrifice of red cloth, or other costly stuff.

Outside the village was the cemetery, or "village of the dead," in which, as the Indians say, the "dead live." On scaffolds, high enough to be out of the reach of dogs and wild animals, lay the bodies, each dressed and painted as for a festival, closely wrapped in fur robes, and provided with bow and arrows, pipe and tobacco, shield, knife, flint and steel, together with food to last until the soul should reach the spirit land. Each body lay on its back upon a separate scaffold, with feet pointing toward the rising sun. Relatives of the dead might be seen at any time lying prostrate under the scaffolds, lamenting with cries and howls, tearing their hair, and gashing themselves with knives or otherwise torturing themselves, as a penance to appease the spirits of the dead.

When the scaffolds decayed and the bodies fell to the ground, relatives buried the remains; but the skulls, bleached white, were placed in circles of a hundred or more on the prairie, at equal distances apart, with the faces all looking to the center, where, upon a little mound at the foot of a "medicine pole" bearing sacrificial objects, were placed two buffalo skulls, a male and a female. Each human skull rested upon a bunch of wild sage which was carefully tended and renewed when faded, as flowers are renewed upon a white man's grave. And food was often placed before each skull, that the former owners might not go hungry in the spirit world.

Although Catlin was inclined to idealize the Mandan in all his writings, his description of their manner of wearing their hair makes no very pleasing picture. He says:

> The stature of the Mandans is rather below the ordinary size of man, with beautiful symmetry of form and proportion, and wonderful suppleness and elasticity; they are pleasingly erect and graceful, both in their walk and their attitudes; and the hair of the men, which generally spreads over their backs, falling down to the hams, and sometimes to the ground, is divided into plaits or slabs of two inches in width, and filled with a profusion of glue and red earth or vermilion, at intervals of an inch or two, which becoming very hard, remains in and unchanged from year to year.
>
> This mode of dressing the hair is curious, and gives to the Mandans the most singular appearance. The hair of the men is uniformly all laid over from the forehead backwards; carefully kept above and resting on the ear, and thence falling down over the back, in these flattened bunches, and painted red, extending oftentimes quite on to the calf of the leg, and sometimes in such profusion as almost to conceal the whole figure from the person walking behind them. . . .
>
> The hair of the women is also worn as long as they can possibly cultivate it, oiled very often, which preserves on it a beautiful gloss and shows its natural colour. They often braid it in two large plaits, one falling down just back of the ear, on each side of the head; and on any occasion which requires them to "put on their best looks," they

PLATE 52

A Pawnee village of earth lodges numbering 2,500 souls which stood in the Loupe fork of Platte River, Nebraska. Deserted in 1875

PLATE 53

A Wichita grass lodge, Kansas. Fifty feet in diameter; smoke hole at the peak

pass their fingers through it, drawing it out of braid, and spreading it over their shoulders. The Mandan women observe strictly the same custom, which I observed amongst the Crows and Blackfeet (and, in fact, all other tribes I have seen, without a single exception), of parting the hair on the forehead, and always keeping the crease or separation filled with vermillion or other red paint.

In mourning, like the Crows and most other tribes, the women are obliged to crop their hair all off; and the usual term of that condolence is until the hair has grown again to its former length.

When a man mourns for the death of a near relation the case is quite different; his long, valued tresses are of much greater importance, and only a lock or two can be spared. Just enough to tell of his grief to his friends, without destroying his most valued ornament, is doing just reverence and respect to the dead.

Vanity and effeminacy among the Mandan were carried to their greatest extreme by a distinct and apparently degenerate class of whom Catlin gives a detailed description:

These gay and tinselled bucks may be seen in a pleasant day in all their plumes, astride of their pied or dappled ponies, with a fan in the right hand made of a turkey's tail—with whip and a fly-brush attached to the wrist of the same hand, and underneath them a white and beautiful and soft pleasure-saddle, ornamented with porcupine quills and ermine, parading through and lounging about the village for an hour or so, when they will cautiously bend their course to the suburbs of the town, where they will sit or recline upon their horses for an hour or two, overlooking the beautiful games where the braves and the young aspirants are contending in manly and athletic amusements;—when they are fatigued with this severe effort, they wend their way back again, lift off their fine white saddle of doe's-skin, which is wadded with buffalo's hair, turn out their pony—take a little refreshment, smoke a pipe, fan themselves to sleep, and doze away the rest of the day.

Having once overcome the native antipathy of the Mandan braves, Catlin found that they were eager to have him paint their portraits and regarded it as a high honor. But when the artist was about to put on canvas a picture of one of the "dandies," which would have been a valuable addition to his portrait gallery, the chiefs became very indignant and informed him, through the interpreter, that if he continued to paint portraits of such "worthless fellows," they should insist on having their own destroyed—a threat which effectually ended the sitting.

The artist, however, painted portraits of many of the more distinguished chiefs of the tribe, among whom perhaps the most interesting was Mah-to-toh-pa. Of this chieftain's dress and adornments and their significance Catlin has left the following account, which is the more valuable since both the dress and robe which Mah-to-toh-pa presented to the artist, after wearing them while his portrait was being painted, were destroyed by fire and water in Philadelphia before the collection came into the possession of the Smithsonian Institution:

Mah-to-toh-pa had agreed to stand before me for his portrait at an early hour of the next morning, and on that day I sat with my palette of colors prepared, and waited till twelve o'clock, before he could leave his toilette with feelings of satisfaction as to the propriety of his looks and the arrangement of his equipments; and at that time it was announced that "Mah-to-toh-pa was coming in full dress!" I looked out of the door of the wigwam and saw him approaching with a firm and elastic step, accompanied by a great crowd of women and children, who were gazing on him with admiration, and escorting him to my room. No tragedian ever trod the stage, nor gladiator ever entered the Roman Forum, with more grace and manly dignity than did Mah-to-toh-pa enter the wigwam, where I was in readiness to receive him. He took his attitude before me, and with the sternness of a Brutus and the stillness of a statue, he stood until the darkness of night broke upon the solitary stillness. His dress, which was a very splendid one, was complete in all its parts, and consisted of a shirt or tunic, leggings, moccasins, head-dress, necklace, shield, bow and quiver, lance, tobacco-sack, and pipe; robe, belt, and knife; medicine-bag, tomahawk, and war-club, or *ro-ko-mo-kon*.

The shirt, of which I have spoken, was made of two skins of the mountain sheep, beautifully dressed, and sewed together by seams which rested upon the arms; one skin hanging in front upon the breast, and the other falling down upon the back; the head being passed between them, and they falling over and resting on the shoulders. Across each shoulder, and somewhat in the form of an epaulette, was a beautiful band, and down each arm from the neck to the hand was a similar one, of two inches in width (and crossing the other at right angles on the shoulder) beautifully embroidered with porcupine quills worked on the dress, and covering the seams. To the lower edge of these bands the whole way, at intervals of half an inch, were attached long locks of black hair, which he had taken with his own hand from the heads of his enemies whom he had slain in battle, and which he thus wore as a trophy, and also as an ornament to his dress. The front and back of the shirt were curiously garnished in several parts with porcupine quills and paintings of the battles he had fought, and also with representations of the victims that had fallen by his hand. The bottom of the dress was bound or hemmed with ermine skins, and tassels of ermines' tails were suspended from the arms and the shoulders.

The *Leggings*, which were made of deer skins, beautifully dressed, and fitting tight to the leg, extended from the feet to the hips, and were fastened to a belt which was passed around the waist. These, like the shirt, had a similar band, worked with porcupine quills of richest dyes, passing down the seam on the outer part of the leg, and fringed also the whole length of the leg, with the scalp-locks taken from his enemies' heads.

The *Moccasins* were of buckskin, and covered in almost every part with the beautiful embroidery of porcupines' quills.

The *Head-dress*, which was superb and truly magnificent, consisted of a crest of war-eagles' quills, gracefully falling back from the forehead over the back part of the head, and extending quite down to his feet; set the whole way in a profusion of ermine, and surmounted on the top of the head, with the horns of the buffalo, shaved thin and highly polished.

The *Necklace* was made of 50 huge claws of nails of the grizzly bear, ingeniously arranged on the skin of an otter, and worn, like the scalp-locks, as a trophy—as an evidence unquestionable, that he had contended with and overcome the desperate enemy in open combat.

His *Shield* was made of the hide of the buffalo's neck, and hardened with the glue that was taken from its hoofs; its boss was the skin of a polecat, and its edges were fringed with rows of eagles' quills and hoofs of the antelope.

His *Bow* was of bone, and as white and beautiful as ivory; over its back was laid, and firmly attached to it, a coating of deer's sinews, which gave it its elasticity, and of course death to all that stood inimically before it. Its string was three stranded and twisted of sinews, which many a time had twanged and sent the whizzing death to animal and to human victims.

The *Quiver* was made of a panther's skin and hung upon his back, charged with its deadly arrows; some were poisoned and some were not; they were feathered with hawks' and eagles' quills; some were clean and innocent, and pure, and others were stained all over, with animal and human blood that was dried upon them. Their blades or points were of flints, and some of steel; and altogether were a deadly magazine.

The *Lance* or spear was held in his left hand; its blade was two-edged and of polished steel, and the blood of several human victims was seen dried upon it, one over the other; its shaft was of the toughest ash, and ornamented at intervals with tufts of war-eagles' quills.

His *Tobacco-sack* was made of the skin of an otter, and tastefully garnished with quills of the porcupine; in it was carried his *k'nick-k'neck* mixture (the bark of the red willow, which is smoked as a substitute for tobacco); it contained also his flint and steel, and spunk for lighting.

His *Pipe*, which was ingeniously carved out of the red steatite (or pipe-stone), the stem of which was three feet long and two inches wide, made from the stalk of the young ash; about half its length was wound with delicate braids of the porcupine's quills, so ingeniously wrought as to represent figures of men and animals upon it. It was also ornamented with the skins and beaks of wood-peckers' heads, and the hair of the white buffalo's tail. The lower half of the stem was painted red, and on its edges it bore the notches he had recorded for the snows (or years) of his life.

His *Robe* was made of the skin of a young buffalo bull, with the fur on one side, and the other finely and delicately dressed, with all the battles of his life emblazoned on it by his own hand.

His *Belt*, which was of a substantial piece of buckskin, was firmly girded around his waist; and in it were worn his tomahawk and scalping-knife.

His *Medicine-bag* was the skin of a beaver, curiously ornamented with hawks' bills and ermine. It was held in his right hand and his *ro-ko-mo-kon* (or war-club) which was made of a round stone, tied up in a piece of rawhide, and attached to the end of a stick, somewhat in the form of a sling, was laid with others of his weapons at his feet.

Such was the dress of Mah-to-toh-pa when he entered my wigwam to stand for his picture; but such I have not entirely represented it in his portrait; having rejected such trappings and ornaments as interfered with the grace and simplicity of the figure. He was beautifully and extravagantly dressed; and in this he was not alone, for hundreds of others are equally elegant. In plumes, and arms, and ornaments, he is not singular; but in laurels and wreaths he stands unparalleled. His breast has been bared and scarred in defense of his country, and his brows crowned with honors that elevate him conspicuous above all of his nation. There is no man amongst the Mandans so generally loved, nor any one who wears a robe so justly famed and honorable as that of Mah-to-toh-pa.

I said his robe was of the skin of a young buffalo bull, and that the

PLATE 54

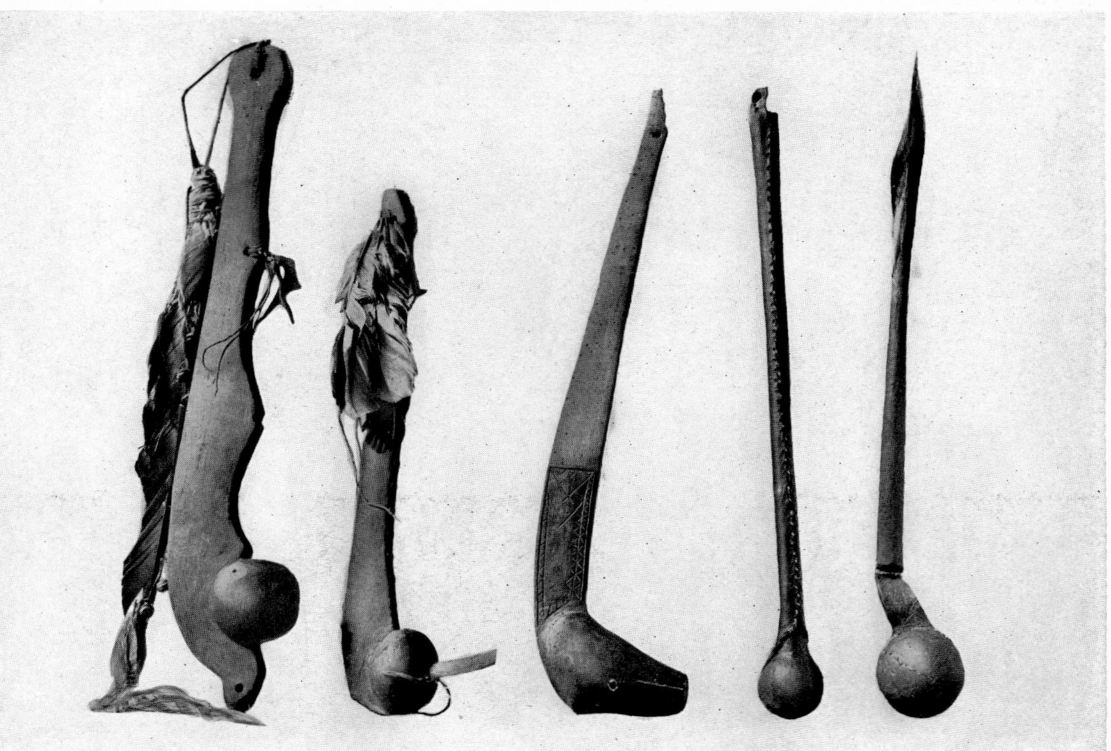

Winnebago war clubs; handles of wood, bare or encased in leather, and stone heads

PLATE 55

A Crow scaffold burial on the plains. Burial took place above ground to protect the body from coyotes

battles of his life were emblazoned on it; and on a former occasion, that he presented me a beautiful robe, containing all the battles of his life, which he had spent two weeks' time in copying from his original one, which he wore on his shoulders.

This robe, with its tracings on it, is the chart of his military life; and when explained, will tell more of Mah-to-toh-pa.

Twelve battle-scenes are there represented, where he has contended with his enemy, and in which he has taken fourteen of their scalps. The groups are drawn according to his own rude ideas of the arts.

One of the battle scenes on the robe (Figure 10) represents the death of Mah-to-toh-pa's brother at the hands of an Arikara chief. Mah-to-toh-pa's vengeance upon the slayer is thus described by Catlin:

The following was, perhaps, one of the most extraordinary exploits of this remarkable man's life, and is well attested by Mr. Kipp, and several white men, who were living in the Mandan village at the time of its occurrence. In a skirmish, near the Mandan village, when they were set upon by their enemies, the Riccarees [Arikara], the brother of Mah-to-toh-pa was missing for several days, when Mah-to-toh-pa found the body shockingly mangled, and a handsome spear left piercing the body through the heart. The spear was by him brought into the Mandan village, where it was recognized by many as a famous weapon belonging to a noted brave of the Riccarees, by the name of Won-ga-tap. This spear was brandished through the Mandan village by Mah-to-toh-pa (with the blood of his brother dried on its blade), crying most piteously, and swearing that he would some day revenge the death of his brother with the same weapon.

It is almost an incredible fact, that he kept this spear with great care in his wigwam for the space of four years, in the fruitless expectation of an opportunity to use it upon the breast of its owner; when his indignant soul, impatient of further delay, burst forth in the most uncontrollable frenzy and fury, he again brandished it through the village, and said, that the blood of his brother's heart which was seen on its blade was yet fresh, and called loudly for revenge. "Let every Mandan (said he) be silent, and let no one sound the name of Mah-to-toh-pa—let no one ask for him, nor where he has gone, until you hear him sound the war-cry in front of the village, when he will enter it and show you the blood of Won-ga-tap. The blade of this lance shall drink the heart's blood of Won-ga-tap, or Mah-to-toh-pa mingles his shadow with that of his brother."

With this he sallied forth from the village, and over the plains, with the lance in his hand; his direction was toward the Riccaree village, and all eyes were upon him, though none dared to speak till he disappeared over the distant grassy bluffs. He travelled the distance of two hundred miles entirely alone, with a little parched corn in his pouch, making his marches by night, and laying secreted by days, until he reached the Riccaree village; where (being acquainted with its shapes and its habits, and knowing the position of the wigwam of his doomed enemy) he loitered about in disguise, mingling himself in the obscure throng; and at last, silently and alone, observed througn the rents of the wigwam the last motions and movements of his victim, as he retired to bed with his wife; he saw him light his last pipe, and smoke it "to its end"—he saw the last whiff, and saw the last curl of blue smoke that faintly steeped from its bowl—he saw the village awhile in darkness and silence, and the embers that were covered in the middle of the wigwam gone nearly out, and the last flickering light which had been gently playing over them; when he walked softly, but not slyly, into the wigwam and seated himself by the fire, over which was hanging a large pot, with a quantity of cooked meat remaining in it; and by the side of the fire, the pipe and tobacco-pouch which had just been used; and knowing that the twilight of the wigwam was not sufficient to disclose the features of his face to his enemy, he very deliberately turned to the pot and completely satiated the desperate appetite, which he had got in a journey of six or seven days, with little or nothing to eat; and then, as deliberately, charged and lighted the pipe, and sent (no doubt, in every whiff that he drew through its stem) a prayer to the Great Spirit for a moment longer for the consummation of his design. Whilst eating and smoking, the wife of his victim, while laying in bed, several times enquired of her husband, what man it was who was eating in their lodge? to which, he as many times replied, "It is no matter; let him eat, for he is probably hungry."

Mah-to-toh-pa knew full well that his appearance would cause no other reply than this, from the dignitary of the nation; for, from an invariable custom amongst these Northern Indians, any one who is hungry is allowed to walk into any man's lodge and eat. Whilst smoking his last gentle and tremulous whiffs on the pipe, Mah-to-toh-pa (leaning back, and turning gradually on his side, to get a better view of the position of his enemy, and to see a little more distinctly the shapes of things) stirred the embers with his toes (readers, I had every word of this from his own lips, and every attitude and gesture acted out with his own limbs), until he saw his way was clear; at which moment, with his lance in his hands, he rose and drove it through the body of his enemy, and snatching the scalp from his head, he darted from the lodge—and quick as lightning, with the lance in one hand, and the scalp in the other, made his way to the prairie! The village was in an uproar, but he was off, and no one knew the enemy who had

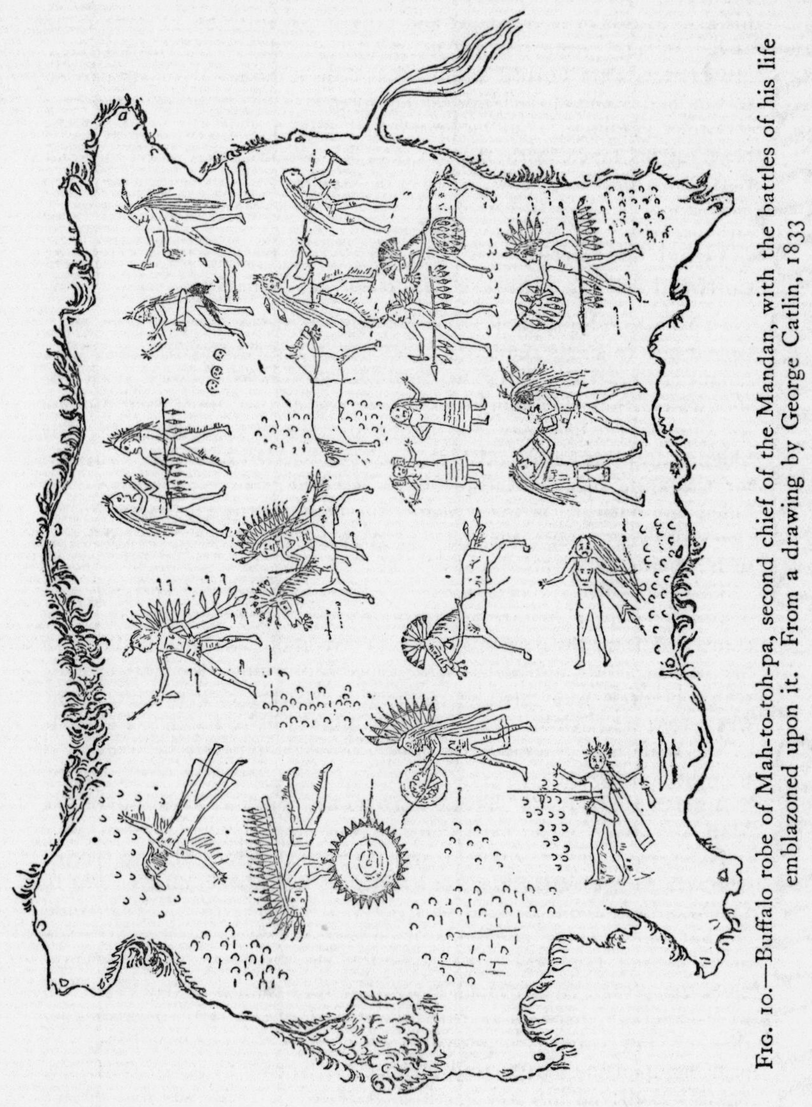

FIG. 10.—Buffalo robe of Mah-to-toh-pa, second chief of the Mandan, with the battles of his life emblazoned upon it. From a drawing by George Catlin, 1833

struck the blow. Mah-to-toh-pa ran all night, and lay close during the days; thanking the Great Spirit for strengthening his heart and his arm to this noble revenge, and prayed fervently for a continuance of his aid and protection till he should get back to his own village. His prayers were heard; and on the sixth morning, at sunrise, Mah-to-toh-pa descended the bluffs, and entered the village amidst deafening shouts of applause, while he brandished and showed to his people the blade of his lance, with the blood of his victim dried upon it, over that of his brother; and the scalp of Won-ga-tap suspended from its handle.

Other important events in Mah-to-toh-pa's life as pictured on the robe are described as follows:

8. Mah-to-toh-pa, or Four Bears, kills a Shienne chief, who challenged him to single combat, in presence of the two war-parties; they fought on horseback with guns, until Mah-to-toh-pa's powder-horn was shot away; they then fought with bows and arrows, until their quivers were emptied, when they dismounted and fought single-handed. The Shienne drew his knife, and Mah-to-toh-pa had left his; they struggled for the knife, which Mah-to-toh-pa wrested from the Shienne, and killed him with it; in the struggle, the blade of the knife was several times drawn through the hand of Mah-to-toh-pa, and the blood is seen running from the wound.

This extraordinary occurrence also, was one which admits of, and deserves a more elaborate description, which I will here give as it was translated from his own lips, while he sat upon the robe, pointing to his painting of it; and at the same time brandishing the identical knife which he drew from his belt, as he was showing how the fatal blow was given; and exhibiting the wounds inflicted in his hand, as the blade of the knife was several times drawn through it before he wrested it from his antagonist.

A party of about 150 Shienne warriors had made an assault upon the Mandan village at an early hour in the morning, and driven off a considerable number of horses, and taken one scalp. Mah-to-toh-pa, who was then a young man, but famed as one of the most valiant of the Mandans, took the lead of a party of fifty warriors, all he could at that time muster, and went in pursuit of the enemy; about noon of the second day, they came in sight of the Shiennes; and the Mandans seeing their enemy much more numerous than they had expected, were generally disposed to turn about and return without attacking them. They started to go back, when Mah-to-toh-pa galloped out in front upon the prairie, and plunged his lance into the ground; the blade was driven into the earth to its hilt—he made another circuit around, and in that circuit tore from his breast his reddened sash,

PLATE 56

A Cheyenne tree burial, Oklahoma. The body was wrapped in a buffalo skin

PLATE 57

A Cheyenne family, showing the travois

which he hung upon his handle as a flag, calling out to the Mandans, "What! have we come to this? We have dogged our enemy two days, and now when we have found them, are we to turn about and go back like cowards? Mah-to-toh-pa's lance, which is red with the blood of brave men, has led you to the sight of your enemy, and you have followed it; it now stands firm in the ground, where the earth will drink the blood of Mah-to-toh-pa! you may all go back, and Mah-to-toh-pa will fight them alone!"

During this maneuver, the Shiennes, who had discovered the Mandans behind them, had turned about, and were gradually approaching, in order to give them battle; the chief of the Shienne war-party seeing and understanding the difficulty, and admiring the gallant conduct of Mah-to-toh-pa, galloped his horse forward within hailing distance, in front of the Mandans, and called out to know "who he was who had stuck down his lance and defied the whole enemy alone?"

"I am Mah-to-toh-pa, second in command of the brave and valiant Mandans."

"I have heard often of Mah-to-toh-pa, he is a great warrior—dares Mah-to-toh-pa to come forward and fight this battle with me alone, and our warriors will look on?"

"Is he a chief who speaks to Mah-to-toh-pa?"

"My scalps you see hanging to my horse's bits, and here is my lance with the ermine skins and the war-eagle's tail!"

"You have said enough."

The Shienne chief made a circuit or two at full gallop on a beautiful white horse, when he struck his lance into the ground, and left it standing by the side of the lance of Mah-to-toh-pa, both of which were waving together their little red flags, tokens of blood and defiance.

The two parties then drew nearer, on a beautiful prairie, and the two full-plumed chiefs, at full speed, drove furiously upon each other, both firing their guns at the same moment. They passed each other a little distance and wheeled, when Mah-to-toh-pa drew off his powder-horn, and by holding it up, showed his adversary that the bullet had shattered it to pieces and destroyed his ammunition; he then threw it from him, and his gun also—drew his bow from his quiver, and an arrow, and his shield upon his left arm! The Shienne instantly did the same; *his* horn was thrown off, and his gun was thrown into the air—his shield was balanced on his arm—his bow drawn, and quick as lightning, they were both on the wing for a deadly combat! Like two soaring eagles in the open air, they made their circuits around, and the twangs of their sinewy bows were heard, and the war-whoop, as they dashed by each other, parrying off the whizzing arrows with their shields! Some lodged in their legs and others in their arms; but both protected their *bodies* with their bucklers of bull's hide.

Deadly and many were the shafts that fled from their murderous bows. At length the horse of Mah-to-toh-pa fell to the ground with an arrow in his heart. His rider sprang to his feet, prepared to renew the combat; but the Shienne, seeing his adversary dismounted, sprang from his horse, and driving him back, presented the face of his shield toward his enemy, inviting him to come on! A few shots more were exchanged thus, when the Shienne, having discharged all his arrows, held up his empty quiver, and dashing it furiously to the ground, with his bow and his shield, drew and brandished his naked knife!

"Yes!" said Mah-to-toh-pa, as he threw *his* shield and quiver to the earth, and was rushing up. He grasped for his knife, but his belt had it not; he had left it at home! His bow was in his hand, with which he parried his antagonist's blow, and felled him to the ground! A desperate struggle now ensued for the knife—the blade of it was several times drawn through the right hand of Mah-to-toh-pa, inflicting the most frightful wounds, while he was severely wounded in several parts of the body. He at length succeeded, however, in wresting it from his adversary's hand, and plunged it to his heart.

By this time the two parties had drawn up in close view of each other, and at the close of the battle Mah-to-toh-pa held up, and claimed in deadly silence, the knife and scalp of the noble Shienne chief.

9. Several hundred Minatarrees and Mandans attacked by a party of Assinneboins—all fled but Mah-to-toh-pa, who stood his ground, fired, and killed one of the enemy, putting the rest of them to flight, and driving off sixty horses! He is here seen with his lance and shield—foot-tracks of his enemy in front, and his own party's horse-tracks behind him, and a shower of bullets flying around his head; here he got the name of "*The Four Bears*," as the Assinneboins said he rushed on like four bears.

10. Mah-to-toh-pa gets from horse and kills two Ojibbeway women and takes their scalps; done by the side of an Ojibbeway village, where they went to the river for water. He is here seen with his lance in one hand and his knife in the other—an eagle's plume head-dress on his horse, and his shield left on his horse's back. I incurred his ill-will for awhile by asking him whether it was manly to boast of taking the scalps of women, and his pride prevented him from giving me any explanation or apology. The interpreter, however, explained to me that he had secreted himself in the most daring manner, in full sight of the Ojibbeway village, seeking to revenge a murder, where he remained six days without sustenance, and then killed the two women in full view of the tribe, and made his escape, which entitled him to the credit of a victory, though his victims were women. . . .

12. Mah-to-toh-pa between his enemy the Sioux, and his own people,

with an arrow shot through him, after standing the fire of the Sioux for a long time alone. In this battle he took no scalps, yet his valor was so extraordinary that the chiefs and braves awarded him the honor of a victory.

This feat is seen in the center of the robe—head-dress of war-eagles' quills on his own and his horse's head—the tracks of his enemies' horses are seen in front of him, and bullets flying both ways all around him. With his whip in hand, he is seen urging his horse forward, and an arrow is seen flying, and bloody, as it has passed through his body. For this wound, and the several others mentioned above, he bears the honorable scars on his body, which he generally keeps covered with red paint.

Such are the battles traced upon the robe of Mah-to-toh-pa, or Four Bears, interpreted by J. Kipp from the words of the hero while sitting upon the robe, explaining each battle as represented.

Through the favor of a medicine-man whose portrait he had painted, Catlin was permitted to view the most secret rites of the chief religious festival of the Mandan, never before witnessed in its entirety by a white man.

This ceremony lasted four days, during which several dances were performed in the village plaza. The rites had, besides their religious significance, three distinct objects: (1) to celebrate the subsiding of the Flood, an important event in the mythology of the Mandan, as it is in that of most river-dwelling peoples; (2) to dance the "bull dance" in honor of the buffalo; and (3) to initiate the youths of the tribe into manhood through an ordeal of privation and torture, which was designed to prepare them for extreme endurance and to make a severe test of their bodily strength. In his vivid descriptions and accurate drawings, Catlin has left a valuable record of this last grotesque and horrible ceremony, the worst terrors of which are happily now a thing of the past.

During the first three days of the festivities, the candidates for the torture, closely guarded in the medicine lodge, were required to observe a rigid fast and vigil, abstaining wholly during that time from food, drink, and sleep. It is possible that by this measure they were rendered to some degree unconscious and consequently less sensitive to the tortures which were inflicted upon them on the fourth day and which brought the ceremonies to a close. This ordeal, which was practiced by many of the Plains tribes, consisted in suspending the candidates by means of skewers passed through the muscles of the back, and in otherwise mutilating and gashing them. After such torments had been borne to the point of producing unconsciousness, the candidates were sent out from the medicine lodge to where, with various heavy accouterments attached to skewers thrust through the flesh of arms and legs, they were dragged over the ground as rapidly as possible, until both the weights and the skewers which held them were broken away through the flesh, and the victim again fainted from pain and loss of blood. No aid could be offered to any victim, but he must be left to the mercy of "The Great Spirit." As soon as he was able to rise and make his way to his lodge, his friends took him in hand and applied remedies to his wounds.

When the buffalo were at last exterminated by means of firearms which the Indian hunters had acquired from the white men, the roving life of the nomads of the plains necessarily came to an end. Even if the buffalo had not been slaughtered, both they and the Indians whose livelihood depended on them must have been driven from their ancient range by the advancing tide of civilization. The former wild tribes of the Plains are now gathered in various reservations where they have adopted an agricultural mode of life and are rapidly being converted into thrifty and civilized citizens of the United States.

There are still old people among them, however, as in the Omaha tribe, who remember the dismay and distress of mind which fell upon them when it was first realized that the buffalo, which was so closely linked with all their traditions and which they had been taught to believe had been given to them as an inexhaustible supply of food forever, had indeed vanished and with it their old free life.

PLATE 58

A bull-boat of the Hidatsa, North Dakota. Buffalo hide on a wooden framework

A Paiute village, Utah. These brush lodges represent the most primitive habitations known to the North American Indians

REFERENCES

CARVER, JONATHAN. Travels through the interior parts of North America in the years 1766, 1767, and 1768. London, 1778.

—— Three years' travels through the interior parts of North America for more than five thousand miles. Philadelphia, 1796.

CATLIN, GEORGE. Letters and notes on the manners, customs, and condition of the North American Indians. Vols. I–II. New York and London, 1844.

—— O-kee-pa: a religious ceremony; and other customs of the Mandans. Philadelphia, 1867.

COUES, ELLIOTT, editor. History of the expedition of Lewis and Clark to the sources of the Missouri River and to the Pacific in 1804–5–6. A new edition. Vols. I–IV. New York, 1893.

DONALDSON, THOMAS. The George Catlin Indian gallery. U. S. Nation. Mus. Ann. Rep. 1885, pp. 399–406. Washington, 1886.

DORSEY, JAMES OWEN. Omaha dwellings, furniture, and implements. 13th Ann. Rep. Bur. Ethnol. Washington, 1896.

—— Siouan sociology. 15th Ann. Rep. Bur. Ethnol. Washington, 1897.

FLETCHER, ALICE C. and LA FLESCHE, FRANCIS. The Omaha Tribe. 27th Ann. Rep. Bur. Amer. Ethnol. Washington, 1911.

IRVING, JOHN T. Indian sketches taken during an expedition to the Pawnee tribes. Vols. I–II. Philadelphia, 1835.

JAMES, EDWIN. Account of an expedition from Pittsburgh to the Rocky Mountains . . . under the command of Major Stephen H. Long. Vols. I–II, and atlas. Philadelphia, 1823.

LA FLESCHE, FRANCIS. The Osage Tribe: rite of vigil. 39th Ann. Rep. Bur. Amer. Ethnol. Washington, 1925.

McGee, W J. The Siouan Indians: a preliminary sketch. 15th Ann. Rep. Bur. Amer. Ethnol. Washington, 1897.

Matthews, W. Ethnography and philology of the Hidatsa Indians. U. S. Geog. Geol. Surv. Misc. Pub. No. 7. Washington, 1877.

Maximilian, Prince of Weid. Travels in the interior of North America. Translated from the German by H. Evans Lloyd. London, 1843.

Parkman, Francis. The Oregon trail: sketches of prairie and Rocky Mountain life. 8th ed. Boston, 1883.

Will, G. F. and Spinden, H. J. The Mandans: a study of their culture, archaeology, and language. Papers Peabody Mus. Amer. Archaeol. Ethnol. Harvard Univ. Vol. 3, No. 4. Cambridge, Mass., 1906.

CHAPTER VII

WEST COAST TRIBES

Cut off from the rest of the mainland by towering mountain ranges and vast tracts of desert land, the tribes of the West Coast, although including representatives of such widely distributed families as the Shoshonean and Athapascan, developed in their isolation a culture distinct from and for the most part inferior to that of the red-skinned statesmen of the East, the pueblo-builders of the Southwest, and the huntsmen of the central Plains region.

The effects of environment are nowhere more clearly shown than in two California tribes, the Mohave and their near neighbors and relatives, the Yuma, who together form a connecting link between the culture of the Southwest and that of the West Coast as represented by the Diegueño and other tribes of southern California.

The Mohave, who lived in scattered dwellings along the Colorado River, were wanderers and warriors to an extent undreamed of by most California tribes. They were athletic and well developed and famous for the artistic painting and tattooing of their bodies. These decorations largely supplied the place of clothing, for on account of the mild climate both the Mohave and Yuma dispensed with all garments except the bark-fiber petticoat of the women and the breechcloth of the men. They built their houses of logs, with four supporting poles at the center, walls only two or three feet high, and nearly flat roofs of brush covered with sand.

The Mohave resembled the Pueblos in practicing a rude sort of agriculture and their granaries were somewhat like kivas, being cylindrical structures with flat roofs. For animal food they depended largely on salmon which they ate broiled or stewed. Although a river tribe, these Indians had no canoes but used instead rafts, or *balsas*, made of bundles of reeds. Their pottery was better, their basketry poorer, than elsewhere in California. They differed from their California neighbors also in using shells as jewelry, not as money.

In social organization, however, as well as in many customs, the Mohave resembled other California Indians. The tribe was divided into gentes, with inheritance in the male line. Chiefs were hereditary but not so important as three other leaders chosen for their ability—the war-leader, the master of entertainments, and the shaman, or medicine man.

The Mohave had no cemeteries, as cremation of the dead was the universal practice throughout California. However, the ashes were buried after a fashion, for the logs on which the body was burned were placed over a trench and as body and fuel were consumed the ashes fell into the excavation and were covered over with sand. Not only was the dead man's body destroyed, but his house, containing all his property was also set on fire. Into the blaze mourners cast their own personal belongings, sometimes even their garments.

Like other tribes of southern California, both the Mohave and the Yuma were familiar with the narcotic properties of the Jimson weed and made use of the drug in their religious observances in order to produce dreams. Such dreams were regarded as the basis of all religion and indeed of all knowledge.

The Diegueño, whose name was derived from the Franciscan mission of San Diego, were among the most primitive of the California Indians. They lived in the southernmost part of the State and were practically the same people as the Cocopa and other tribes of the northern part of Lower California.

The Diegueño resembled the Mohave in their gentile system, by which descent was traced through the father's line, and in a number of other customs. Like the Mohave, for example, they took not only the scalp lock from a fallen foe, but the entire scalp including the ears. These gruesome trophies are said to have adorned the heads of the dancers in the scalp-dance which followed a victory.

A braided girdle of agave fiber for carrying burdens was the sole article worn by the men, while the women were clad only in the two-piece petticoat popular among all California tribes. The rear portion of this garment was of willow bark; the front apron of the same material or of strings closely netted or braided. Sandals made of agave fiber about half an inch thick were sometimes worn. Both men and women wore their hair long, the men bunching it on the crown of the head, the women letting it hang loose but trimmed across the forehead into a deep "bang" to the eyebrows.

Just north of the Diegueño were the Luiseño who were likewise named for a mission, that of San Luis Rey de Francis. Although of Shoshonean stock they resembled their relatives east of the mountain ranges even less than did the Diegueño their Yuman kinsfolk. Because of the similarity of environment, the Luiseño and Diegueño were, in fact, much alike, although the Luiseño were even more primitive than were the Diegueño. These southern Californians raised no crops but lived chiefly on acorns and various bulbous plants, supplemented by a variety of animal foods including not only fish and game but also reptiles, insect larvae, and worms—almost everything, in fact, except dogs and men.

For religious ceremonies the southern California Indians used the *wamkish* or "temple," which was merely a circular plot of ground inclosed within a fence or *hotshish* of brush. This unroofed ceremonial inclosure was associated with the generally practiced rites of mourning and the *toloache* or Jimson-weed religion.

A very definite link between the West Coast Shoshoneans and the Pueblo Indians is found in the sand paintings which both used as part of their religious ceremonials. The painting was made in the *wamkish* or ceremonial inclosure and was a part of the Luiseño Jimson-weed initiation for boys, the *Yunish Matakish* or death rite, and the adolescence ceremony for girls. As with the Pueblos, these sand paintings were conventionalized religious symbols, the knowledge of which was confined to the initiates of the Jimson-weed cult and was imparted secretly by the elders to the younger members of the tribe.

The toloache ritual, by which boys were initiated into the Jimson-weed or Chingishnish religion, had as its most important proceeding the taking of the drug, which is very powerful and has been known to produce fatal results.

The ceremony of initiation concluded with the ant ordeal, in which the victim was fastened down on an ant hill, and the insects allowed to bite him at will. This novel form of torture was ended by releasing the sufferer and whipping the ants from his body with nettles.

The girls' ceremony was also a characteristic rite among the Shoshoneans of southern California. Its central feature was the "roasting." Several girls were usually treated at once, thereby making the ceremony more general and increasing its importance. A few tribes, however, as the Yurok, Hupa, and Mohave, made the rite individual and an affair for kinsmen rather than the whole community. Kroeber gives the following description of the roasting ordeal:

> The first step in the ceremony was to make the girls swallow balls of tobacco as an ordeal. Only those who did not vomit were considered virtuous. As the Indians say, this was a hard test.

The girls were then placed on their backs in a pit that had previously been lined with stones, heated, and then carpeted with tussock grass and sedge. Two warmed flat stones were put on the abdomen of each maiden. The girls lay as still as possible for three days. At night men and in the day women danced around the pit. Each girl had her head covered with an openwork basket to keep the flies off, the Luiseño say—perhaps to prevent undue and prejudicial movements. . . .

The girls did not wholly fast, but refrained from meat, fish, and salt. Once every 24 hours they left the pit, which was then reheated.

When finally taken out the girls had their faces painted by the wife of the officiating chief. Bracelets and anklets of human hair and necklaces of *Echinocystis macrocarpa*, a variety of prickly "sea-urchin," were put upon them. They were now free to go about.

There is one southern Californian tribe of whom mention should be made, although they are practically extinct and very little can now be learned about them. These are the Chumash who formerly occupied the coast and three large islands of the Santa Barbara region. They were among the first of the California Indians to be discovered by the Spaniards who came to their shores toward the middle of the sixteenth century, and finding them peaceable and friendly, established several missions among them. They were more maritime in their way of life than any other Californian tribe and seem to have been the only ones to construct seaworthy canoes. These were made of planks lashed together and cemented with asphalt, which occurs in large quantities along the coast.

The art of decorating wooden vessels with an inlay of *haliotis* was known to the Chumash, but no specimen of their work is now extant. They were also skilled in basketry, which was an art very highly developed in California. They did not, however, manufacture pottery, but used soapstone for their pots and vessels as did the far-northern Eskimo. The Chumash used metates, mortars, and pounding slabs of stone. Other remains include large stone rings, sometimes beautifully polished, supposed to have been used to slip over the women's digging sticks to give the stroke more force. Such, at least, is the explanation of their use given by the natives. Pipes have also been found made of stone tubes, doubtless employed chiefly by shamans. Pipes of wood or cane were probably used by the people generally, although their remains have perished. The Chumash used clam-shell disk beads as money, and probably furnished most of the supply for the southern tribes. They employed the usual method of measuring the strung beads on the circumference of the hand.

Some distance farther north on the coast, separated from the Chumash by various intervening tribes, was a related nation, the Pomo. They are still in existence and are today the second most populous of the California tribes, numbering more than 1,200 and exceeded only by the Mono. It is estimated that they numbered originally nearly 8,000. About three-fourths of the present population are said to be of unmixed blood.

There were several distinct geographical divisions of the Pomo who together formed a continuous and comparatively compact body. The heart of their land was the valley of Russian River. To the east of this valley and separated from it by a range of mountains is a basin containing one of the few large bodies of fresh water in California—Clear Lake; this formed another center for the Pomo population. Still farther east and north, and cut off from Clear Lake by another range of mountains, were the Sacramento Valley Pomo, sometimes called the Salt Pomo from their ownership of a famous deposit of salt.

Attempts of neighboring tribes to steal the salt led to numerous conflicts, including one or two with the Clear Lake Pomo. Comparatively few of the Pomo lived on the coast. Fewer still occupied the redwood district; aside from deer and acorns these gloomy forests furnished little food.

The political unit among the Pomo was the village and there were about seventy-five of these, besides many

PLATE 60

Mohave Indian chief in ceremonial paint, National Museum

smaller clusters of dwellings and camping places, most of which were grouped around some one of the principal villages. These were inhabited by a people who had little to fear from danger of famine. They had no need to cultivate the soil, for food supplies were to be found on every hand.

Pomo customs in dress, house-building, and such matters, differed in certain details according to the habitat. The double skirt of the women, for instance, was made of such materials as might be at hand in any particular locality. Where deer were to be had, it was made of skin; on the coast, of shredded inner redwood bark; in Russian River Valley, of willow bark; and on Clear Lake, of tule rush. Of these materials, fiber seems to have been the favorite. Basketry caps were not worn. The only headgear was supplied by the carrying net which was woven into a broad band in front to ease the strain on the forehead. As for the men, they did not bother with clothes at all except perhaps a skin wrapped around the hips.

California moccasins and other footgear were so clumsily made that the Indians usually preferred to go about barefoot. This, indeed was the usual practice of the North American tribes except when on long expeditions. Soft moccasins were occasionally worn, however, and sometimes sandals and leggings of tule or of netted twine formed part of the Pomo costume. Men wore ear tubes of long, incised bird bones, or wooden rods tipped with a bead and small brilliant feathers. Nosepins of *haliotis* were also worn. The women had a variety of beads and other ornaments.

Types of houses also depended on the climate and vegetation of each district. Along the shore and in the adjacent belt of heavy timber the living house was built of slabs of redwood bark leaned together into a cone from six to eight feet high and from ten to fifteen feet across, without any covering of earth. A central post suggests the possible evolution of the semisubterranean house. This type of dwelling was made also by other tribes who lived in the neighborhood of the redwood trees. Such houses were necessarily small and accommodated only single families.

The Pomo had a true sweat-house, distinct from the assembly or dance house, though the two were identical in plan and differed only in size, use, and name. A diameter of 15 or 20 feet sufficed for this sudatory or "fire lodge," *ho shane* or *holi shane*. The men, besides sweating daily, usually slept in this structure, which was peculiarly theirs and spent much of their spare time during winter within it. Evidently the *cha* or *gha*, the living house, was for women, children, property, cooking, and eating; a man's normal place was in one of the two *shane*.

What Kroeber calls "the makeshift character of central California culture" is perhaps most apparent in the failure to use the redwood, with which the coast people were abundantly supplied, for building seaworthy canoes such as were common farther north. These California tribes seem to have been content with rafts of a few logs for crossing streams and visiting mussel and sea-lion rocks offshore. On Clear Lake the rafts, although made of bundled tule rush, were often boat-shaped, with rising sharp prow, a stern, and gunwales to prevent the waves from washing over the top.

In basketry, on the other hand, the Pomo excelled. Their baskets are accounted the finest made in California—perhaps in the world. In certain features they are unique. In order to appreciate these points, some understanding of the technique of basket-making is necessary.

The typical basketry of the Indians of the East was simply plaited and made by intertwining two strands of like material, such as corn-husks. This produced a stiff, inflexible shape. The materials and methods of the California Indians were altogether different and much more varied and adaptable. Consequently they were able to secure a remarkable variety and a high degree of beauty in their products.

In making their baskets the California Indians used chiefly two methods—twining and coiling. In the twined work the heavy foundation is vertical from the center to the rim of the basket and the woof of lighter material is horizontal. Twined work is done with two strands carried simultaneously, alternating above and below each other, completely hiding the foundation. The product is usually quite flexible, but returns to and maintains its proper shape. In coiled work the heavy foundation is laid in horizontal coils around the basket with the filling run spirally around the heavy twigs. Such baskets are usually rigid and firm.

The Pomo are the only California Indians who understand "lattice twining" or wickerwork, and the only ones who use the methods of twining and of coiling equally well. In northernmost California coiling is never practiced. To the south, twining is employed only for the coarser forms of basketry, for burden baskets, seed beaters, parching trays, cradles, traps, and the like. Baskets of the finer sort, intended for caps, for cooking utensils, or for holding water, all, indeed, which are intended for decoration or permanent use, are invariably coiled. The Pomo employ both methods, although their boiling receptacles are usually twined and their feathered and gift baskets chiefly coiled.

The special expertness of the Pomo in basketry is shown by the fact that they use diagonal as well as plain twining, and coil over three rods or one with nearly equal frequency. Another feature which distinguishes their work is the method of ornamentation. In the North, where twining is best understood, the only means of introducing color into the pattern is by overlaying or facing; that is, using a double thread for twining, so that the colored thread shows only on one side. This method is unknown to the Pomo. Their favorite means of ornamentation is by the use of feathers. A description of this work is given by Kroeber:

> Black, wavy quail plumes may be scattered over the surface of a basket, or fine bits of scarlet from the woodpecker's scalp worked into a soft, brilliant down over the whole of a coiled receptacle; or both be interspersed, or small woven-in-beads be included among the feathers. The height of display is reached in the basket whose entire exterior is a mass of feathers, perhaps with patterns in two or three lustrous colors. A gently flaring bowl of this sort, a luminous scarlet intersected by lines of soft, brilliant yellow, with a solid edge of beads and fringe of evenly cut pendants of haliotis, the whole 12, 15, or 18 inches across, radiates a genuine magnificence that appeals equally to the savage and the civilized eye. It is not inappropriately that American fancy has denominated these masterpieces "sun baskets"; although the native has learned the designation from the white man. To him they served as gifts and treasures; and above all they were destroyed in honor of the dead. It is impressive and representative not only of the gentle melancholy sentiments of the Pomo but of the feelings of the California Indians as a whole, that these specimens of the highest artistic achievement that their civilization has been able to produce were dedicated to purposes of mourning their kindred.

Of the amazing skill of the Pomo women Kroeber says:

> The perfection with which the Pomo woman combines fineness and evenness of stitch, especially in her coiled wares, is truly remarkable. . . . Elsewhere, 30 wrappings per linear inch make an unusually fine basket; among the Pomo this is rather common, and 60 stitches, and even more, can be found.

One sort of basket which was universally used among the California Indians was the carrying basket, always conical in shape and woven in varying ways according to locality. Throughout California, on account of the scarcity of boats and the absence of suitable dogs, transportation was by human carriers alone, who bore their burdens always on the back, and usually hung them from the forehead, only occasionally from the chest.

The cradle used by the Pomo was of the sitting type found among the tribes to the north of them. It was a basket made of rather heavy sticks laid close and united by the twining method. The bottom in which

PLATE 61

"Sitting" type of cradle used by the Wintun Indians of Northern California

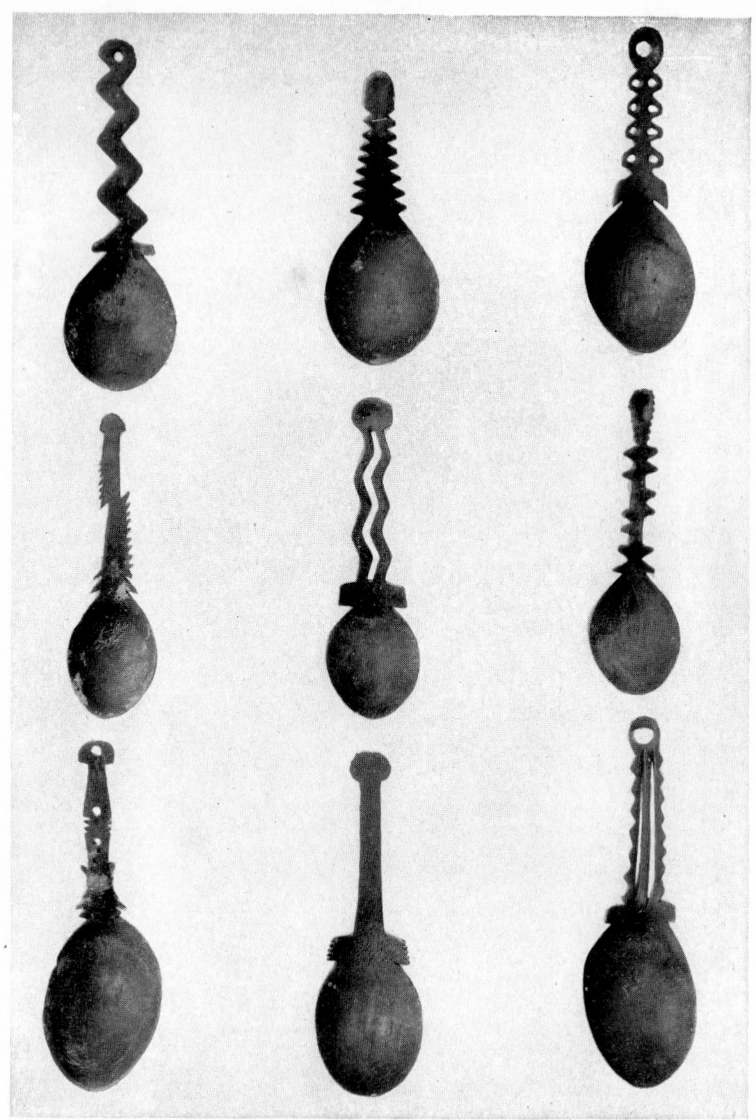

Carved elk-antler spoons for acorn gruel made by the Yurok Indians of California

the child is set is round, the sides straight. A hood is sometimes fashioned of a separate little cone of openwork basketry on which may be placed a piece of skin or a mat to protect the child's face.

Although these Indians had only the most primitive sort of fire-drill, they used another device for producing fire which seems to have been unique; two lumps of quartz were struck against each other and the shower of sparks thus produced was caught on tinder. The Pomo were the chief manufacturers of shell money in California. A certain large clam which was found in great abundance in the region was used for this purpose. The shells were broken up and ground on sandstone until the pieces were nearly round, then bored, strung, and given a finish by being rolled on a slab. The value of these coins varied according to their size and degree of polish. Since constant handling gave the shell a gloss not to be obtained in any other way, the older the money became the more highly it was prized. Not only did the Pomo prepare the shell money, but they were expert in making long strings consisting of definite numbers of the beads. These Indians developed a mathematical sense far in advance of their neighbors. They were a wealthy people and liked to calculate the amount of their riches.

Although thus commercially minded, the Pomo were not without a vein of mysticism which expressed itself in their elaborate religious ceremonies consisting of two sets of rituals, the *Hahluigak*, or "ghost ceremony," and a still more important festival known as the *Guksu* rites. The former must be distinguished from certain recent modifications known as the "ghost-dance movement," the earlier wave of which originated in Nevada about 1870 to 1872 and swept over northern California including the Pomo within its influence.

Pomo impersonators in the ghost dances (from some of which women were excluded) were of two kinds—the *Hahluigak*, or ghosts, and the *No-hahluigak*, or "ash" ghosts. The ordinary ghosts, attended by the ash ghosts, gave their performances by day. The exhibitions of the ash ghosts, who appear to have been the higher class, possessing special power over fire, were usually conducted at night. Kroeber gives the following description of both classes of performers:

> On his head the ghost dancer wore a net filled with down, a feather tuft, a band of yellow-hammer quills that followed the crown and hung down behind, and a circlet of pepperwood leaves. No other regalia were worn except a girdle and sometimes a necklace of the same foliage. The entire body was covered with paint. . . .
>
> The ash ghosts were more simply dressed. Their ornaments were restricted to a few feathers on the head, and a screen of leaves to hide the face. The body was completely painted.
>
> The badge of authority of the ash ghosts was a crooked stick, the butt of which was fashioned to represent the head of a crane. . . .
>
> At times the ghosts carried living rattlesnakes, and on approaching the dance house at night they are reported to have worn on their heads some sort of flaming device. . . .
>
> Even the ordinary ghost dancers would scatter coals of fire about the house when angered, but outright exhibitions, such as eating live coals and plunging the hands into the fire, were reserved to the ash ghosts. . . .

The most important of all the ceremonials was the *Guksu* rite. The old men in charge of the *Guksu* also directed the ghost ritual; the head one of the initiates was the custodian of the feathers and other paraphernalia used in the ghost ceremony, while the others helped to dress and paint the ghost dancers.

The *Guksu* was the chief of the spirits impersonated by the Pomo in this ceremony. He wore the "big head" ornament of radiating feather-tipped sticks which terminated in front in a Cyrano nose of red feathers, and carried a double bone whistle and a long staff tipped with feathers. Another spirit impersonated in these rites was called *Shalnis*, whose costume consisted of a feather-covered mantle of network which fell from the crown of his head, entirely enveloping his form. He was painted black and carried a plain black staff.

According to Powers, the Pomo possessed a definite and characteristic conception of heaven:

> They believe that in some far, sunny island of the Pacific—an island of fadeless verdure; of cool and shining trees, looped with clinging vines; of bubbling fountains; of flowery and fragrant savannas, rimmed with lilac shadows, where the purple and wine-stained waves shiver in a spume of gold across the reefs, shot through and through by the level sunbeams of the morning—they will dwell forever in an atmosphere like that around the Castle of Indolence; for the deer and the antelope will joyously come and offer themselves for food, and the red-fleshed salmon will affectionately rub their sides against them, and softly wriggle into their reluctant hands. It is not by any means a place like the Happy Hunting Grounds of the lordly and eagle-eyed Dokotas, where they are "drinking delight of battle" with their peers, or running in the noble frenzy of the chase; but a soft and a forgetting land, a sweet oblivious sleep, awaking only to feast and then to sleep again.

In northern California, the Yurok were the center of a remarkable civilization affiliated with that of the tribes of the northwest coast rather than with the more primitive cultures of central and southern California. They shared in many of the customs and beliefs of the alien tribes immediately surrounding them, chief of whom were the Karok to the northeast and the Hupa to the southeast. Together with the Yurok these tribes were the leaders in a culture which reached a higher level than was to be found elsewhere in California; in the technical excellence of their arts they were rivaled only by the far-distant Chumash.

Money was even more essential to Yurok institutions than to those of the Pomo, and consisted, among these northern tribes, of dentalium shells. Two species of this mollusk occur in California, *D. hexagonum* in the south and *D. indianorum* in the north. Since both species live in comparatively deep water, however, their presence was unknown to the Indians. So the Yurok, instead of depending on their own supply, imported the tapering, tubular shells from the north. Every shell which they received had doubtless traveled many miles, probably hundreds, and had passed from nation to nation on the way. Had any Yurok thought to look for the source of supply on his own coast, he might have unearthed untold wealth for himself and his nation.

Almost as much as these shells the Yurok prized woodpecker scalps, which besides forming a medium of exchange were used as material for dance head-dresses and the trimming of other regalia. Kroeber says that they represent the Yurok idea of the acme of splendor. Dentalia, on the other hand, were used solely as money. When large sums changed hands, however, the shell money was usually supplemented by various other objects possessing intrinsic value, such as deerskins of rare colors and large blades of obsidian and flint.

Social standing and influence among the Yurok was chiefly a question of wealth. A great deal depended on the price paid for a woman in marriage, for not only was the dignity of both husband and wife, but also the social standing of their children enhanced thereby. A poor man was despised chiefly for the small sum he had been able to pay for the mother of his children, and for the cheapness of his own mother. Children for whom no price had been paid were regarded as illegitimate and stood at the bottom of the social scale. A girl's father, in arranging for her marriage, did not always consult her wishes, but made the best bargain he could, both for his own profit and for her honor.

Marriage being by purchase, it logically followed that divorce entailed the refunding of the money paid for the bride. A man was not expected to divorce his wife except for good cause, such as laziness or sterility. With regard to this, Kroeber says:

> An implied condition of purchase of a wife was that she bear children. Sterility therefore meant nonfulfillment of contract, and was perhaps the most frequent cause of divorce. If a couple with children separated, the woman could take them with her only on full repayment of her original price. On the other hand, each child left with the husband reduced the repayment, and several canceled it altogether. Theoretically, therefore, the average middle-aged or elderly

Karok plank house, showing double pitch and ragged shingling of roof. Northern California

Boat of Yurok manufacture on Trinity River at Hupa, California

PLATE 64

The Karok center of the world; sacred town of Katimin on left bank of the Klamath River, California; beyond, the ridge up which go the souls of the dead

woman with adult children was free to return to her parents' house, and remained with her husband from choice alone. . . .

Similarly, it might be inferred that a wife was bought for a natural span of life. If she died young a sister or kinswoman was due the husband. If he passed away first his equity did not lapse but remained in the family, and she was married by his brother. In either event, however, a payment, smaller than the original one, was made to her family . . . [since] no union could take place without a payment. . . .

Unfaithfulness on the part of the wife does not appear to have been a cause for divorce, but entailed the payment of a fine to the husband of from one to five strings of money. Since the payment of money was the only way in which an offense might be atoned for, a man who was unable to pay the required fine often became the slave of the one whom he had wronged. Except among these more advanced northwestern tribes, the institution of slavery was unknown in California.

One of the most gainful occupations among the Yurok was the healing art, which was, as a rule, monopolized by the women, whose power to cure disease was believed to depend on the possession of one or more "pains" which enabled the shaman to see and extract similar pains from sick people. These pains, acquired by the shaman from a spirit, usually of a dead ancestor, were supposed to be animate, material objects which operated after the fashion of a homeopathic remedy. I quote in part Kroeber's transcription of a shaman's story:

I began with a dream. At that time I was already married at Sregon. In the dream I was on Bald Hills. There I met a Chilula man who fed me deer meat which was black with blood. . . .

In the morning I was ill. A doctor was called in to treat me and diagnosed my case. Then I went to the sweat house to dance for 10 nights. This whole time I did not eat. Once I danced until I became unconscious. They carried me into the living house. When I revived I climbed up the framework of poles for drying fish, escaped through the smoke hole, ran to another sweat house, and began to dance there.

On the tenth day, while I was dancing, I obtained control of my first "pain." It came out of my mouth looking like a salmon liver, and as I held it in my hands blood dripped from it to the ground. This is what I had seen in my dreams on Bald Hills. I then thought that it was merely venison. It was when I ate the venison that the pain entered my body.

Once, while the others slept, I dreamed I saw an *uma'a* [magician] coming. One of his legs was straight, the other bent at the knee, and he walked on this knee as if it were his foot, and had only one eye. Then I shouted, dashed out, and ran down along the river. My male relatives pursued me and brought me back unconscious. Then I danced for three nights more. At this time I received my four largest pains. One of these is blue, one yellowish, another red, and the fourth white. Because I received these in dreaming about the *uma'a* they are the ones with which I cure sickness caused by an *uma'a*.

My smaller pains are whitish and less powerful. It is they that came to me in my first period of training. The pains come and go from my body. I do not always carry them in me. Today they are inside of me. . . .

Gradually I obtained more control over my pains, until finally I could take them out of myself, lay them in a basket, set this at the opposite end of the sweat house, and then swallow them from where I stood. . . .

When I am summoned to a patient, I smoke and say to myself: "I wish you to get well because I like what they are paying me." If the patient dies, I must return the payment. Then I begin to doctor. After I have danced a long time I can see all the pains in the sick person's body. . . . Sometimes a doctor really wishes to kill people. Then she blows her pains out through her pipe, sending them into the person that she hates.

Money was as important in healing the scars of war as in restoring sick people to health. Among the commercially minded Yurok, war was not considered an honorable pursuit, as among so many of the Eastern tribes, but simply murder on a large scale. Their wars were merely feuds that involved large groups of people. All avoided being drawn into such a war, as they avoided taking sides in private quarrels. Settlement took the form of compensation for damages. Such compensation was mutual and not confined to the losing side, with the paradoxical result that the winner, who usually inflicted the greater damage, had to bear the chief burden of making "reparations!"

The Yurok fought usually with bows and arrows. In close fighting they used a short stone club for cracking the heads of their enemies. Spears were only occasionally employed. They took no scalps but sometimes decapitated a fallen foe to make sure he was dead. No shields were carried, but body armor was sometimes used in the shape of jackets made either of thick elk hide or of rods wound together with string. The latter sort was not very popular, being as stiff and unyielding as a strait-jacket. The women were almost as warlike as the men, sometimes rushing into a fight and laying hold of some of the enemy in order that the men might kill them.

In times of peace the Yurok dispensed not only with their armor, but with nearly all clothing. Kroeber's account of their dress is as follows:

> The dress of northwestern California was essentially that of all the tribes of the State. Young men usually folded a deerskin about the hips. Their elders did not scruple to go naked. A breechclout was not worn. Women put on a buckskin apron, about a foot wide, its length slit into fringes, which were wrapped with a braid of lustrous *Xerophyllum* [a kind of snail-shell], or strung with pine nuts. From the rear of the waist a much broader apron or skirt was brought around to meet the front piece. The rear apron was again fringed, but contained a considerable area of unslit skin. Women also habitually wore neat, round, snugly fitting caps of basketry. These were modeled with a nearly flat top, but degenerated after some months into a peak. In cold weather both sexes threw over the shoulders a blanket or cape, normally of two deer hides sewn together. . . .
>
> Rich women ornamented their dress heavily. Haliotis and clam shells jangled musically from the ends of the fringes; and occasionally a row of obsidian prisms tinkled with every step. Poor women contented themselves with less. They sometimes had recourse to a simple skirt of fringed inner bark of the maple, which was standard wear for adolescent girls and novitiate shamans.
>
> All women had the entire chin, from the corners of the mouth downward, tattooed solidly except for two narrow blank lines. . . . This style is universal in northwestern California.

The Yurok construct their houses of planks split from logs with wedges. These they set endwise in the ground usually two rows thick to form the walls. Two plates are laid across the end walls to serve as ridge-poles, that is, if the house is the home of a man of wealth. A single-ridged house is a sign of poverty.

The interior of the house consists of a square room, which is on two levels, the central portion being dug out from two to five feet deep, forming a pit which serves to mark the sites of ancient houses. The fireplace is a shallow depression in the middle of the pit, usually bordered by stones. Above it is a frame of poles for drying salmon and other provisions.

The "shelf" area which surrounds the central pit is used for storage and if the family is prosperous is usually filled with huge baskets of acorns covered with inverted conical baskets. The rest of the space is often crowded with various other provisions as well as baskets and utensils temporarily out of commission. Most of the occupations of the family when indoors are carried on in the pit. Many houses have also a sort of stone-flagged porch, which serves as an outdoor living room.

The sweat-house was an important institution among the Yurok, as it served not only for the sleeping quarters of the men and boys but also as a temple where the most sacred religious rites were held. It was a smaller structure than the dwelling house, accommodating only seven regular occupants. The interior was entirely instead of only partially excavated, and the side walls did not reach above the surface of the ground.

The porch is even more important to the sweat-house than to the dwelling. A considerable space in front of the main entrance is paved with stones. Here the old men gather to sun themselves and to talk. Except in the northeastern part of the State the method of producing steam by pouring water over heated stones is unknown in California. When the Yurok wish to indulge in the luxury of a sweat bath, they kindle a wood fire in the stone pit and tightly close both the entrance and the small exit at the back, so that an intense heat is soon produced, as well as volumes of smoke. The sweater lies on the ground in order to avoid suffocation. After the fire has burned itself out, he opens the exit, wriggles out, and plunges into the nearby river or ocean.

The Yurok, with their neighbors, the Tolowa and Wiyot, were manufacturers of canoes which were sold to other neighboring tribes, including the Hupa and Karok. The Yurok canoe was dug out of half a redwood log and was a clumsy but symmetrical boat. Although used on the ocean, this canoe is especially adapted for navigating a rushing river full of rocks, having a square prow and rounded bottom without a stern. The paddles are stout poles six to eight feet long, spreading into narrow, heavy blades, and used by standing men. The helmsman, who is seated, wields a short paddle.

Although the Yurok, like all California Indians, depended on the acorn as a staple food, they ate more fish, particularly salmon, than was customary among the other tribes. The large ocean mussel, too, was commonly used by the people on the coast, while salt was furnished by seaweed dried in round blackish cakes. The flesh of the whale was greatly prized as food, but, as the Yurok did not attempt to hunt sea animals, except the sea-lion, their supply was limited to such whales as might be stranded on the beach. The food supply of these people was usually ample enough to make it unnecessary for them to eat the grasshoppers, angle-worms, and yellow-jacket larvae popular elsewhere in the State. In times of scarcity, however, they fell back on almost anything, particularly availing themselves of the large yellow slugs common in California. Both reptiles and dogs, however, were considered poisonous.

The Yurok were accustomed to eat but two meals a day—breakfast, which came late, after the greater part of the day's work was over, and supper in the evening, about sunset. They were light eaters and gluttony was frowned upon as the vice of a poor and shiftless man.

Fish were taken usually with dip nets, although seines and other set nets, as well as harpoons, were sometimes used. For their nets the Yurok used a heavy two-ply twine made from the fibers of an iris leaf. It was the women's duty to gather the leaves and extract two fine silky fibers from each by means of an artificial thumbnail of mussel shell. The string was usually twisted and the nets always knotted by men, who used implements made of elk antler. The nets were weighted by means of stones which were grooved, pierced, or naturally perforated.

In hunting the sea-lion, the Yurok disguised themselves in bear- or deerskins and awaited the animals at their haunts on the rocks. As the sea-lions clambered up, the hunters attracted their attention by barking and wriggling and otherwise "playing sea-lion," much as the Eskimo hunters "play seal." They then leaped up and harpooned them. As the sea-lion dived into the water, it was followed by boat, the harpoon regained by means of the line, and the animal speared again. In this way a canoe might be dragged far out to sea before the sea-lion had ceased its struggles.

The acorns used as food by the Yurok as by all other California tribes, would have been inedible except for the process of leaching employed. They were first gathered, dried, and stored away in great baskets, and later shelled and pounded into meal. For this purpose a stone pestle, usually a foot long, was used on a hard, smooth slab or rock. The Yurok used pestles that were carefully dressed and shaped and sometimes ornamented with a raised ring or flange on the handle, whereas most of the other Californians were satisfied with a rough cobble. The Yurok had no mortar, but the acorn fragments and meal were kept from scattering by a flaring basketry hopper, while a brush made of soaproot fibers was used to sweep up whatever escaped this container. Ancient mortars have occasionally been brought to light in the Yurok country, but their use seems to be wholly unknown to the present inhabitants.

After being pulverized the meal was spread out in a hollow in a mound of clean sand, and hot water poured over it in order to remove the bitter taste of the tannic acid. This was the quick method of leaching. Sometimes acorns were buried for a year in swampy mud, and were purplish when taken out ready to be roasted on hot coals; usually, however, they were prepared by pounding and leaching as described above.

After the hot water had drained off through the sand the acorn meal was ready to be cooked. This was usually done by stirring it, together with a quantity of hot stones, in closely woven baskets used as pots. The stirring was necessary to prevent the hot stones from burning holes in the basket. As in the case of the pestles, we find the stirring paddles of the Yurok and their nearest neighbors much better shaped and more highly ornamented than were the "mush paddles" of other California tribes. The Yurok paddle is always made of some hard wood, and is sometimes nearly four feet long. When prepared, the acorn gruel of the California Indian is almost as tasteless as wheat flour cooked in water would be, and about as nourishing, being usually richer in starch and in some cases decidedly oily.

Almost the only crop raised by the Yurok was tobacco for smoking. Those who grew tobacco sold to those farther south, who did not. The same species grows wild also, but is never used by the Yurok for fear it may have sprouted in a graveyard, although it grows chiefly along sandy bars close to the river. The natives of California seem to have used their tobacco undiluted with bark, and to have smoked chiefly at bedtime in the sweat house in order to induce drowsiness. Their pipes were slightly curved tubes made of polished hardwood, the bowl sometimes lined with soapstone. They were kept in little pouches of deerskin in which tobacco was also carried. To fill a pipe one had only to press it down into the tobacco at the bottom of the pouch.

The Yurok's only method of making baskets was that of twining, and in this style of basketry they excelled. They made a great variety, from the coarse burden and storage baskets to small trays and bowls for serving individual portions of fish and acorn mush. Perhaps the finest work was lavished on the basket caps worn by the women.

Various objects which the Yurok made of wood included head-rests and stools; cylindrical boxes or trunks hollowed out from the smaller logs of the redwood and closed with a lid that was lashed on; rectangular platters or trays for deer meat; huge finger bowls for cleaning the deer meat from the hand before it could come in contact with any sea animal; and the standard fire-drill.

The points of cutting instruments and other implements were made of elk horn, which was also used for spoons having rather flat bowls and carved handles. Most Californians dipped up their acorn gruel with their fingers, but the Yurok were more fastidious in their habits. Elk or deer horn was also used for making purses or money boxes, which were cylindrical in shape, like the large wooden boxes for valuables, but only six or seven inches long, and would hold several folded strings of dentalia.

Considering the tools with which the Yurok artisan was obliged to work, the results achieved were truly remarkable. Logs and planks were split with wedges of elk horn, curved or nearly flat according to the intended use, the edges of which had been sharpened by rubbing on stone. The wedges were driven by pear-shaped mauls, from six to eight inches long, of basalt or other rock. These were carefully made and shaped, usually quite symmetrical, and sometimes beautifully finished. In

PLATE 65

Family group of the Hupa Indians of California in the National Museum. Showing method of fire making and various stages in the preparation of acorn gruel, the favorite food of these Indians

the care they bestowed on the manufacture of these tools the Yurok differed from most Californians, who were content with unshaped stones. Another tool on which the Yurok lavished great pains was the stone handle of the adz, the blade of which consisted of heavy mussel shell lashed on with thongs.

Religion among the Yurok centered about certain localities which were regarded as hallowed by having been the scene from time immemorial of sacred rites performed in honor of some mythological person or spirit. The most sacred rite connected with the ceremonials was the recitation of a long formula, usually given by an old man accompanied by an assistant, who also performed the prescribed symbolic acts, such as fasting and secluding themselves from the ordinary dwellings and occupations of men. Certain ceremonies in the sweat-house preceded the public recitation. These occupied several nights, during which offerings of tobacco or angelica root were thrown on the fire.

After the recitation of the formula, the sacred dance began and was repeated every afternoon, sometimes both afternoon and morning, for five, ten, or more days. Women did not join in the performance but were onlookers only. Any man, however, might take part. The dancers' regalia consisted of the most precious possessions of the Yurok, and so eager were the rich men of the town to display their wealth that they readily supplied the performers with their greatest treasures—all except dentalium money. The largest obsidian and flint blades, the whitest deerskins, and the most gorgeous bands of woodpecker scalps were handed over to the dancers for display. The performers were men noted for their ability to sing and dance, and constantly composed new words that were sung to the old dance melodies. The two most famous dances are known as the White Deerskin and the Jumping dance.

A local dance of a less solemn nature was the so-called

Kepel Dam dance, which was a Deerskin dance associated with the building of a salmon dam at the village of Kepel in early autumn. None of these ceremonies, however, has been performed for many years.

Since the love of money is the ruling passion among the Yurok it is not surprising to find that one of their deities is Pelintsiek, "Great Dentalium," who appears to be the Indian prototype of our "Almighty Dollar." A greater god than Pelintsiek, however, is the mighty Pulekukwerek for whom the Yurok have the greatest veneration. The creator of all things was Wohpekumen, who was less noble and more inclined to play tricks than the great Pulekukwerek.

Other characters in Yurok mythology are Megwomets, a bearded dwarf, who carries acorns on his back and is the giver of vegetable foods; Segep, the coyote, less praised than among other California tribes; Wertspit, the locust larva, who wished death into the world; and Kego'or, the porpoises, who dwelt at Kenek until men were created. Thunder and Earthquake also lived at Kenek, until Earthquake was beaten at his favorite game of shinny. The house sites of many of these great ones of old are still shown at the little town.

The Yurok believe that the world floats on water—a river which has its source in the sky. There the Deerskin dance is danced nightly, and there live the gigantic white coyote and his yellow mate, who are the parents of all coyotes on earth.

The Yurok civilization, superior in many ways to the culture of either southern or central California, was shared by a group of neighboring tribes, who spoke different languages but were much alike in traditions and customs. On the north were the Athapascan Tolowa; on the east, the Karok (the "upstream people"), who lived on the banks of the Klamath River just above the Yurok (the "down-stream people"); while on the south were more Athapascan tribes, and the Wiyot. Of the southern Athapascans, the nearest to the Yurok and the most closely associated both with them and with the Karok were the Hupa. These three nations were on the most friendly terms with one another; trading, intermarrying, and taking part in one another's religious celebrations.

Trade between the Yurok and the Hupa was especially active; the one being a coast-dwelling nation of fishermen and manufacturers, and the other living in a region which abounded in game and vegetable products, they were able to supply each other's needs to a considerable extent. From the Yurok the Hupa bought canoes, salt-water fish, mussels, and seaweed, in exchange for acorns and other inland food. The two tribes looked upon each other as relatives and friends.

The Hupa occupy a beautiful valley some six or eight miles long through which flows the Trinity River together with a number of smaller streams from the high mountain ranges on either side. So secluded were these people that they knew nothing of the coming of the white men until 1850 when they were suddenly overrun by both whites and Chinese in the first mad rush for gold. Hunted from their homes like wild animals, it was not until the majority of their persecutors had left for richer fields that the unfortunate Hupa ventured to return and take up the broken threads of their existence in their old home, which was finally secured to them as a reservation in 1864.

Their houses, built of planks like those of the Yurok, were grouped in villages on the banks of the river, usually near a spring. The larger dwellings, called *xonta*, were used as sleeping places for the women and as storehouses for the family possessions, while the men occupied the smaller sweat-houses or "taikyūw."

These inland people were habitually better clothed than were those of the warmer coast region. For dress occasions the men wore tunics made of two deerskins with the hair on, which were joined along one side with the necks meeting over the left shoulder and were held in place by a belt at the waist; sometimes these picturesque garments were made of panther skins. Ordinarily only a breechclout of skins was worn, supplemented by leggings sewed up the front with sinew and ornamented with fringes and sometimes with paintings. Moccasins of buckskin with elk-hide soles were also sometimes worn. The long hair of the men was tied in two clubs on either side of the head or in one at the back and was held in place by a fillet sometimes ornamented with red woodpecker scalps. In their ears they wore dentalium-shell earrings with tassels of woodpecker feathers. Ornamental skin quivers full of arrows were a part of "full dress." Other skin bags or pockets as well as sacks made of netting were carried when needed.

The women wore the double petticoat and apron popular with all the California tribes. These were made of buckskin, fringed and ornamented with strands of shells and beads. In cold weather a long cape of various kinds of skins was worn around the shoulders. A close-fitting cap of basketwork and moccasins similar to those worn by the men completed the woman's costume. Her favorite ornaments were shell or bead earrings and necklaces. Her hair was worn in two long pigtails on either side of the face, ornamented with strands of leather, sometimes covered with red woodpecker crests, and perfumed with sprays of the *yerba buena*, a kind of mint. A heavily tattooed chin added the final touch to a woman's beauty.

Mighty hunters were the Hupa, bringing down elk, deer, panthers, and other big game with no other weapon than the flint-tipped arrows they shot with unerring skill from their stout yew bows. Stalking the game to get within bowshot was no easy task. To do so required much watchful waiting and senses scarcely less keen than those of the hunted wild things. In order to deceive the

PLATE 66

Ceremonial of the Kwakiutl Indians of British Columbia called "The Return of the Cannibal" in which an initiate is freed from the cannibal spirit

PLATE 67

Chilkat family group, southeastern Alaska. Man in ceremonial costume, women weaving blanket and baskets

sensitive nostrils of the elk and deer, the Hupa hunter would carefully bathe and perfume his body with fragrant incense from smoking fir-tree boughs or sweet-smelling herbs of various kinds. He would then conceal himself within a mask of the head and antlers, sometimes the entire skin, of an elk. Thus disguised he would trot along on all fours, playing elk so successfully that he might even deceive a panther crouching in a tree overhead ready for a spring. Leaping upon his prey and seeking to sink his teeth in its neck, the unwary beast would find his jaws impaled upon the projecting points of long pins which the hunter, in anticipation of just such an emergency, always thrust through the masses of his hair worn coiled upon his neck underneath the elk skin.

The Hupa depended upon the elk and deer for many things besides food. Their efficiency in adapting every portion of the animal to a variety of uses was scarcely less, indeed, than that of the Chicago pork packers, who are famous for utilizing all parts of the hog "except the squeal." In his memoir on "The Life and Culture of the Hupa," Goddard illustrates the cleverness of the Indians in this respect:

> The man who succeeded in securing an elk had a large quantity of welcome food, a skin which, when properly tanned, would defend him in battle from the arrows of the enemy, and antlers which furnished him material for spoons and wedges.
>
> The deerskins were also very valuable. They were in constant demand for clothing and bedding. The hides were retained by the master of the hunt. . . . The carcass was cut in accordance with prescribed rules. Some portions were not eaten at all, among them the flesh on the floating ribs and the breast bone. Other parts were forbidden to women. None of the animal was wasted save from religious scruples. The blood was drunk at once. The stomach, in which other parts were put, was buried in the ashes until cooked and then eaten. The ears were a delicacy to be roasted in the camp-fire and eaten after the hunt. The bone of the leg was saved with its marrow, which was of service in mixing paint. The sinews were saved for bowstrings. The brain was removed and dried that it might be used in dressing the hide. The meat which was not needed for immediate consumption was cut into strips by the women and cured over a fire.

The Hupa bill-of-fare included, besides venison, many small animals such as squirrels and woodrats, and a variety of birds such as the grouse, pheasant, and mountain quail. Fish also formed an important article of diet, particularly the salmon, which during the spring and fall runs were caught in great quantities by means of nets and traps. In olden times, before the clean waters of the Trinity had been muddied by mining operations, the salmon were taken by means of spears. These were long poles ending in two prongs tipped with barbs of bone or horn which, like the harpoon heads of the Eskimo, were detachable and controlled by a long line fastened to the shaft of the spear.

Sturgeon was another fish greatly prized by the Hupa not only as food but also for the glue obtained from the head. Trout and other small fish, including great numbers of lamprey eels, were also taken, usually in dip nets. The favorite food for a long journey was dried salmon roe, which was eaten without cooking, as were also all kinds of dried fish.

The staple vegetable food of the Hupa was acorn mush, which was sometimes eaten hot, sometimes baked as bread and eaten cold. This is still a favorite food. Dried hazelnuts, ripe chinquapin, and roasted nuts of the pepperwood are also eaten, as well as seeds of pines and grasses, various lily bulbs, particularly those of the soaproot, and the fresh shoots of many plants. These last are eaten raw, but the bulbs are cooked in much the same fashion as the Apache prepares his mescal—that is, they are roasted in a pit for about two days and when cooked in this manner are said to be an agreeable and nourishing food. As for fruits, it is hard to realize that wild grapes and berries were all that were known to the natives of California, so famous now for its oranges, apples, grapes, figs, and almost every other kind of fruit, all of which have been introduced by the white invaders of the land.

The only plant cultivated by the Hupa was tobacco. Like the Yurok, they believed that the wild variety was poisonous, particularly if it had grown on a grave. Their pipes were usually of wood having the bowl faced with serpentine or sandstone and decorated with an inlay of mother-of-pearl. Occasionally the entire pipe would be made of sandstone.

The manufacture of pipes, bows and arrows, and other implements and utensils of wood or horn, the cultivation of tobacco, and the dressing of hides, were considered the duties of the men. On the women devolved the fine arts of cooking, sewing, and basketry. Hupa basketry is of twined work, the simplest example of which is found in the lattices used in the fish dams, while finer types are seen in the closely woven cooking and burden baskets and in the ornamental ones used as hats by the women. The designs are usually geometrical, the most popular figure being the triangle or modifications of it obtained by combining a number in various ways. The favorite colors are black and red.

In many of their customs, such as marriage by purchase, the religious dances, and the use of dentalium shells for money, the Hupa were very much like their neighbors, the Yurok. In their social organization, too, they followed the Yurok very closely. Wealth was greatly respected and the head man in a village was invariably the richest person there. Wrongdoing was punishable by a fine, but in the case of murder the money might be rejected by the murdered man's relatives and life for life exacted instead—not necessarily the life of the murderer, but that of some member of his family. Even an accidental death might be atoned for in this way. Goddard mentions an instance of the accidental death of a child who was burned to death in a fire a woman had built for heating wash-water out of doors. Although the woman was in no way at fault, the life of her son was sought as a recompense. With regard to the further extension of this principle, Goddard says:

If the feud was between villages or tribes, the death of any male member of the village or tribe atoned for the injury. This principle was applied to the whole white race. If a white man killed an Indian, a white man's life was due in return. Wanton killing of Indians by the first white men caused many an innocent white man's death. This small regard for the mere individual and the great regard for the family is a point to be kept well in mind when dealing with or studying the Indians.

Since the Hupa valley was converted into a reservation, the history of the natives seems to have been far from happy. Goddard gives the following survey of the situation:

H. L. Knight, an attorney at law, of Eureka, who spent some months on the Reservation in 1871, has this to say concerning the treatment they [the Hupa] had received and were receiving from the men in charge:

"If the Reservation was a plantation, the Indians were the most degraded slaves. I found them poor, miserable, vicious, degraded, dirty, naked, diseased, and ill-fed. The oldest men, or stout middle-aged fathers of families, were spoken to just as children or slaves. They know no law but the will of the Agent; no effort has been made to teach them any, and where it does not conflict with this dictation, they follow the old forms of life—polygamy, buying and selling of women, and compounding crime with money *ad libitum*." (*Report of the Indian Commissioner*, 1871, p. 158.)

The Reservation was abandoned as a failure in 1877, but with a change at Washington it was afterwards decided to continue it. Army officers were put in charge and the industrial affairs of the Reservation were straightened out. In 1892 the soldiers were removed, but great harm had already been done by their long-continued presence after all need for it had passed. Goddard says of this phase of Government control:

Nothing could have been worse for these Indians than the maintenance of these men in comparative indleness in their midst. It may be said in all truth that if the Government in 1864 had resolved to do all that lay in its power to demoralize this people, it could hardly have taken a course more sure to reach that end than the one followed.

Upper—Medicine-man's wand from the Kwakiutl Indians, British Columbia. Lower—Carved and inlaid dish of sheep's horn from the Haida Indians of southeastern Alaska. In the National Museum

Since the removal of the military element, however, the situation of the Hupa has greatly improved. They are becoming self-supporting through farming, stock raising, and other useful occupations and trades. They are acquiring some education and are as a rule law-abiding. In 1904 Goddard reported the tribe as numbering 450 with a nearly equal birth and death rate.

The degree of civilization attained by the West Coast tribes is found to increase steadily as the warm and enervating climate of the south is replaced by the more stimulating conditions of life farther north. Of the inhabitants of the Northwestern coasts and islands, Boas gives the following general account:

> The Pacific Coast of America between Juan de Fuca Strait and Yakutat Bay is inhabited by a great many Indian tribes distinct in physical characteristics and distinct in languages, but one in culture. Their arts and industries, their customs and beliefs, differ so much from those of all other Indians that they form one of the best defined cultural groups of our continent.
>
> While a hasty glance at these people and a comparison with other tribes emphasize the uniformity of their culture, a closer investigation reveals many peculiarities of individual tribes which prove that their culture has developed slowly and from a number of distinct centers, each people adding something to the culture which we observe at the present day.
>
> The region inhabited by these people is a mountainous coast intersected by innumerable sounds and fiords and studded with islands, large and small. Thus intercourse along the coast by means of canoes is very easy, while access to the inland is difficult on account of the rugged hills and the density of the woods.

Dense forests along the coast furnish wood, particularly the red cedar, of which the natives make houses, canoes, implements, and utensils, utilizing the bark for clothing and rope. Garments and blankets were formerly made of the skins of various animals. Today they are more often woven of mountain-goat wool, dog's hair, feathers, or a mixture of these.

Carvings in wood and stone are usually of characteristically grotesque designs executed with great skill.

The most artistic products of the handiwork of these people, however, are the baskets of which a great variety are made, from the large, open-mesh carrying basket to the closely woven, water-tight pots of basketry in which water is boiled by means of heated stones.

The animal food furnished by the abundant supply of land and sea animals, fish, and shellfish, is supplemented by roots, berries, seaweed and sea grass. The sea grass and berries, as well as fish roe and other kinds of animal food, are dried for winter use and eaten mixed with fish oil which is kept in bottles of dried kelp. Fish oil, in fact, furnishes the invariable sauce for winter foods, even for preserved crabapples and other fruits. Fresh meat in winter is supplied by the elk, deer, and various other game, which are hunted today with guns, but were formerly shot with arrows tipped with stone, bone, or copper, or caught in large nets made of cedar bark, deer sinews, or nettles.

Many different languages are spoken by the North Pacific tribes, including the Tlingit, Haida, and Wakashan tongues. The last named—the Wakashan—is represented by two groups of dialects spoken respectively by the Nootka and the Kwakiutl, both of whom inhabit parts of Vancouver Island and the adjacent mainland.

The Kwakiutl are described by Boas as having a remarkable and distinct type of face—much longer than that of the average Indian, with a high, hooked nose. They are divided into various tribes having many subdivisions. Each of these groups traces its origin to a mythical ancestor who descended from heaven, or emerged from the underworld or the ocean, built his house, and founded his family at a certain place—actually some old village site, showing that the group was originally a village community. Each group claims a distinct rank and certain privileges based on the adventures of its mythological ancestor. These privileges and distinctions descend to the children through the mother, but are bestowed upon the father also at the time of his marriage as a kind of dowry. A curious custom gave the name and rank of a man to his slayer, who might put his own successor in place of his killed enemy. In this way names spread from tribe to tribe. Not all the individuals of a clan enjoyed the same rank. As with all the tribes of the Northwest coast, the Kwakiutl were divided into three classes—the nobility, common people, and slaves.

One of the most distinctive institutions among the tribes of the North Pacific is the potlatch, which is the name given to festivals at which great quantities of property are either given away or destroyed as evidence of the owner's wealth. As practiced among the Kwakiutl, however, according to Boas, the property thus given away is always returned with interest and constitutes an investment rather than a gift. In his memoir on the Kwakiutl Indians, published in 1897, Boas gives the following explanation of the potlatch:

The child when born is given the name of the place where it is born. This name it keeps until about a year old. Then his father, mother, or some other relative, gives a paddle or a mat to each member of the clan and the child receives his second name. When the boy is about 10 or 12 years old, he obtains this third name. In order to obtain it, he must distribute a number of small presents, such as shirts or single blankets, among his own clan or tribe. When the youth thus starts out in life, he is liberally assisted by his elders, particularly by the nobility of the tribe.

I must say here that the unit of value is the single blanket. . . . When a native has to pay debts and has not a sufficient number of blankets, he borrows them from his friends and has to pay the following rates of interest:

For a period of a few months, for 5 borrowed blankets 6 must be returned; for a period of six months, for 5 borrowed blankets 7 must be returned; for a period of twelve months or longer, for 5 borrowed blankets 10 must be returned. . . .

When a boy is about to take his third name, he will borrow blankets from the other members of the tribe, who all assist him. . . . The next June he pays his debts in a festival, at which all the clans from whom he borrowed blankets are present. The festival is generally held on the street or at an open place near the village. Up to this time he is not allowed to take part in feasts. But now he may distribute property in order to obtain a potlach name. . . .

Still more complicated is the purchase or the gift, however one chooses to name it, of a "copper." All along the North Pacific Coast . . . curiously shaped copper plates are in use, which in olden times were made of native copper . . . but which nowadays are worked out of imported copper. . . . The front of the copper is covered with black lead, in which a face, representing the crest animal of the owner, is graven. These coppers have the same function which bank notes of high denominations have with us. The actual value of the piece of copper is small, but it is made to represent a large number of blankets and can always be sold for blankets. The value is not arbitrarily set, but depends upon the amount of property given away in the festival at which the copper is sold.

The only valid measure of a man's wealth, according to Kwakiutl ideas, is the amount of property that he is willing to destroy. Boas thus describes the working out of this principle:

The rivalry between chiefs and clans finds its strongest expression in the destruction of property. A chief will burn blankets, a canoe, or break a copper, thus indicating his disregard of the amount of property destroyed and showing that his mind is stronger, his power greater, that that of his rival. If the latter is not able to destroy an equal amount of property without much delay, his name is "broken." He is vanquished by his rival and his influence with the tribe is lost, while the name of the other chief gains correspondingly in renown. . . .

In by far the greater number of cases where coppers are broken the copper is preserved. . . . Finally, somebody succeeds in buying up all the broken fragments, which are riveted together, and the copper has attained an increased value. Since the broken copper indicates the fact that the owner has destroyed property, the Indians pride themselves upon their possession.

During their festivals the Kwakiutl wore masks representing the face and deeds of an ancestor. One of these masks, now in the Berlin Museum, is double and is opened and closed by means of strings. It represents Nolis, an ancestor of a certain group, the outer mask showing him in a state of rage vanquishing his rivals, the inner one picturing him as kindly disposed, distributing property in a friendly way. On top of the mask is the image of a bear's head, which refers to a legendary bear who broke the dam that prevented Nolis from sending his property up the river.

The Kwakiutl passion for destroying property found expression in their feasts at which not only was a great quantity of food consumed but the house itself was frequently threatened with destruction, as well as the lives of both host and guests. These festivities were known as "grease feasts" and are thus described by Boas:

> When a person gives a grease feast, a great fire is lighted in the center of the house. The flames leap up to the roof and the guests are almost scorched by the heat. Still the etiquette demands that they do not stir, else the host's fire has conquered them. Even when the roof begins to burn and the fire attacks the rafters, they must appear unconcerned. The host alone has the right to send a man up to the roof to put out the fire. While the feast is in progress the host sings a scathing song ridiculing his rival and praising his own clan, the feats of his forefathers and his own. Then the grease is filled in large spoons and passed to the rival chief first. If a person thinks he has given a greater grease feast than that offered by the host, he refuses the spoon. Then he runs out of the house to fetch his copper "to squelch with it the fire." The host proceeds at once to tie a copper to each of his house posts. If he should not do so, the person who refused the spoon would on returning strike the posts with the copper, which is considered equal to striking the chief's face.

In his pride on such an occasion a chief would risk not only his own home but that of several other related families who might be occupying the same house. Such houses are large and well built. They are thus described by Boas, in part:

> The houses of the Kwakiutl form a square, the sides of which are from 40 to 60 feet long. The door is generally in the center of the side nearest the sea, which forms the front of the house. The latter has a gable roof, the ridge of which runs from the front to the rear. The walls consist of boards which are fastened to a framework of poles. . . .
>
> The house is inhabited by several families, each of whom has a fireplace of its own. The corners belonging to each family are divided off from the main room by a rough framework of poles, the top of which

is used for drying fish or other sorts of food. On each side of the fire stands the immense settee, which is large enough for the whole family. . . . The houses generally face the beach and are built in a row. . . . Opposite to the houses, on the side of the street toward the sea, there are platforms; summer seats, on which the Indians pass most of their time, gambling and conversing.

Besides the family totems, which are hereditary animals, the Kwakiutl had a complicated tribal mythology, the chief figures of which were impersonated in the ceremonies conducted by the various secret societies which were as numerous and as powerful among these northwestern tribes as among the Pueblos of the Southwest. Here, too, they formed a bond of union among peoples of such alien tongues as the Kwakiutl and their more northern neighbors, the Haida and the Tlingit Indians.

On the Queen Charlotte Islands, a group about seventy-five miles northwest of Vancouver Island, live the Haida, whose nearest relatives are found distributed along the coast to the north, on the Aleutian Islands and on the Siberian coast of Asia. These Indians form a distinct type, being, as a rule, larger, more stalwart, and of lighter complexion than other American tribes. This difference is especially marked in the women, who are tall and athletic, while the typical Indian woman is short and apt to be fat, especially in middle age.

Living so far from the mainland, the Haida made long voyages in dug-out canoes of red cedar, sometimes large enough to carry as many as a hundred persons, together with the necessary equipment. Ordinarily, canoes were made to accommodate from twenty to thirty people. In these the Haida were accustomed to travel as far as to Victoria on Vancouver Island, and thence to the various towns on Puget Sound.

The Haida brought with them, for sale or traffic, furs, seal oil, silver ornaments such as bracelets, rings, and earrings, and carvings in wood and stone. The stone carvings were made of a peculiar kind of slate-stone found on the Queen Charlotte Islands, very soft when first quarried and easily carved into fanciful figures of various kinds, but growing very hard upon exposure to air after being rubbed with oil which seems to harden as well as polish it.

The wood carvings of the Haida were most often displayed on the totem poles which usually formed part of the front walls of their dwellings. The houses were built with planks around a central excavation after the usual fashion of the northwest coast, but were rendered distinctive by the presence of these posts, which were usually made from a single cedar tree hollowed out at the back. They were sometimes from fifty to sixty feet high and were elaborately carved and painted in brilliant shades of red, yellow, and green. A circular opening near the ground served as the entrance to the house. The carvings represented the totems or heraldic designs of the families occupying the dwelling. As each lodge usually housed several families, the carvings might be said to indicate the family names of the different occupants, serving the same purpose as personal cards in the entrance of the modern apartment house. Of one of their mythological creatures, the thunder bird, Swan says:

> The belief in the thunder bird is common with all the tribes of the northwest coast. . . It is a belief in a supernatural being of gigantic stature, who resides in the mountains and has a human form. When he wishes for food he covers himself with wings and feathers as one would put on a cloak. Thus accoutered, he sails forth in search of prey. His body is of such enormous size that it darkens the heavens, and the rustling of his wings produces thunder.
>
> The lightning is produced by a fish, like the Hypocampus, which he gets from the ocean and hides among his feathers. When he sees a whale he darts one of these animals down with great velocity, and the lightning is produced by the creature's tongue, which is supposed to be like that of the serpent.

The Tlingit inhabit a great archipelago on the southern coast of Alaska, which possesses a comparatively mild and equable climate.

Their villages number a score or more and are occupied by closely related tribes, including the Stickeens, the Sitkas, the Yakutat, the Chilkat, and others less well known than these. All these tribes are divided into two groups of clans known as the Raven and the Wolf families and speak dialects of the same language—the Tlingit tongue. Members of clans belonging to the same family or phratry were forbidden to marry one another, with the exception of the Eagle clan, the members of which, although they belonged to the Raven Phratry, might marry on either side.

The Tlingit traced descent through the mother's line and the children belonged to the clan of the mother. Since the father and all his relatives belonged to a different clan, however, there was nothing to prevent the intermarriage of relatives on the paternal side of the house.

Most of the native manners and customs of these Indians are rapidly dying out with the advance of civilization. Totem poles are no longer erected, but the art of carving still survives and miniature totem poles, canoes, paddles, and trinket boxes are manufactured for sale among the tourists. The Chilkat are famous for the blankets they weave from the wool of the mountain goats.

The old method of constructing canoes is still used to some extent. This consists in splitting a log of the required length, roughly hollowing it out, and then filling it with water into which hot stones are thrown. When the wood has become sufficiently pliable through this process of steaming, braces are put in to hold it in shape. The canoe is then completed by patient chipping and sandpapering to give it a smooth finish. The braces are left in to serve as seats, although formerly the occupants sat in the bottom to paddle. This is said to have caused most of the men to have misshapen legs. Since the introduction of oars, both oars and paddles have

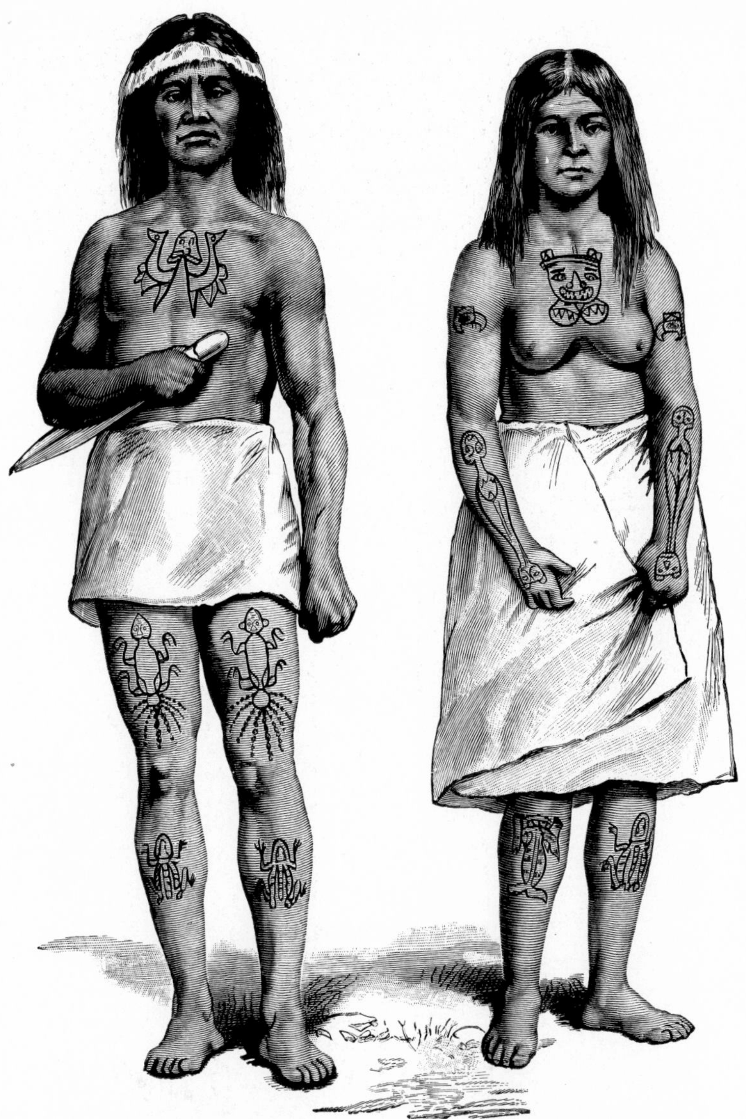

Haida man and woman. British Columbia. The tattoo designs resemble those used in totem poles

PLATE 70

Left—A Haida pole, supposed to be the most elaborate column in Alaska, in the Territorial Park, Sitka. Right—A Tlingit pole

been used in conjunction and a sail is also used whenever possible.

Basketry is the principal industry of the Tlingit women and is carried on in practically every home, chiefly by the older women, who are experts in the art. Native dyes of many brilliant tints, chiefly yellow, green, and red, are used, combined of course with the black so frequently found in northwest color schemes, which is produced by the use of black straws found in the bottom of certain lakes.

The importance of the totem in the life of these people is explained in detail by Jones as follows:

> The totem pole is but one of the many expressions of totemism. Everything the native possesses, in many instances even his person, carries totemic designs. He does not make a common halibut hook, or a paddle, a spoon, a bracelet, or scarcely any other object, without etching his totem on it. Why? Because everything he uses is associated with his patron friend and protector, be it eagle, crow, bear, or wolf. If he puts the image of his patron on his halibut hook, it will help him to have good success; on his paddle, to go safely over the deep; on his spoon, to protect him from poisonous foods; on his house, to bless his family. . . .
>
> All handiwork in wood, stone, bone, horn, copper, gold, and silver bears totemic designs. So with moccasins, baskets, and blankets. In this age even marble tombstones are ordered to bear the same. In the burial grounds of natives may now be seen marble monuments (white man totem) with the salmon, the grampus, and other totemic figures chiselled on them. Not a few natives have tatooed on their person their totemic patron. . . .
>
> The memorial or mortuary pole is a monument erected in the burial ground to the memory of the dead. It usually carries the single image of the patron animal of the deceased. When cremation was the universal custom of disposing of the dead, cavities were made in the back of the mortuary tablets in which to deposit the ashes of the deceased. . . .
>
> Totem poles vary in height from a few feet to fifty or more. They are usually very costly, not because of their intrinsic, but for their sentimental, value. In some instances they are valued at three or four thousand dollars each. They are carved out of a solid tree trunk (usually yellow cedar), and by tools of the natives' own make, a rude adz being the principal one used.

Certain aspects of this distinctive culture of the Northwest coast were shared, as we have seen, by the Eskimo of Alaska. Like their southern neighbors, however, the Alaska Eskimo are abandoning their old customs and manner of life for the doubtful blessings of the white man's civilization. The native tongues are fast vanishing before the all-conquering English; the old religion is being replaced by a curious sort of pseudo-Christianity; and the tribal laws must in time be discarded for the white man's method of dispensing justice.

REFERENCES

Boas, Franz. The social organization and the secret societies of the Kwakiutl Indians. U. S. Nation. Mus. Ann. Rep. 1895, pp. 311–738. Washington, 1897.

—— The Kwakiutl of Vancouver Island. Mem. Amer. Mus. Nat. Hist. Jesup North Pacific Expedition. Vol. 5, Part 2. New York, 1909.

—— The social organization of the Kwakiutl. Amer. Anthrop. (N. S.) Vol. 22, pp. 111–126, 1920.

Goddard, Pliny Earle. Life and culture of the Hupa. Univ. Calif. Pub. Amer. Archaeol. Ethnol. Vol. 1, No. 1, Berkeley, 1903.

—— Hupa texts. Univ. Calif. Pub. Amer. Archaeol. Ethnol. Vol. 1, No. 2. Berkeley, 1904.

Jones, Livingston F. A study of the Thlingets of Alaska. London, [1914].

Krause, Aurel. Die Tlinkit Indianer. Auftrage der Bremer geographichan Gesellschaft, 1880–81. Jena, 1885.

Kroeber, A. L. Handbook of the Indians of California. Bur. Amer. Ethnol. Bull. 78. Washington, 1925. [Contains a bibliography of 415 titles.]

Mason, Otis T. The Ray collection from Hupa Reservation. Smithsonian Inst. Ann. Rep. 1886, Part 1, pp. 205–239. Washington, 1889.

Powers, Stephen. Tribes of California. Cont. N. Amer. Ethnol. Vol. 3. Washington, 1897.

Swan, James G. The Haidah Indians of Queen Charlotte's Islands, British Columbia. Smithsonian Cont. Knowl. 267. Washington, 1874.

Swanton, John R. Contributions to the ethnology of the Haida. Mem. Amer. Mus. Nat. Hist. Jesup North Pacific Expedition, Vol. 5, Part 1, New York, 1905.

Waterman, T. T. Some conundrums in Northwest Coast Art. Amer. Anthrop. (N. S.) Vol. 25, pp. 435–451, 1923.

CHAPTER VIII

MYTHS AND LEGENDS

ESKIMO

Sedna and the Fulmar[1]

Once upon a time there lived on a solitary shore an Inung with his daughter Sedna. His wife had been dead for some time and the two led a quiet life. Sedna grew up to be a handsome girl and the youths came from all around to sue for her hand, but none of them could touch her proud heart. Finally, at the breaking up of the ice in the spring a fulmar[2] flew from over the ice and wooed Sedna with enticing song. "Come to me," it said, "come into the land of the birds, where there is never hunger, where my tent is made of the most beautiful skins. You shall rest on soft bearskins. My fellows, the fulmars, shall bring you all your heart may desire; their feathers shall clothe you; your lamp shall always be filled with oil, your pot with meat." Sedna could not long resist such wooing and they went together over the vast sea. When at last they reached the country of the fulmar, after a long and hard journey, Sedna discovered that her spouse had shamefully deceived her. Her new home was not built of beautiful pelts, but was covered with wretched fishskins, full of holes, that gave free entrance to wind and snow. Instead of soft reindeer skins her bed was made of hard walrus hides and she had to live on miserable fish, which the birds brought her. Too soon

[1]Franz Boas. The Central Eskimo, *6th Ann. Rep. Bur. Ethnol.*, pp. 583-585.

[2] An Arctic sea bird of the petrel family.

she discovered that she had thrown away her opportunities when in her foolish pride she had rejected the Inuit youth. In her woe she sang: "Aja. O father, if you knew how wretched I am you would come to me and we would hurry away in your boat over the waters. The birds look unkindly upon me the stranger; cold winds roar about my bed; they give me but miserable food. O come and take me back home. Aja."

When a year had passed and the sea was again stirred by warmer winds, the father left his country to visit Sedna. His daughter greeted him joyfully and besought him to take her back home. The father hearing of the outrages wrought upon his daughter determined upon revenge. He killed the fulmar, took Sedna into his boat, and they quickly left the country which had brought so much sorrow to Sedna. When the other fulmars came home and found their companion dead and his wife gone, they all flew away in search of the fugitives. They were very sad over the death of their poor murdered comrade and continue to mourn and cry until this day.

Having flown a short distance they discerned the boat and stirred up a heavy storm. The sea rose in immense waves that threatened the pair with destruction. In this mortal peril the father determined to offer Sedna to the birds and flung her overboard. She clung to the edge of the boat with a death grip. The cruel father then took a knife and cut off the first joints of her fingers. Falling into the sea they were transformed into whales, the nails turning into whalebone. Sedna holding on to the boat more tightly, the second finger joints fell under the sharp knife and swam away as seals; when the father cut off the stumps of the fingers they became ground seals. Meantime the storm subsided, for the fulmars thought Sedna was drowned. The father then allowed her to come into the boat again. But from that time she cherished a deadly hatred against him and swore bitter revenge. After they got ashore, she called her dogs and let them gnaw off the feet and hands of her father while he was asleep. Upon this he cursed himself, his daughter, and the dogs which had maimed him; whereupon the earth opened and swallowed the hut, the father, the daughter, and the dogs. They have since lived in the land of Adlivun, of which Sedna is the mistress.

IROQUOIAN

Cherokee

How the World Was Made [1]

The earth is a great island floating in a sea of water, and suspended at each of the four cardinal points by a cord hanging down from the sky vault, which is of solid rock. When the world grows old and worn out, the people will die and the cords will break and let the earth sink down into the ocean, and all will be water again. The Indians are afraid of this.

When all was water, the animals were above in Gălûñ'lătĭ, beyond the arch; but it was very much crowded, and they were wanting more room. They wondered what was below the water, and at last Dâyuni'si, "Beaver's Grandchild," the little Water-beetle, offered to go and see if it could learn. It darted in every direction over the surface of the water, but could find no firm place to rest. Then it dived to the bottom and came up with some soft mud, which began to grow and spread on every side until it became the island which we call the earth. It was afterward fastened to the sky with four cords, but no one remembers who did this.

At first the earth was flat and very soft and wet. The animals were anxious to get down, and sent out different birds to see if it was yet dry, but they found no place

[1] James Mooney. Myths of the Cherokee. *19th Ann. Rep. Bur. Amer. Ethnol.*, pp. 239–240.

to alight and came back again to Gălûñ'lătĭ. At last it seemed to be time, and they sent out the Buzzard and told him to go and make ready for them. This was the Great Buzzard, the father of all the buzzards we see now. He flew all over the earth, low down near the ground, and it was still soft. When he reached the Cherokee country, he was very tired, and his wings began to flap and strike the ground, and wherever they struck the earth there was a valley, and where they turned up again there was a mountain. When the animals above saw this, they were afraid that the whole world would be mountains, so they called him back, but the Cherokee country remains full of mountains to this day.

When the earth was dry and the animals came down, it was still dark, so they got the sun and set it in a track to go every day across the island from east to west, just overhead. It was too hot this way, and Tsiska'gĭlĭ', the Red Crawfish, had his shell scorched a bright red, so that his meat was spoiled; and the Cherokee do not eat it. The conjurers put the sun another handbreadth higher in the air, but it was still too hot. They raised it another time, and another, until it was seven handbreadths high and just under the sky. Then it was right, and they left it so. This is why the conjurers call the highest place Gûlkwâ'gine Di'gălûñ'lătiyûñ', "the seventh height," because it is seven handbreadths above the earth. Every day the sun goes along under this arch, and returns at night on the upper side to the starting place.

There is another world under this, and it is like ours in everything—animals, plants, and people—save that the seasons are different. The streams that come down from the mountains are the trails by which we reach this underworld, and the springs at their heads are the doorways by which we enter it, but to do this one must fast and go to water and have one of the underground people for a guide. We know that the seasons in the underworld are different from ours, because the water in the springs is always warmer in winter and cooler in summer than the outer air.

When the animals and plants were first made—we do not know by whom—they were told to watch and keep awake for seven nights, just as young men now fast and keep awake when they pray to their medicine. They tried to do this, and nearly all were awake through the first night, but the next night several dropped off to sleep, and the third night others were asleep, and then others, until on the seventh night, of all the animals only the owl, the panther, and one or two more were still awake. To these were given the power to see and to go about in the dark, and to make prey of the birds and animals which must sleep at night. Of the trees, only the cedar, the pine, the spruce, the holly, and the laurel were awake to the end, and to them it was given to be always green and to be greatest for medicine, but to the others it was said: "Because you have not endured to the end you shall lose your hair every winter."

Men came after the animals and plants. At first there were only a brother and sister until he struck her with a fish and told her to multiply, and so it was. In seven days a child was born to her, and thereafter every seven days another, and they increased very fast until there was danger that the world could not keep them. Then it was made that a woman should have only one child in a year, and it has been so ever since.

The First Fire[1]

In the beginning there was no fire, and the world was cold, until the Thunders (Ani′-Hyûñ′tĭkwălâ′skĭ), who lived up in Gălûñ′lătĭ, sent their lightning and put fire into the bottom of a hollow sycamore tree which grew on an island. The animals knew it was there,

[1]James Mooney. Myths of the Cherokee. *19th Ann. Rep. Bur. Amer. Ethnol.*, pp. 241–242.

PLATE 71

Western Eskimo at their storage house for fish

because they could see the smoke coming out at the top, but they could not get to it on account of the water, so they held a council to decide what to do. This was a long time ago.

Every animal that could fly or swim was anxious to go after the fire. The Raven offered, and because he was so large and strong they thought he could surely do the work, so he was sent first. He flew high and far across the water and alighted on the sycamore tree, but while he was wondering what to do next, the heat had scorched all his feathers black, and he was frightened and came back without the fire. The little Screech-owl (*Wa'huhu'*) volunteered to go, and reached the place safely, but while he was looking down into the hollow tree a blast of hot air came up and nearly burned out his eyes. He managed to fly home as best he could, but it was a long time before he could see well, and his eyes are red to this day. Then the Hooting Owl (*U'guku'*) and the Horned Owl (*Tskĭlĭ'*) went, but by the time they got to the hollow tree the fire was burning so fiercely that the smoke nearly blinded them, and the ashes carried up by the wind made white rings about their eyes. They had to come home again without the fire, but with all their rubbing they were never able to get rid of the white rings.

Now no more of the birds would venture, and so the little Uksu'hĭ snake, the black racer, said he would go through the water and bring back some fire. He swam across to the island and crawled through the grass to the tree, and went in by a small hole at the bottom. The heat and smoke were too much for him, too, and after dodging about blindly over the hot ashes until he was almost on fire himself he managed by good luck to get out again at the same hole, but his body had been scorched black, and he has ever since had the habit of darting and doubling on his track as if trying to escape from close quarters. He came back, and the great blacksnake,

Gûle'gĭ, "The Climber," offered to go for fire. He swam over to the island and climbed up the tree on the outside, as the blacksnake always does, but when he put his head down into the hole the smoke choked him so that he fell into the burning stump, and before he could climb out again he was as black as the Uksu'hĭ.

Now they held another council, for still there was no fire, and the world was cold, but birds, snakes, and four-footed animals, all had some excuse for not going, because they were all afraid to venture near the burning sycamore, until at last Kănăne'skĭ Amai'yĕhĭ (the Water Spider) said she would go. This is not the water spider that looks like a mosquito, but the other one with black downy hair and red stripes on her body. She can run on top of the water or dive to the bottom, so there would be no trouble to get over to the island, but the question was, how could she bring back the fire? "I'll manage that," said the Water Spider; so she spun a thread from her body and wove it into a *tusti* bowl, which she fastened on her back. Then she crossed over to the island and through the grass to where the fire was still burning. She put one little coal of fire into her bowl, and came back with it, and ever since we have had fire, and the Water Spider still keeps her tusti bowl.

Iroquois

Creation Myth

A Seneca Version[1]

There were, it seems, so it is said, man-beings dwelling on the other side of the sky. So, just in the center of their village the lodge of the chief stood, wherein lived

[1]J. N. B. Hewitt. Iroquoian Cosmology. (First Part.) *21st Ann. Rep. Bur. Amer. Ethnol.*, pp. 221–254.

his family, consisting of his spouse and one child, a girl, that they two had.

He was surprised that then he began to become lonesome. Now, furthermore, he, the Ancient, was very lean, his bones having become dried; and the cause of this condition was that he was displeased that they two had the child, and one would think, judging from the circumstances, that he was jealous.

So now this condition of things continued until the time that he, the Ancient, indicated that they, the people, should seek to divine his Word; that is, that they should have a dream feast for the purpose of ascertaining the secret yearning of his soul. So now all the people severally continued to do nothing else but to assemble there. Now they there continually sought to divine his Word. They severally designated all manner of things that they severally thought that he desired. After the lapse of some time, then, one of these persons said: "Now, perhaps, I myself have divined the Word of our chief, the excrement. And the thing that he desires is that the standing tree belonging to him should be uprooted, this tree that stands hard by his lodge." The chief said: "Gwă'" [expressing his thanks].

So now the man-beings said: "We must be in full number and we must aid one another when we uproot this standing tree; that is, there must be a few to grasp each several root." So now they uprooted it and set it up elsewhere. Now the place whence they had uprooted the tree fell through, forming an opening through the sky earth. So now, moreover, all the man-beings inspected it. It was curious; below them the aspect was green and nothing else in color. As soon as the man-beings had had their turns at inspecting it, then the chief said to his spouse: "Come now, let us two go to inspect it." Now she took her child astride of her back. Thither now he made his way with difficulty. He moved slowly. They two arrived at the place where the cavern was.

Now he, the Ancient, himself inspected it. When he wearied of it, he said to his spouse: "Now it is thy turn. Come." "Age'," she said, "myself, I fear it." "Come now, so be it," he said, "do thou inspect it." So now she took in her mouth the ends of the mantle which she wore, and she rested herself on her hand on the right side, and she rested herself on the other side also, closing her hand on either side and grasping the earth thereby. So now she looked down below. Just as soon as she bent her neck, he seized her leg and pushed her body down thither. Now, moreover, there [*i.e.*, in the hole] floated the body of the Fire-dragon with the white body, and, verily, he it was whom the Ancient regarded with jealousy. Now Fire-dragon took out an ear of corn, and verily he gave it to her. As soon as she received it she placed it in her bosom. Now, another thing, the next in order, a small mortar and also the upper mortar [pestle] he gave to her. So now, again, another thing he took out of his bosom, which was a small pot. Now, again, another thing, he gave her in the next place, a bone. Now, he said: "This, verily, is what thou wilt continue to eat."

Now it was so, that below [her] all manner of otgon [malefic] male man-beings abode; of this number were the Fire-dragon, whose body was pure white in color, the Wind, and the Thick Night.

Now, they, the male man-beings, counseled together, and they said: "Well, is it not probably possible for us to give aid to the woman-being whose body is falling thence toward us?" Now every one of the man-beings spoke, saying: "I, perhaps, would be able to aid her." Black Bass said: "I, perhaps, could do it." They, the man-beings, said: "Not the least, perhaps, art thou able to do it, seeing that thou hast no sense [reason]." The Pickerel next in turn said: "I, perhaps, could do it." Then the man-beings said: "And again we say, thou canst not do even a little, because thy throat is too long [thou art a glutton]." So now Turtle spoke, saying: "Moreover, perhaps I would be able to give aid to the person of the woman-being." Now all the man-beings confirmed this proposal. Now, moreover, Turtle floated there at the point directly toward which the body of the woman-being was falling thence. So now, on the Turtle's carapace, she, the woman-being, alighted. And she, the woman-being, wept there. Some time afterward she remembered that seemingly she still held [in her hands] earth. Now she opened her hands, and, moreover, she scattered the earth over Turtle. As soon as she did this, then it seems that this earth grew in size. So now she did thus, scattering the earth very many times [much]. In a short time the earth had become of a considerable size. Now she herself became aware that it was she herself, alone seemingly, who was forming this earth here present. So now, verily, it was her custom to travel about from place to place continually. She knew, verily, that when she traveled to and fro the earth increased in size. So now it was not long, verily, before the various kinds of shrubs grew up and also every kind of grass and reeds.... Indeed, it did thus come to pass, and the cause that brought it about is that she, the Ancient-bodied, is, as a matter of fact, a controller, [a god].

PUEBLO

Zuñi

The Trial of Lovers

or

The Maiden of Mátsaki and the Red Feather [1]

[In this charming tale of an Indian *Orpheus and Eurydice*, the hero has the misfortune to slay unwittingly his beautiful and beloved bride. To comfort him, the spirit of the maiden allows him to follow her on her jour-

[1]Frank H. Cushing. Zuñi Folk Tales, New York (Putnam), 1901, pp. 1–33.

ney to the Land of the Dead. As she will be invisible during the daytime, she bids him bind upon her brow a sacred red feather which shall be his guide.]

So at sunrise the young man went away and gathered feathers of the summer birds, and cut many prayer-sticks, whereon he bound them with cotton, as gifts to the Fathers. Then he found a beautiful downy feather plucked from the eagle, and dyed it red with ocher, and tied to it a string of cotton wherewith to fasten it over the forehead of the spirit maiden. When night came, he took meal made from parched corn and burnt sweet-bread, and once more went down to the plaza and sat by the grave-side.

When midnight came and the light glowed forth through the grave-sands, lo! the maiden-spirit came out and stood by his side. She seemed no longer sad, but happy, like one going home after long absence. Nor was the young man sad or single-thoughted like one whose mind errs; so they sat together and talked of their journey till the dayland grew yellow and the black shadows gray, and the houses and hills came out of the darkness.

"Once more would I tell thee to go back," said the maiden's spirit to the young man; "but I know why thou goest with me, and it is well. Only watch me when the day comes, and thou wilt see me no more; but look whither the plume goeth, and follow, for thou knowest that thou must tie it to the hair above my forehead."

Then the young man took the bright red plume out from among the feathers of sacrifice, and gently tied it above the maiden-spirit's forehead.

As the light waved up from behind the great mountain the red glow faded out from the grave-sands and the youth looked in vain for the spirit of the maiden; but before him, at the height of one's hands when standing, waved the light downy feather in the wind of the morning. Then the plume, not the wife, rose before him, like the plumes on the head of a dancer, and moved through the streets that led westward, and down through the fields to the river. And out through the streets that led westward, and down on the trail by the river, and on over the plains always toward the land of evening, the young man followed close to the red feather; but at last he began to grow weary, for the plume glided swiftly before him, until at last it left him far behind, and even now and then lost him entirely. Then, as he hastened on, he called in anguish:

"My beautiful bride! My beautiful bride! Oh, where art thou?"

But the plume, not the wife, stopped and waited....

[Thus day after day the young man followed the red plume, the trail getting rougher and more difficult and the youth growing ever more and more weary, until he reached one day the edge of a deep canyon, "the walls of which were so steep that no man could pass them alive."]

For a moment the red plume paused above the chasm, and the youth pressed on and stretched his hand forth to detain it; but ere he had gained the spot, it floated on straight over the dark cañon, as though no ravine had been there at all; for to spirits the trails that once have been, even though the waters have worn them away, still are.

Wildly the young man rushed up and down the steep brink, and despairingly he called across to the plume: "Alas! ah, my beautiful wife! Wait, only wait for me, for I love thee and cannot turn from thee!" Then, like one whose thoughts wandered, he threw himself over the brink and hung by his hands as if to drop, when a jolly little striped Squirrel, who was playing at the bottom of the cañon, happened to see him, and called out: "*Tsithl! Tsithl!*" and much more, which meant "*Ah hai! Wananí!*" "You crazy fool of a being! You have not the wings of a falcon, nor the hands of a Squirrel, nor the feet of a spirit, and if you drop you will be broken to pieces and the moles will eat up the fragments! Wait! Hold hard, and I will help you, for though I am but a Squirrel, I know how to think!"

Whereupon the little chit ran chattering away and called his mate out of their house in the rock-nook: "Wife! Wife! Come quickly; run to our corn room and bring me a hemlock, and hurry! hurry! Ask me no questions; for a crazy fool of a man over here will break himself to pieces if we don't quickly make him a ladder."

So the little wife flirted her brush in his face and skipped over the rocks to their store-house, where she chose a fat hemlock and hurried to her husband who was digging a hole in the sand underneath where the young man was hanging. Then they spat on the seed, and buried it in the hole, and began to dance round it and sing,—

"Kiäthlä tsilu,
Silokwe, silokwe, silokwe;
Ki'ai silu silu,
Tsithl! Tsithl!"

Which meant, as far as any one can tell now (for it was a long time ago, and partly squirrel talk),

"Hemlock of the
Tall kind, tall kind, tall kind,
Sprout up hemlock, hemlock,
Chit! Chit!"

And every time they danced around and sang the song through, the ground moved, until the fourth time they said "*Tsithl! Tsithl!*" the tree sprouted forth and kept growing until the little Squirrel could jump into it, and by grabbing the topmost bough and bracing himself against the branches below, could stretch and pull it, so that in a short time he made it grow as high as the young man's feet, and he had all he could do to keep the

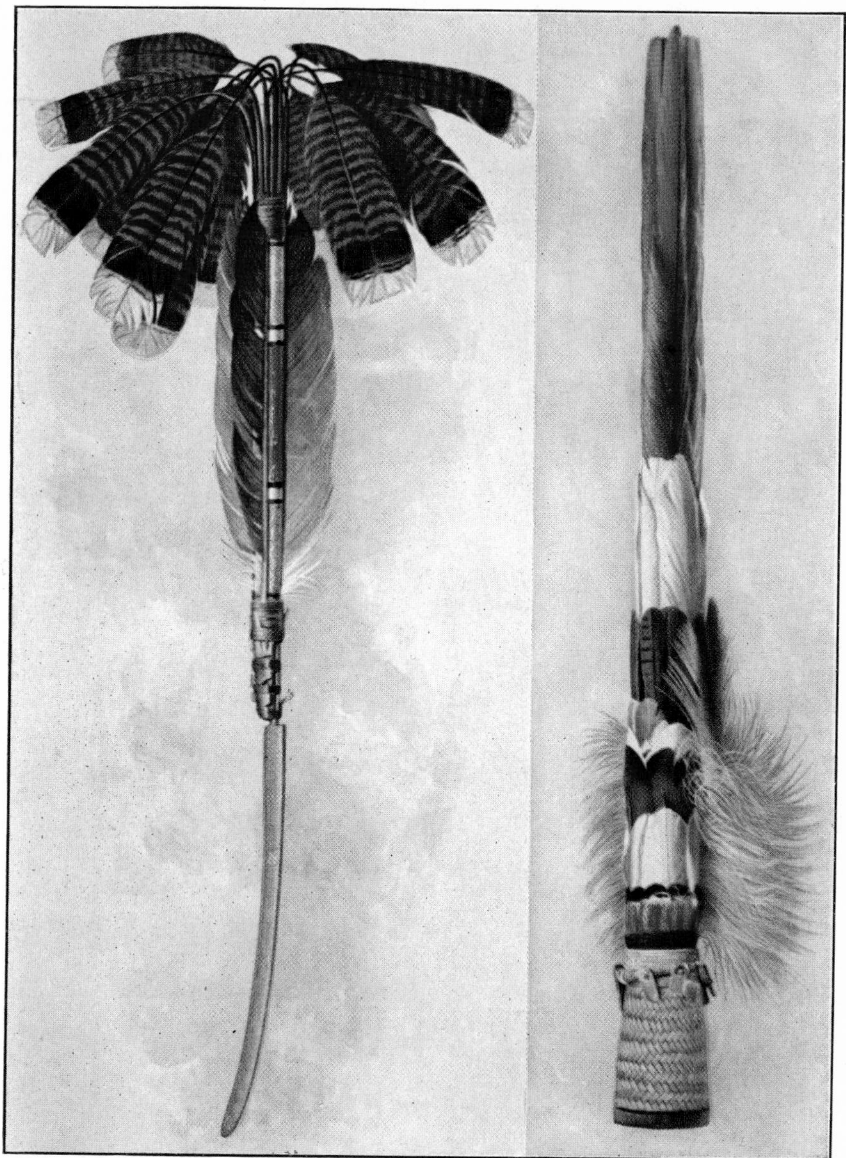

Left—Sword of ᵗHle′wekwe, the Zuñi order of Sword Swallowers. Right—Mi′li (ear of corn covered with plumes), insignia of the Zuñi order of O′naya′naᵗkia (Life Giver's)

poor youth from jumping right into it before it was strong enough to hold him. Presently he said "*Tsithl! Tsithl!*" and whisked away before the young man had time to thank him. Then the sad lover climbed down and quickly gained the other side, which was not so steep; before he could rest from his climb, however, the plume floated on, and he had to get up and follow it.

[Later the sad youth was obliged to leave his wife in the land of departed spirits, which was at the bottom of a great lake whither he could not follow her.]

Then with a cry of despair and anguish he crawled to the lake-shore and buried his face in the sands and rank grasses. Suddenly he heard a low screech, and then a hoarse voice seemed to call him. He looked, and a great Owl flew over him, saying: "*Muhai! Hu hu! Hu hu!*"

"What wilt thou?" he cried, in vexed anguish.

Then the Owl flew closer, and, lighting, asked: "Why weepest thou, my child?"

He turned and looked at the Owl and told it part of his trouble, when the Owl suddenly twisted its head quite around—as owls do—to see if anyone were near; then came closer and said: "I know all about it, young man. Come with me to my house in the mountain, and if thou wilt but follow my counsel, all will yet be well." Then the Owl led the way to a cave far above and bade him step in. As he placed his foot inside the opening, behold! it widened into a bright room, and many Owl-men and Owl-women around greeted him happily, and bade him sit down and eat.

The old Owl who had brought him, changed himself in a twinkling, as he entered the room, and hung his owl-coat on an antler. Then he went away, but presently returned, bringing a little bag of medicine. "Before I give thee this, let me tell thee what to do, and what thou must promise," said he of the owl-coat.

The young man eagerly reached forth his hand for the magic medicine.

"Fool!" cried the being; "were it not well, for that would I not help thee. Thou art too eager, and I will not trust thee with my medicine of sleep. Thou shalt sleep here, and when thou awakest thou shalt find the morning star in the sky, and thy dead wife before thee on the trail toward the Middle Ant Hill. With the rising sun she will wake and smile on thee. Be not foolish, but journey preciously with her, and not until ye reach the home of thy fathers shalt thou approach her or kiss her; for if thou doest this, all will be as nothing again. But if thou doest as I counsel thee, all will be well, and happily may ye live one with the other."

He ceased, and, taking a tiny pinch of the medicine, blew it in the face of the youth. Instantly the young man sank with sleep where he had been sitting, and the beings, putting on their owl-coats, flew away with him under some trees by the trail that led to Mátsaki and the Ant Hill of the Middle.[1]

Then they flew over the lake, and threw the medicine of sleep in at the windows, and taking the plumed prayer-sticks which the young man had brought with him, they chose some red plumes for themselves, and with the others entered the home of the *Kâkâ*. Softly they flew over the sleeping fathers and their children (the gods of the *Kâkâ* and the spirits) and, laying the prayer-plumes before the great altar, caught up the beautiful maiden and bore her over the waters and woodlands to where the young man was still sleeping. Then they hooted and flew off to their mountain.

As the great star came out of the dayland, the young man awoke, and lo! there before him lay his own beautiful wife. Then he turned his face away that he might not be tempted, and waited with joy and longing for the coming out of the sun. When at last the sun came out, with the first ray that brightened the beautiful maiden's

[1] The ancient pueblo of Zuñi itself was called Hálonawan, or the Ant Hill, the ruins of which, now buried beneath the sands, lie opposite the modern town.

face, she opened her eyes and gazed wildly around at first, but seeing her lonely lover, smiled, and said: "Truly, thou lovest me!"

Then they arose and journeyed apart toward the home of their fathers, and the young man forgot not the counsel of the Owl, but journeyed wisely, till on the fourth day they came in sight of the Mountain of Thunder and saw the river that flows by Salt City.

As they began to go down into the valley, the maiden stopped and said: "*Hahuá*, I am weary, for the journey is long and the day is warm." Then she sat down in the shadow of a cedar and said: "Watch, my husband, while I sleep a little; only a little, and then we will journey together again." And he said: "Be it well."

Then she lay down and seemed to sleep. She smiled and looked so beautiful to the longing lover that he softly rose and crept close to her. Then, alas! he laid his hand upon her and kissed her.

Quickly the beautiful maiden started. Her face was all covered with sadness, and she said, hastily and angrily: "Ah, thou shameless fool! I now know! Thou lovest me not! How vain that I should have hoped for thy love!"

With shame, indeed, and sorrow, he bent his head low and covered his face with his hands. Then he started to speak, when an Owl flew up and hooted mournfully at him from a tree-top. Then the Owl winged her way to the westward, and ever after the young man's mind wandered.

Alas! alas! Thus it was in the days of the ancients. Maybe had the young man not kissed her yonder toward the Lake of the Dead, we would never have journeyed nor ever have mourned for others lost. But then it is well! If men and women had never died, then the world long ago had overflown with children, starvation, and warring.

Thus shortens my story.

PLAINS INDIANS

Omaha

The Sacred Pole [1]

Tradition states that the Sacred Pole was cut before the "Ponca gens broke away [from the Omaha] and became the Ponca tribe." Other evidence indicates that the tribes had already become more or less distinct when the Sacred Pole was cut.

There are two versions of the story of the finding of the Sacred Pole. . . .

The account in the Omaha Sacred Legend is as follows:

During this time a young man who had been wandering came back to his village. When he reached his home he said: "Father, I have seen a wonderful tree!" And he described it. The old man listened but he kept silent, for all was not yet settled between the tribes.

After a little while the young man went again to visit the tree. On his return home he repeated his former tale to his father about the wonderful tree. The old man kept silent, for the chiefs were still conferring. At last, when everything was agreed upon between the tribes, the old man sent for the chiefs and said: "My son has seen a wonderful tree. The Thunder birds come and go upon this tree, making a trail of fire that leaves four paths on the burnt grass that stretch toward the Four Winds. When the Thunder birds alight upon the tree it bursts into flame and the fire mounts to the top. The tree stands burning, but no one can see the fire except at night."

When the chiefs heard this tale they sent runners to see what this tree might be. The runners came back and told the same story—how in the night they saw the tree standing and burning as it stood. Then all the people held a council as to what this might mean, and the chiefs said: "We shall run for it; put on your ornaments and prepare as for battle." So the men stripped, painted themselves, put on their ornaments, and set out for the tree, which stood near to a lake. They ran as in a race to attack the tree as if it were a warrior enemy. All the men ran. A Ponca was the first to reach the tree, and he struck it as he would an enemy.

[1] Fletcher and La Flesche. The Omaha Tribe, *27th Ann. Rep. Amer. Bur. Ethnol.*, pp. 217–219.

PLATE 73

Bowls with symbolic designs from the ancient pueblo of Sikyatki, Arizona. In the National Museum

Then they cut the tree down and four men, walking in line, carried it on their shoulders to the village. The chiefs sang four nights the songs that had been composed for the tree while they held a council and deliberated concerning the tree. A tent was made for the tree and set up within the circle of lodges. The chiefs worked upon the tree; they trimmed it and called it a human being. They made a basket-work receptacle of twigs and feathers and tied it about the middle. Then they said: "It has no hair!" So they sent out to get a large scalp lock and they put it on the top of the Pole for hair. Afterward the chiefs bade the herald tell the people that when all was completed they should see the Pole.

Then they painted the Pole and set it up before the tent, leaning it on a crotched stick, which they called *imongthe* (a staff). They summoned the people, and all the people came—men, women, and children. When they were gathered the chiefs stood up and said: "You now see before you a mystery. Whenever we meet with troubles we shall bring all our troubles to him [the Pole]. We shall make offerings and requests. All our prayers must be accompanied by gifts. This [the Pole] belongs to all the people, but it shall be in the keeping of one family (in the Ho^{n}'ga gens), and the leadership shall be with them. If anyone desires to lead (to become a chief) and to take responsibility in governing the people, he shall make presents to the Keepers [of the Pole] and they shall give him authority." When all was finished the people said: "Let us appoint a time when we shall again paint him [the Pole] and act before him the battles we have fought." The time was fixed; it was to take place in "the moon when the buffaloes bellow" (July). This was the beginning of the ceremony of Waxthe'xe xigithe, and it was agreed that this ceremony should be kept up.

Sioux

The Adventures of Ictinike[1]

Many tales are told by the Iowa Indians regarding Ictinike, the son of the sun-god, who had offended his father, and was consequently expelled from the celestial regions. He possesses a very bad reputation among the Indians for deceit and trickery. They say that he taught them all the evil things they know, and they seem to regard him as a Father of Lies. The Omahas state that he

[1] Lewis Spence. The Myths of the North American Indians, London, 1914, pp. 266–268.

gave them their war-customs, and for one reason or another they appear to look upon him as a species of war-god. A series of myths recount his adventures with several inhabitants of the wild. The first of these is as follows:

One day Ictinike encountered the Rabbit, and hailed him in a friendly manner, calling him "grandchild," and requesting him to do him a service. The Rabbit expressed his willingness to assist the god to the best of his ability and inquired what he wished him to do.

"Oh, grandchild," said the crafty one, pointing upward to where a bird circled in the blue vault above them, "take your bow and arrow and bring down yonder bird."

The Rabbit fitted an arrow to his bow, and the shaft transfixed the bird, which fell like a stone and lodged in the branches of a great tree.

"Now, grandchild," said Ictinike, "go into the tree and fetch me the game."

This, however, the Rabbit at first refused to do, but at length he took off his clothes and climbed into the tree, where he stuck fast among the tortuous branches.

Ictinike, seeing that he could not make his way down, donned the unfortunate Rabbit's garments, and, highly amused at the animal's predicament, betook himself to the nearest village. There he encountered a chief who had two beautiful daughters, the elder of whom he married. The younger daughter, regarding this as an affront to her personal attractions, wandered off into the forest in a fit of the sulks. As she paced angrily up and down she heard some one calling her from above, and, looking upward, she beheld the unfortunate Rabbit, whose fur was adhering to the natural gum which exuded from the bark of the tree. The girl cut down the tree and lit a fire near it, which melted the gum and freed the Rabbit. The Rabbit and the chief's daughter compared notes, and discovered that the being who had tricked the one and affronted the other was the same. Together they proceeded to the chief's lodge, where the girl was laughed at because of the strange companion she had brought back with her. Suddenly an eagle appeared in the air above them. Ictinike shot at and missed it, but the Rabbit loosed an arrow with great force and brought it to earth. Each morning a feather of the bird became another eagle, and each morning Ictinike shot at and missed this newly created bird which the Rabbit invariably succeeded in killing. This went on until Ictinike had quite worn out the Rabbit's clothing and was wearing a very old piece of tent skin; but the Rabbit returned to him the garments he had been forced to don when Ictinike had stolen his. Then the Rabbit commanded the Indians to beat the drums, and each time they were beaten Ictinike jumped so high that every bone in his body was shaken. At length, after a more than usually loud series of beats, he leapt to such a height that when he came down it was found that the fall had broken his neck. The Rabbit was avenged.

Ictinike and the Buzzard[1]

One day Ictinike, footsore and weary, encountered a buzzard, which he asked to oblige him by carrying him on its back part of the way. The crafty bird immediately consented, and, seating Ictinike between its wings, flew off with him.

They had not gone far when they passed above a hollow tree, and Ictinike began to shift uneasily in his seat as he observed the buzzard hovering over it. He requested the bird to fly onward, but for answer it cast him headlong into the tree-trunk, where he found himself a prisoner. For a long time he lay there in want and wretchedness, until at last a large hunting-party struck camp at the spot. Ictinike chanced to be wearing some raccoon skins, and he thrust the tails of these through the cracks in the tree. Three women who were standing

[1] Lewis Spence. The Myths of the North American Indians, 1914, p. 268.

near imagined that a number of raccoons had become imprisoned in the hollow trunk, and they made a large hole in it for the purpose of capturing them. Ictinike at once emerged, whereupon the women fled. Ictinike lay on the ground pretending to be dead, and as he was covered with the raccoon-skins the birds of prey, the eagle, the rook, and the magpie, came to devour him. While they pecked at him the buzzard made his appearance for the purpose of joining in the feast, but Ictinike, rising quickly, tore the feathers from its scalp. That is why the buzzard has no feathers on its head.

WEST COAST TRIBES

Karok

Karok Fables [1]

There are many apologues and fables in vogue among the Karok, which gifted squaws relate to their children on winter evenings and through the weary days of the rainy season, while they are cooped up in their cabins; and some of them are not entirely unworthy of a place in that renowned old book written by one Æsop. A few specimens are given here.

FABLE OF THE ANIMALS

A great many hundred snows ago, Kareya, sitting on the Sacred Stool, created the world. First, he made the fishes in the big water, then the animals on the green land, and last of all, The Man. But the animals were all alike yet in power, and it was not yet ordained which should be for food to others, and which should be food for The Man. Then Kareya bade them all assemble together in a certain place, that The Man might give each his power and his rank. So the animals all met together, a great many hundred snows ago, on an evening

[1] Stephen Powers. Tribes of California, *Cont. N. Amer. Ethnol.*, Vol. 3, pp. 35–40.

PLATE 74

Games of Kiowa children, including spinning top, dart and disk, and keeping house. Group in the National Museum

when the sun was set, that they might wait over night for the coming of The Man on the morrow. Now Kareya commanded The Man to make bows and arrows, as many as there were animals, and to give the longest to the one that should have the most power, and the shortest to the one that should have the least. So he did, and after nine sleeps his work was ended, and the bows and arrows which he made were very many.

Now the animals being gathered together in one place, went to sleep, that they might rise on the morrow and go forth to meet The Man. But the coyote was exceedingly cunning, above all the beasts that were, he was so cunning. So he considered within himself how he might get the longest bow, and so have the greatest power, and have all animals for his meat. He determined to stay awake all night, while the others slept, and so go forth first in the morning and get the longest bow. This he devised within his cunning mind, and then he laughed to himself, and stretched out his snout on his fore-paws, and pretended to sleep, like the others. But about midnight he began to get sleepy, and he had to walk around camp and scratch his eyes a considerable time to keep them open. But still he grew more sleepy, and he had to skip and jump about like a good one to keep awake. He made so much noise this way that he woke up some of the other animals, and he had to think of another plan. About the time the morning star came up, he was so sleepy that he couldn't keep his eyes open any longer. Then he took two little sticks and sharpened them at the ends, and propped open his eyelids, whereupon he thought he was safe, and he concluded he would take just a little nap, with his eyes open, watching the morning star. But in a few minutes he was sound asleep, and the sharp sticks pierced through his eyelids, and pinned them fast together.

So the morning star mounted up very swiftly, and then there came a peep of daybreak, and the birds began to sing, and the animals began to rise and stretch themselves, but still the coyote lay fast asleep. At last it was broad daylight, and then the sun rose, and all the animals went forth to meet The Man. He gave the longest bow to the cougar, so he had the greatest power of all; and the second longest to the bear; and so on, giving the next to the last to the poor frog. But he still had the shortest one left, and he cried out, "What animal have I missed?" Then the animals began to look about, and they soon spied the coyote lying fast asleep, with the sharp sticks pinning his eyelids together. Upon that all the animals set up a great laugh, and they jumped on the coyote and danced upon him. Then they led him to The Man—for he could see nothing because of the sticks—and The Man pulled out the sticks, and gave him the shortest bow of all, which would shoot an arrow hardly more than a foot. And all the animals laughed very much.

But The Man took pity on the coyote, because he was now the weakest of all animals, weaker even than the frog, and he prayed to Kareya for him, and Kareya gave him cunning, ten times more than before, so that he was cunning above all the animals of the wood. So the coyote was a friend to The Man and to his children after him, and helped him, and did many things for him, as we shall see hereafter.

In the legendary lore of the Karok the coyote plays the same conspicuous part that Reynard does in ours, and the sagacious tricks that are accredited to him are endless. When one Karok has killed another, he frequently barks like the coyote in the belief that he will thereby be endued with so much of that animal's cunning that he will be able to elude the punishment due to his crime.

THE COYOTE DANCING WITH THE STARS

After Kareya gave the coyote so much cunning he became very ambitious, and wanted to do many things which were very much too hard for him, and which Kareya never intended he should do. One of them once got so conceited that he thought he could dance with the stars, and so he asked one of them to fly close to the top of a mountain and take him by the paw, and let him dance once around through the sky. The star only laughed at him and winked its eye, but the next night when it came around, it sailed close to the mountain and took the coyote by the paw, and flew away with him through the sky. But the foolish coyote soon grew tired of dancing this way, and could not wait for the star to come around to the mountain again. He looked down at the earth and it seemed quite near to him, and as the star could not wait or fly low just then, he let go and leaped down. Poor coyote! he was ten whole snows in falling, and when he struck the earth he was smashed as flat as a willow mat.

Another one, not taking warning from this dreadful example, asked a star to let him dance once round through the sky. The star tried to dissuade him from the foolhardy undertaking, but it was of no avail; the silly animal would not be convinced. Every night when the star came around, he would squat on top of a mountain and bark until the star grew tired of his noise. So one night it sailed close down to the mountain and told the coyote to be quick for it could not wait, and up he jumped and caught it with his paw, and went dancing away through the great blue heaven. He, too, soon grew tired, and asked the star to stop and let him rest a little while. But the star told him it could not stop, for Kareya had made it to keep on moving all the while. Then he tried to get on the star and ride, but it was too small. Thus he was compelled to keep on dancing, dangling down from one paw, and one piece of his body after another dropped off until there was only one paw left hanging to the star.

Haida

The Birth of Sîñ[1]

The Haida of British Columbia and the Queen Charlotte Islands possess a striking myth relating to the incarnation of the Sky-god, their principal deity. The daughter of a certain chief went one day to dig in the beach. After she had worked some time she dug up a cockle-shell. She was about to throw it to one side when she thought she heard a sound coming from it like that of a child crying. Examining the shell she found a small baby inside. She carried it home and wrapped it in a warm covering, and tended it so carefully that it grew rapidly and soon began to walk.

She was sitting beside the child one day when he made a movement with his hand as if imitating the drawing of a bowstring, so to please him she took a copper bracelet from her arm and hammered it into the shape of a bow, which she strung and gave him along with two arrows. He was delighted with the tiny weapon, and immediately set out to hunt small game with it. Every day he returned to his foster mother with some trophy of his skill. One day it was a goose, another a woodpecker, and another a blue jay.

One morning he awoke to find himself and his mother in a fine new house, with gorgeous door-posts splendidly carved and illuminated in rich reds, blues and greens. The carpenter who had raised this fine building married his mother, and was very kind to him. He took the boy down to the sea-shore, and caused him to sit with his face looking toward the expanse of the Pacific. And so long as the lad looked across the boundless blue there was fair weather.

His father used to go fishing, and one day Sîñ, for such

[1] Lewis Spence. The Myths of the North American Indians, London, 1914, pp. 314-316.

PLATE 75

Shoshoni women and child in a tipi. The blankets are of their own weaving

was the boy's name, expressed a wish to accompany him. They obtained devil fish for bait, and proceeded to the fishing ground, where the lad instructed his father to pronounce certain magical formulae, the result of which was that their fishing-line was violently agitated and their canoe pulled around an adjacent island three times. When the disturbance stopped at last they pulled in the line and dragged out a monster covered with piles of halibut.

One day Sîñ went out wearing a wren-skin. His mother beheld him rise in stature until he soared above her and brooded like a bank of shining clouds over the ocean. Then he descended and donned the skin of a blue jay. Again he rose over the sea, and shone resplendently. Once more he soared upward, wearing the skin of a woodpecker, and the waves reflected a colour as of fire.

Then he said: "Mother, I shall see you no more; I am going away from you. When the sky looks like my face painted by my father there will be no wind. Then the fishing will be good."

His mother bade him farewell, sadly, yet with the proud knowledge that she had nurtured a divinity. But her sorrow increased when her husband intimated that it was time for him to depart as well. Her supernatural son and husband, however, left her a portion of their power. For when she sits by the inlet and loosens her robe the wind scurries down between the banks and the waves are ruffled with tempest; and the more she loosens the garment the greater is the storm. They call her in the Indian tongue Fine-weather-Woman. But she dwells mostly in the winds, and when the cold morning airs draw up from the sea landward she makes an offering of feathers to her glorious son. The feathers are flakes of snow, and they serve to remind him that the world is weary for a glimpse of his golden face.

Tlingit

Notes on Tlingit Legends [1]

Many of their legends assume to explain the origin of things and the mysteries of existing phenomena. One tells of the creation of the world. *Yalkth* (the immense imaginary bird) is the mighty Creator.

Other legends claim to give us the origin of man, of the sun, moon, and stars, of the whale-killer and of other animals.

For example, the origin of the iniquitous little mosquito is thus given:

There was in ancient times a great giant,[2] cruel and very bloodthirsty. His passion was to kill men, drink their blood and eat their hearts.

Many men tried to kill the giant, but were unable to do so until this plan was conceived: A man pretended to be dead and lay down on his blanket. The giant came along and saw him. He felt of the man's flesh and found that he was still warm. Then he began to gloat over him and say, "I will eat his heart and drink his blood." So he lifted up the man, who allowed his head to hang down just as if he were dead, and carrying him into his house laid him down, and then went on some errand.

Immediately the man jumped up and seized a bow and arrow. Just then the son of the giant came in, and he pointed the arrow at the boy's head and asked him where his father's heart was, and threatened to kill him if he did not tell. The boy answered that his father's heart was in his heel.

Then the giant came in and the man shot the arrow through his heel. Just as the giant lay dying, he said: "Though you burn me, I will still eat you."

[1] Livingston F. Jones. A Study of the Thlingets of Alaska, London, pp. 183–187.

[2] In some versions, an old woman.

After the giant was dead the body was cremated. Then the man, in derision, took the ashes and threw them to the winds. But each particle of the ashes became a mosquito.

The Son of the Wolf Chief [1]

Once upon a time a town near the North Pacific Ocean suffered greatly from famine and many of the Indians who lived there died of hunger. It was terrible to see them sitting before their doors, too weak and listless to move, and waiting silently and hopelessly for death to come. But there was one boy who behaved quite differently from the rest of the tribe. For some reason or other *he* seemed quite strong on his legs, and all day long he would go into the fields or the woods, with his bow and arrows slung to his back, hoping to bring back a supper for himself and his mother.

One morning when he was out as usual, he found a little animal that looked like a dog. It was such a round, funny little thing that he could not bear to kill it, so he put it under his warm blanket, and carried it home, and as it was very dirty from rolling about in the mud and snow, his mother washed it for him. When it was quite clean, the boy fetched some red paint which his uncle who had died of famine had used for smearing over their faces, and put it on the dog's head and legs so that he might always be able to trace it when they were hunting together.

The boy got up early next morning and took his dog into the woods and the hills. The little beast was very quick and sharp, and it was not long before the two got quite a number of grouse and birds of all sorts; and as soon as they had enough for that day and the next, they returned to the wigwam and invited their neighbors to supper with them. A short time after, the boy was out on the hills wondering where the dog had gone,

[1] Mrs. Lang. The Strange Story Book, London, 1913, pp. 110–115.

for, in spite of the red paint, he was to be seen nowhere. At length he stood still and put his ear to the ground and listened with all his might, and that means a great deal, for Indian ears are much cleverer at hearing than European ones. Then he heard a whine which sounded as if it came from a long way off, so he jumped up at once and walked and walked till he reached a small hollow, where he found that the dog had killed one of the mountain sheep.

"Can it really *be* a dog?" said the boy to himself. "I don't know; I wish I did. But at any rate, it deserves to be treated like one," and when the sheep was cooked, the dog—if it was a dog—was given all the fat part.

After this, never a day passed without the boy and the dog bringing home meat, and thanks to them the people began to grow fat again. But if the dog killed many sheep at once, the boy was always careful to give it first the best for itself.

Some weeks later the husband of the boy's sister came to him and said:

"Lend me your dog, it will help me greatly." So the boy went and brought the dog from the little house he had made for it, and painted its head and its feet, and carried it to his brother-in-law.

"Give it the first thing that is killed as I always do," observed the boy, but the man answered nothing, only put the dog in his blanket.

Now the brother-in-law was greedy and selfish and wanted to keep everything for himself; so after the dog had killed a whole flock of sheep in the fields, the man threw it a bit of the inside which nobody else would touch, exclaiming rudely:

"Here take that! It is quite good enough for you."

But the dog would not touch it either, and ran away to the mountains yelping loudly.

The man had to bring back all the sheep himself, and it was evening before he reached the village. The first

Upper—Ancient ceremonial basket of exquisite workmanship from Santa Barbara County, California. Lower—Tulare trinket basket from the Tulare Indian Reservation, California. In the National Museum

person he saw was the boy who was waiting about for him.

"Where is the dog?" asked he, and the man answered:

"It ran away from me."

On hearing this the boy put no more questions, but he called his sister and said to her:

"Tell me the truth. What did your husband do to the dog? I did not want to let it go, because I guessed what would happen."

And the wife answered:

"He threw the inside of a sheep to it, and that is why it ran off."

When the boy heard this, he felt very sad, and turned to go into the mountains in search of the dog. After walking some time he found the marks of its paws, and smears of red paint on the grass. But all this time the boy never knew that the dog was really the son of the Wolf Chief and had been sent by his father to help him, and he did not guess that from the day that he painted red paint round its face and on its feet a wolf can be told far off by the red on its paws and round its mouth.

The marks led a long, long way, and at length they brought him to a lake, with a town on the opposite side of it, where people seemed to be playing some game, as the noise that they made reached all the way across.

"I must try if I can get over there," he said, and as he spoke, he noticed a column of smoke coming right up from the ground under his feet, and a door flew open.

"Enter!" cried a voice, so he entered, and discovered that the voice belonged to an old woman, who was called "Woman-always-wondering."

"Grandchild, why are you here?" she asked, and he answered:

"I found a young dog who helped me to get food for the people, but it is lost and I am seeking it."

"Its people live right across there," replied the woman,

"it is the Wolf Chief's son, and that is his father's town where the noise comes from."

"How can I get over the lake?" he said to himself, but the old woman guessed what he was thinking and replied:

"My little canoe is just below here."

"It might turn over with me," be thought, and again she answered him:

"Take it down to the shore and shake it before you get in, and it will soon become large. Then stretch yourself in the bottom and, instead of paddling, wish with all your might to reach the town."

The boy did as he was told, and by and by he arrived on the other side of the lake. He shook the canoe a second time, and it shrunk into a mere toy-boat which he put in his pocket, and after that he went and watched some boys who were playing with a thing that was like a rainbow.

"Where is the Chief's house?" he asked when he was tired of looking at their game.

"At the other end of the village," they said, and he walked on till he reached a place where a large fire was burning, with people sitting round it. The chief was there too, and the boy saw his little wolf playing about near his father.

"There is a man here," exclaimed the Wolf Chief. "Vanish all of you!" and the wolf people vanished instantly, all but the little wolf, who ran up to the boy and smelt him and knew him at once. As soon as the Wolf Chief beheld that, he said:

"I am your friend; fear nothing. I sent my son to help you because you were starving, and I am glad you have come in quest of him." But after a pause, he added:

"Still, I do not think I will let him go back with you; but I will aid you in some other way," and the boy did not guess that the reason the chief was so pleased to see him was because he had painted the little wolf. Yet, as he glanced at the little beast again, he observed with surprise that it did not look like a wolf any longer, but like a human being.

"Take out the fish-hawk's quill that is hanging on the wall, and if you should meet a bear, point the quill straight at it, and it will fly out of your hand. I will also give you this," and he opened a box and lifted out a second quill stuck in a blanket. "If you lay this side on a sick person, it will cure him; and if you lay the other side on your enemy, it will kill him. Thus you can grow rich by healing sick people."

So the boy and the Wolf Chief made friends, and they talked together a long time, and the boy put many questions about things he had seen in the town, which puzzled him.

"What was the toy the children were playing with?" he asked at last.

"That toy belongs to me," answered the chief. "If it appears to you in the evening it means bad weather, and if it appears in the morning it means fine weather. Then we know that we can go out on the lake. It is a good toy."

"But," continued he, "you must depart now, and before you leave eat this, for you have a long journey to make and you will need strength for it," and he dropped something into the boy's mouth.

And the boy did not guess that he had been absent for two years, and thought it was only two nights.

Then he journeyed back to his own town, not a boy any more, but a man. Near the first house he met a bear and he held the quill straight towards it. Away it flew and hit the bear right in the heart; so there was good meat for hungry people. Further on, he passed a flock of sheep, and the quill slew them all and he drew it out from the heart of the last one. He cooked part of a sheep for himself and hid the rest where he knew he could find them. After that he entered the town.

It seemed strangely quiet. What had become of all his friends and of the children whom he had left behind him when he left to seek for his dog? He opened the door of a hut and peeped in: three or four bodies were stretched on the floor, their bones showing through their skin, dead of starvation; for after the boy had gone to the mountains there was no one to bring them food. He opened another door, and another and another; everywhere it was the same story. Then he remembered the gift of the Wolf Chief and he drew the quill out of his blanket and laid one side of it against their bodies, so that they all came to life again, and once more the town was full of noise and gaiety.

"Now come and hunt with me," he said; but he did not show them his quill lest he should lose it as he had lost the dog. And when they beheld a flock of mountain sheep grazing, he let fly the quill so quickly that nobody saw it go, neither did they see him pull out the quill and hide it in his blanket. After that they made a fire and all sat down to dine, and those who were not his friends gave him payment for the meat.

For the rest of his life the man journeyed from place to place, curing the sick and receiving payment from their kinsfolk. But those who had been dead for many years took a long while to get well, and their eyes were always set deep back in their heads, and had a look as if they had seen something.

MYTHS AND LEGENDS

REFERENCES

BOAS, FRANZ. Kwakiutl tales. Columbia Univ. Cont. Anthrop. Vol. 2. New York, 1910.

JUDSON, KATHERINE B., editor. Myths and legends of Alaska. Chicago (A. C. McClurg), 1911.

—— Myths and legends of California and the Old Southwest. Chicago (A. C. McClurg), 1912.

—— Myths and legends of the Great Plains. Chicago (A. C. McClurg), 1913.

LANG, MRS. The strange story book. Edited by Andrew Lang. London and New York (Longmans, Green), 1913.

LUMMIS, CHARLES F. The man who married the moon, and other Pueblo Indian folk-stories. New York, 1894.

MOONEY, JAMES. Myths of the Cherokee. 19th Ann. Rep. Bur. Amer. Ethnol. Washington, 1902.

SPENCE, LEWIS. The myths of the North American Indians. London (Harrap), 1914.

SWANTON, JOHN R. Haida texts and myths. Bur. Amer. Ethnol. Bull. 29. Washington, 1905.

—— Tlingit Myths and Texts. Bur. Amer. Ethnol. Bull. 39. Washington, 1909.

CHAPTER IX

THE INDIANS IN HISTORY

Except for legends of semi-mythical heroes, no records have come down to us of the deeds of individual Indians of America north of Mexico prior to the coming of the white men in 1492. Before that epoch-making voyage of Columbus, the red men, to be sure, had inhabited the continent of North America for many centuries; but because of the Babel of tongues and the lack of a written language, their story during all that time is forever lost, except as it can be read in the rough by those skilled in interpreting archeology and folklore.

It was not until their white foes became their chroniclers that the Indians began really to live in history. The records of the colonies show that in their dealings with the invaders the "savages" often prove themselves, in statecraft and in strategy, the equals of their civilized opponents. Nevertheless, the superiority of the whites in equipment, discipline, and knowledge, could not but give them the ultimate victory. Every brief triumph of Indian cunning and Indian prowess served only to prolong a futile struggle against the invincible march of civilization. But the struggle, though hopeless, was desperate and determined, and sufficed to give many an Indian name a permanent place in colonial history.

To Columbus, and indeed to most of the early explorers, the Indians offered nothing but kindness until events taught them to do otherwise. The whites, coming in great ships from beyond the outermost limits of the Indian world, armed with terrible weapons, bringing strange animals, and offering in barter bright and glittering objects never before seen by the red men, had to the savage mind all the characteristics of gods. Their advent was easily the most wonderful event in Indian history. It was therefore natural that these extraordinary beings should be both attractive and awe-inspiring to the natives, who welcomed them with offerings of deer meat and of tobacco sacred to the gods, and were ready to fall down and worship them.

Too soon came disillusionment, when events revealed that the new gods had the intention and the power of supplanting their dusky worshipers in the land. Even had the Indians remained personally unmolested by the whites, it would have been well-nigh intolerable to them to behold their sheltering forests destroyed, their game animals slaughtered or dispersed, their waterways obstructed, and their lands usurped by the all-powerful strangers. When, in addition to these inescapable injuries, they saw their warriors wantonly shot down or enslaved, their women debauched, and their homes destroyed, it is small wonder that they began to harry and plunder, to burn and massacre, in a vain attempt to rid the land of the invader.

For the Indians were no mild-mannered people to be treated thus with impunity. Wary statesmen, skillful war leaders they had, and loyally they did their bidding. No fear of torture or punishment could deter them. They were familiar with bloodshed under the most revolting circumstances. Such a race does not submit without a struggle to domination by invaders.

The white men, however, had deadly aids which turned the scale against the Indians. Not only were they provided with muskets and cannon, protected with steel armor practically impenetrable to Indian weapons, and mounted in some instances on armored horses which struck terror to the savage heart; but they brought in their train pestilences, such as the smallpox, which decimated the Indian villages, and strong drink, which stole away the judgment of their statesmen.

The Europeans, for the most part, felt only contempt for the natives, whom they regarded as an inferior race and whose rights they considered themselves in no way bound to respect. Moreover, many of the colonizers looked upon themselves as a new holy people, invading a new promised land, whose pagan inhabitants it was the will of the Almighty that they should exterminate. Franklin quotes one of the Indian orators as saying: "The Great Spirit, who made all things, made everything for some use. Now, when he made rum he said, 'Let this be for the Indians to get drunk with; and it must be so.'" And Franklin, Quaker and peace lover, adds: "Indeed, if it be the design of Providence to extirpate these savages in order to make room for the cultivators of the earth, it seems not impossible that rum may be the appointed means. It has already annihilated all the tribes who formerly inhabited the seacoast."

When the colonists, through encroachments and misunderstandings which led to acts of violence, became familiar with the horrors of Indian warfare, fury and hatred were added to their original feelings of contempt and arrogance. They now looked upon the Indians not merely as inferior beings but as dangerous wild beasts that it was their duty to destroy. Thus arose those savage Indian wars which raged for so long in New England, Virginia, and the Carolinas.

Not only were there natural local causes of antagonism between the Indians and the whites, but European quarrels of long standing led the English, French, Spanish, and Dutch to play off against each other the forces of the savages. Thus in New England both the French and the Dutch were instrumental in inciting Indian warfare, the one on the northern, the other on the southwestern border. Besides frequent Indian forays in the remoter districts, there were two serious wars between

Powhatan's mantle of deerskin with figures worked in shells, obtained by early Virginia colonists 300 years ago. In the Ashmolean Museum, Oxford

the New England colonists and the Indians in the seventeenth century.

In 1637 the colony of Connecticut, aided by a few men from Massachusetts, waged a war of extermination against the Pequot Indians, by which the entire tribe was reduced to an impotence almost equivalent to annihilation. For forty years thereafter the Indians made no determined stand against the whites, although Connecticut was involved to some extent in a struggle between the Narraganset and the Mohegan, both of whom had signed a treaty of peace with the English in 1638, at the close of the Pequot War. The Mohegan treacherously murdered the Sachem of the Narraganset at the instigation of the commissioners of the United Colonies, thereby cementing an alliance between their chief, Uncas, and the colony of Connecticut, which lasted for forty years. Because of the jealousy it created among other tribes, this pact between the Mohegan and the English became one of the chief causes of the final struggle between the Indians and the whites for the possession of New England territory, known as King Philip's War.

King Philip, as the English called him, was the second son of Massasoit, chief of the Wampanoag tribe, who had always maintained friendly relations with the white men. On the death of his father and elder brother, Philip, or Metacom, became chief.

He was the most remarkable of all the Indians of New England. For nine years after his elevation to the chieftaincy, although accused of plotting against the colonists, he seems to have devoted his energies to observation and preparation rather than to overt actions of a warlike nature. He even acknowledged himself the King's subject. But war with the English was inevitable, and the struggle called King Philip's War (1675–76) broke out, resulting in the practical extermination of the Indians after they had inflicted great losses upon the whites.

The ability of King Philip is seen in the plans he made before the war began, the confederacy he formed, and the havoc he wrought among the white settlements. Of ninety towns, fifty-two were attacked and twelve were completely destroyed. The bravery of the Indians was in many cases remarkable. Only treachery among the natives in all probability saved the colonists from extinction. In a decisive battle in a swamp in Rhode Island on August 12, 1676, the last force of the Indians was defeated with great slaughter, King Philip himself being among the slain. His body was subjected to the indignities usual at that time, and his head is said to have been exposed at Plymouth for twenty years. His wife and little son were sold as slaves in the West Indies.

Widely divergent estimates of King Philip's character and achievements have been entertained by different authorities, but he can not but be considered a man of marked abilities. Weeden says: "History has made him 'King Philip' to commemorate the heroism of his life and death. He almost made himself a king by his marvelous energy and statecraft put forth among the New England tribes. Had the opposing power been a little weaker, he might have founded a temporary kingdom on the ashes of the colonies." King Philip has furnished the inspiration for several poems, tales, and histories.

Meantime, somewhat similar struggles, with the inevitable outcome of victory for the whites and defeat for the Indians, were taking place farther south. Though oft-told, the story of the colony of Virginia and its dealings with Powhatan and his family is too interesting and appropriate to be omitted. The settlement at Jamestown, Virginia, in 1607, was made in spring, when beautiful flowers filled the woods and beguiled the newcomers into fancying that all would go easily and well. They took no care to raise food, but wasted the warm months without serious

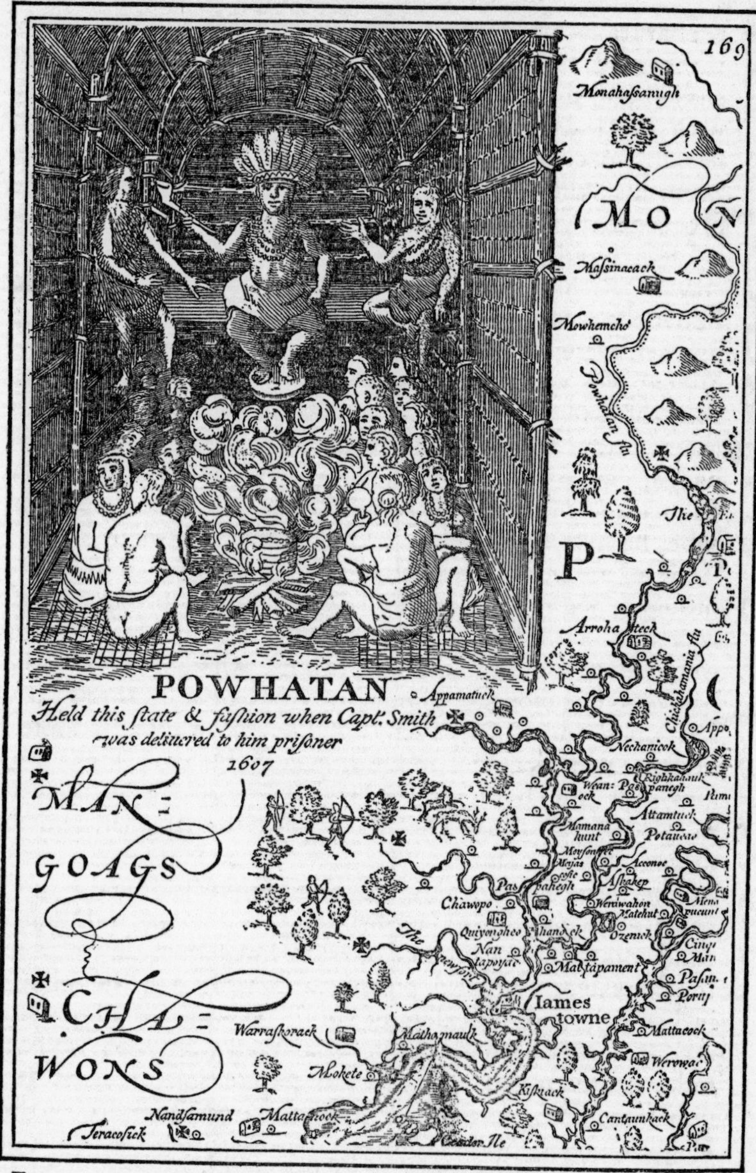

FIG. 11. A map published in Captain John Smith's History of Virginia

preparation for winter. When sickness and starvation threatened them, the bold Captain John Smith, though envied and disliked by many, undertook to trade for corn with the Indians of the great confederation of the Powhatan. Ascending the River Chickahominy in December 1607, his skiff was at length stopped by shallows, but he proceeded by canoe with two companions and an Indian guide. Landing in White Oak Swamp, near the present city of Richmond, they were attacked by 200 Indians under the chief Opecancanough, and captured. Two Englishmen were killed, but Smith, as he says, so astonished his captors with his pocket compass and his knowledge that they, regarding him as a magician, carried him about the country, and at length to their great "emperor," Powhatan, who received them at Werowocomoco (now Gloucester on the York River), where, clad in a coonskin robe, he held his court in a kind of long wigwam.

Here, as Smith says, after some time two stones were brought before the emperor, and Smith, being bound, was laid with his head thereon. Warriors with clubs were about to dash out his brains, when it is said the princess Pocahontas, about 13 years of age, threw herself upon him and saved his life. Powhatan adopted Smith as his son and made him a chief, gave him corn, and sent him back to the settlement, where he arrived in good time to save the remnant of the English, and to discomfit his enemies.

The princess Pocahontas became very friendly and came often to Jamestown bringing food. She was sometimes dressed in a robe of doeskin lined with down from the breast of the wild pigeon, and wore a white plume in her hair, and bracelets of coral. Powhatan, who ruled a confederacy of many tribes scattered over 8,000 square miles of territory, with a total population of 8,000 Indians including 2,500 warriors, remained friendly to the English, even in their lowest distress of starvation and sickness. So also did his son Mantauquas.

PLATE 78

Pocahontas
From a copy of the Booton Hall portrait, courtesy of
Mr. Fairfax Harrison

Captain John Smith made many expeditions of trade and exploration among the rivers of Virginia and Maryland, during which he mapped the country with surprising accuracy; he showed great tact in dealing with the Indians, and great firmness in controlling the English. After two years, however, sick and wounded, he returned to England. His successor, Captain Argall, equally bold, but without tact or scruple, treacherously seized Pocahontas and held her at Jamestown as a hostage for claims against Powhatan. While there she loved and married John Rolfe, and bore him a son named Thomas Rolfe, from whom several prominent Virginian families, including John Randolph of Roanoke, trace descent. When Pocahontas visited England with her husband and son, she was received with much honor; but her romantic adventures soon came to a tragic end. Just as she was about to set sail for Virginia she was stricken with smallpox and died, being then only twenty-two years of age.

The peaceable attitude of Powhatan lulled to rest any fears of the colonists, so that by 1620 the Indians were allowed to go freely into the settlements, and even into the settlers' houses, were employed as servants, and had learned to use the English weapons. When Powhatan died his brothers, Opitchapan and Opecancanough in succession ruled in his stead. This last chief, far from cherishing the friendly views of Powhatan, prepared for the extirpation of the English invaders. His plans were kept so secret, that, except for a warning given by friendly Indians to the village of Jamestown, no suspicion of his purpose was felt by the settlers. Suddenly, on a concerted day and hour of April, 1622, the Indians fell upon the unsuspecting colonists simultaneously from the Chesapeake to the farthest settlements inland. A few of the English successfully defended themselves, and Jamestown was saved by the warning; but 347 of the whites were butchered.

A grim revenge, not less bloodthirsty than the attack, was taken by the survivors, breaking the power of the Powhatan. The colony grew and prospered till it far outnumbered the Indian population. Yet Opecancanough nourished his hatred. At length, in 1644, when an old man of nearly 100 years of age, a second time he fomented a sudden massacre in which 300 English were slain. Governor Berkeley took the field against him with a body of horsemen, and at length captured the aged chief, who was so emaciated and feeble as to require to be carried in a litter, and even to need aid to open his eyes. Opecancanough was taken to Jamestown and displayed to the people. This he resented, and asking that his eyelids be raised, he said sternly to his captors, "Had it been Opecancanough's fortune to take Sir William Berkeley a prisoner, he would have disdained to make a show of him." A soldier who had lost relatives in the massacre shot the aged chief in revenge. The Indians were harried and never again in the tidewater section of Virginia made a stand against the whites.

The Tuscarora, an Iroquoian tribe of North Carolina, narrowly escaped a similar fate of persecution and extinction. The first authentic information concerning this people is given by Lawson, sometime Surveyor General of North Carolina, in his *History of Carolina*, written about 1709 and published in 1718. He knew these Indians well, having lived in close contact with them for many years.

Although the Tuscarora were originally a peaceable and industrious people, they were speedly brutalized by the vices of the colonists with whom they came in contact; their women were debauched by the whites and both men and women were kidnapped and sold into slavery. The colonists of North Carolina, like their Puritan brethren of New England, did not concede to the Indian any right to the soil; hence the lands of the Tuscarora and of their Indian neighbors and allies were appropriated without thought of purchase. It is not strange, therefore, that such conduct on the part of the whites should eventually have awakened distrust and jealousy in the minds of the erstwhile amiable Tuscarora, which, fomented by these and other grievances, finally ripened into a hatred that led to resistance and reprisal.

Perhaps the most lucid and condensed statement of the wrongs suffered by the Tuscarora is contained in a petition which they made to the Provincial Government of Pennsylvania in 1710. They officially formulated a number of proposals embodying their grievances and their desire to have these adjusted or removed by the conclusion of peace, and to this end they sent, through another Iroquoian tribe, the Conestoga (Susquehanna), an embassy with these pacific overtures to the people and government of Pennsylvania. The governor and provincial council dispatched two commissioners to meet this embassy at Conestoga on June 8, 1710, where, in addition to the Tuscarora emissaries, they found Civility and four other Conestoga chiefs, and Opessa, the head chief of the Shawnee. In the presence of these officials the Tuscarora ambassadors delivered their proposals, attested by eight wampum belts, at the same time informing the Pennsylvania commissioners that these were sent as an overture for the purpose of asking for a cessation of hostilities until the following spring, when their chiefs and head men would come in person "to sue for the peace they so much desired." By the first belt, the elder women and the mothers besought the friendship of the Christian people, the Indians, and the government of Pennsylvania, so that they might fetch wood and water without risk of danger. By the second, the children born and those about to be born, implored for room to sport and play without the fear of death or slavery. By the third, the young men asked for the privilege of leaving their towns, without the fear of death or slavery, to hunt for meat for their mothers, their children, and the aged ones. By the fourth, the old men, the elders of the people, asked for the consummation of a lasting peace, so that the forest (the paths to other tribes) might be as safe for them as their palisaded towns. By the fifth, the entire tribe asked for a firm peace. By the sixth, the chiefs asked for the establishment of a lasting peace with the government, people, and Indians of Pennsylvania, whereby they would be relieved from "those fearful apprehensions they have these several years felt." By the seventh, the Tuscarora begged for a "cessation from murdering and taking them," so that thereafter they would not fear "a mouse, or anything that ruffles the leaves." By the eighth, the tribe, being strangers to the people and government of Pennsylvania, asked for an official path or means of communication between them.

It was the statement of a tribe at bay, who desired to remove to a more just and friendly government than that whence they came. At this time there was no war between them and the white people; there had been no massacre by the Tuscarora, no threat of hostility on the part of the Indians, yet to maintain peace and to avoid the impending shedding of blood, they were even then willing to forsake their homes. The petition not meeting with a favorable reception by the commissioners of Pennsylvania, the Conestoga chiefs present at the conference determined to send these belts, brought by the Tuscarora, to the Iroquois confederation. It was the reception of the belts with their pitiful messages by the Five Nations that eventually moved the latter to take steps to shield and protect the Tuscarora.

Disappointed in their attempt to escape peacefully from their persecutors, the Tuscarora sought revenge by massacring about 130 of the colonists on September 22, 1711. Colonel Barnwell, sent by South Carolina to the aid of North Carolina, drove the Tuscarora into

PLATE 79

Indian arrowheads and spearheads

PLATE 79

Indian arrowheads and spearheads

a palisaded town, defeated them, and offered them a treaty of peace. This treaty the English later violated by seizing some Indians and sending them away into slavery. This was the beginning of the second war between the Tuscarora and their allies and the people of North Carolina. Aid was again sent by South Carolina and the Tuscarora were again defeated.

After their second defeat at the hands of the English, the Tuscarora resolved to accept the hospitality of their kinsmen and began a migration to the north which was not completed until nine years later. In 1722 the last of the exiles were received into the "extended lodge" of the Five Nations of the Iroquois, who were thereafter known as the Six Nations. The numbers of those who remained in their homes gradually fell off till the tribe died out in North Carolina altogether.

It is a relief to turn from these tragic stories to the history of the colonies of Pennsylvania and Georgia, in both of which peace was long preserved by a mild and scrupulously just treatment of the Indians. The Quaker, William Penn, first proprietor in Pennsylvania, lived among the Indians and learned their ways. In founding his colony, although he held the territory as owner under a grant from the English crown, he was careful to make treaties with the Indians which constituted purchases of lands. These agreements, made with suitable solemnity and recorded by the Indians in their belts of wampum, were scrupulously kept on both sides. Consequently the Pennsylvania colonists suffered little or nothing from Indian raids for about seventy years, while terrible petty wars were raging in Virginia and New England. Indians helped white families with food in winter time, and white children were left in Indian care. The Quakers lived among them unarmed.

It was not until the great French and Indian War of 1755 that real trouble came to Pennsylvania. After Braddock's defeat organized bodies of French and

Indians harried the whole frontier of the colony, and the usual horrors of scalping, burning, and massacre were perpetrated by the Hurons, Shawnee, and other Indian partisans of the French. This led to reprisals by some of the colonists, who failed in many instances to distinguish the peaceable from the hostile.

Georgia was colonized under the benevolent proprietorship of James Oglethorpe, a man who sought to ameliorate the condition of the wretched by giving them an opportunity in a New World. It was quite in his character to make a just treaty with the Indians and to keep it. Thus Georgia, too, for a long time enjoyed peaceful relations with the red men.

The Spaniards, although their policy toward the Indians was less relentless than that of the majority of the English colonists, nevertheless had several notable conflicts with the natives of the South and West. The battle of Mavilla (in what is now southern Alabama), October 15, 1540, between the Indians and the Spaniards of De Soto's army, has been described by the historian Bancroft as probably the greatest Indian battle ever fought within the United States. The Indians were commanded by Tascalusa, a powerful chief of the Mobile tribe, whose name signifies "Black Warrior."

Tascalusa is described by the historians of the expedition, at his first meeting with De Soto, as very tall and strongly built, symmetrical and handsome in appearance, with an air of haughty dignity, seated upon a raised platform with his son beside him and his principal men around, one of whom held erect a sort of banner of deerskin curiously painted. His head was covered with a turban in the fashion of the Gulf tribes, and over his shoulders was thrown a feather mantle which reached to his feet. He looked on with contempt at the equestrian exercises with which the Spaniards strove to impress him, and gave unwilling ear to their demands for burden carriers and provisions, but when threatened by De Soto replied that he would send messengers ahead to his principal town, Mavilla, to order all to be prepared. Instead of this, however, he instructed the messengers to call in all the fighting men of his tribe to Mavilla, a stockaded town between the Alabama and Tombigbee rivers, to attack the Spaniards.

On the arrival of the advance guard of Spaniards, they unloaded their baggage in the public square, the Indians being apparently friendly and receiving them with a dance of welcome; but while this was going on some of the soldiers noticed them concealing bundles of bows and arrows under branches of trees, and on entering one of the houses the upper platforms near the roof were found filled with armed warriors. De Soto, on being warned, at once made preparations for defense and sent for the chief, who refused to come. An attempt to seize him precipitated the battle, in which the Spaniards were at first driven out of the town, followed by the Indians, who had freed the Indian burden carriers of the Spaniards from their chains and given them bows and arrows to use against the white men. In the open country outside the town the Spaniards were able to use their cavalry, and although the Indians desperately opposed their naked bodies, with bow and arrow, to the swords, long lances, and iron armor of the Spanish horsemen for a whole day, the town was at last set on fire and those who were not cut down outside were driven back into the flames. Men, women, and children fought, and many deliberately committed suicide when they saw that the day was lost. Of about 580 Spaniards engaged, some 20 were killed outright, and 150 wounded, despite their horses and protective armor, besides which they lost a number of horses, all their baggage, and some 200 pounds of pearls. De Soto himself was wounded and his nephew was among the killed. The lowest estimate of the Indian loss was 2,500 men, women, and children killed. The fate of Tascalusa was never known, but the body of his son was found thrust through with a lance.

The troubles of the Spaniards farther west in the Pueblo country have already received attention. Once the foreigners were installed in the region, the uprisings of the Indians against them seem to have differed from those in other parts of the continent in that their inspiration was as much religious as economic. The Spaniards did not usurp the uninviting Pueblo lands nor attempt to expel the owners. They did strive to gather them into Holy Church, however, and to control their civil lives. And so, much blood came to be spilled.

The leader of the great Pueblo revolt of 1680 was Pope (pronounced *Po-Pé*), a celebrated Tewa medicine-man of the pueblo of San Juan. He took up his headquarters at Taos and began quietly to fan the flames of civil and religious revolt, appealing for the restoration of the old Pueblo life. This developed into a plot to murder or drive from the country the 2,400 Spanish colonists and priests. The plot quickly spread among the Pueblos, meeting with enthusiasm as it went. August 13, 1680, was the day set for the onslaught, and the news was communicated by runners, even to the far-off Hopi in Arizona, by means of a knotted string; but for some reason the Piros of the lower Rio Grande were not invited to join in the massacre. Every precaution was taken to keep from the Spaniards all news of the proposed revolt; no woman was permitted to know of it, and, because suspected of treachery, Pope put his own brother-in-law to death. Nevertheless the news leaked out, and Pope's only hope of success was to strike at once. The blow came on August 10. Four hundred Spanish colonists, including 21 priests, were murdered, and Santa Fé was besieged, its thousand inhabitants taking refuge with governor Antonio de Otermin in the official buildings. Here they remained until the 20th, when a sortie made by 100 of the men resulted in the rout of

PLATE 80

Chief Joseph, (*c.* 1830-1904). Commander of the Nez Percés in the masterly retreat to the Canadian border, 1877

Pushmataha (1764-1824). Noted Choctaw chief and ally of the Americans in the War of 1812

the Indians, 200 being killed and 47 captured and hanged in the plaza of the town. The following day the Spaniards abandoned Santa Fé and began their long retreat down the Rio Grande to El Paso.

Having accomplished this much, Pope set about to realize the rest of his dream. Those who had been baptized as Christians were washed with yucca suds; the Spanish language and all baptismal names were prohibited; where not already consumed by the burning of the churches, all Christian objects were destroyed, and everything done to restore the old order of things. This project of obliterating everything Spanish from the life and thought of the Indians met with the same enthusiasm as that with which the plan of revolt had been received, and for a time Pope, dressed in ceremonial garb as he went from pueblo to pueblo, was everywhere received with honor. His success, however, had been more than he could stand. Assuming the rôle of a despot, he put to death those who refused to obey his commands, and took the most beautiful women for himself and his captains. Then the old enemies of the Pueblos intervened—drought, and the Apache and the Ute, who took advantage of the absence of the Spaniards to resume their forays. Internal dissension also arose. The Keresan tribes and the Taos and Pecos people fought against the Tewa and the Tano, and the latter deposed Pope on account of his lordly demands, electing to his place Luis Tupatú, who ruled the Tewa and the Tano until 1688, when Pope was again elected. He did not live to see his work destroyed by the reconquest of the province by Vargas in 1692.

The English and the Dutch, the French and the Spanish, did not, of course, all pursue an identical policy toward the Indians. Their several attitudes seem to have agreed, however, in a common sense of superiority over the red man. Perhaps the French came nearer to accepting him on terms of personal equality than did the others, but if this is true it did not prevent the French from crushing the Indian where the conquest of territory or economic security necessitated it. Thus the history of French settlement along the lower Mississippi reads not unlike the history of English settlement in New England or the Carolinas,—encroachments on the one hand, creating friction which led to massacres on the other, which in turn called for reprisals in the nature of partial or complete extermination. The fate of the Natchez tribe in the 18th century inspired two of the great works of Chateaubriand, *Les Natchez* and *Atala*, and has surrounded these Indians with a legendary aura.

The Natchez constituted the largest tribe on the lower Mississippi, having an estimated strength of 4,500 souls in 1650. A strongly centralized government distinguished them from other tribes, as their head chief seems to have had absolute power over the property and lives of his subjects. According to an early historian, as soon as anyone had the misfortune to displease him or his mother, they ordered their guards to kill him. "Go and rid me of that dog," said they; and they were immediately obeyed. On the chief's death his wives committed suicide and parents sacrificed children at his bier. Friction which may have been inspired in part by English traders from the Atlantic led to three wars with the French, in 1716, 1722, and 1729. The first two were minor affairs involving some deaths and destruction of homes on both sides, but they seem to have left bitterness which sought only an excuse to find expression. A political blunder committed by the French in exacting the head of one of their principal Suns (chiefs), Old-hair, to avenge the outbreak of 1722, rankled in the breasts of the Natchez.

A brutal and inefficient French governor, Chopart, brought on the final war by attempting to occupy the site of the principal Natchez village as a private plantation. The Indians decided that the only way to escape French exactions was to destroy the French entirely, and they secretly invited the Chickasaw and the Choctaw to fall upon all the white settlements on the same day. In order to strike their blows at the same time, each of the parties to the conspiracy was given a bundle of sticks, one of which was to be withdrawn and destroyed each day. According to Swanton, in some manner one or two of the sticks in the Natchez bundle were destroyed in addition to the ones abstracted by agreement, so that this tribe struck their blow two days before the time agreed upon. Probably either the great chief's mother who was friendly to the French, or "Stel-o-na, the beautiful daughter of White Apple," who loved a French officer, abstracted the sticks.

Friendly Indians repeatedly warned Governor Chopart of the impending attack, a service which he rewarded by putting the informers in irons. On the day they supposed was the right one the Natchez appeared at Fort Rosalie and offered to dance for the entertainment of some distinguished visitors lately arrived. At a given signal they interrupted the dance to seize their firearms and kill the garrison. Contemporary historians state that the Natchez had too much contempt for Governor Chopart to kill him themselves and had a slave club him to death. A conservative estimate places the number of French killed at 250 and prisoners captured at 150 children and 80 women, and the same number of negro slaves.

Disgruntled at the premature attack of the Natchez and the failure of their own part of the program, the Choctaw held out a hand for a large slice of French plunder. When the Natchez failed to satisfy their greed they turned traitor and joined forces with the whites against their erstwhile allies. Eventually, the French troops from New Orleans and elsewhere arrived with the Choctaw to storm the Natchez in Fort Rosalie. This part of the engagement came to an end with the release by the Natchez of their prisoners in return for the withdrawal of the French forces which permitted the

Indians to escape. They abandoned their villages and split into three sections, one of which was attacked by the French in 1831, resulting in many killed and the capture of 450 who were sold into slavery in Santo Domingo. A small section remained near their former homes and were unmolested, while the third and largest group were received by the Chickasaw and built a village near them in northen Mississippi.

Almost from the beginning of French activity in northern North America the settlers and the government of New France came into more or less sympathetic contact with several tribes of the country, thanks to the peaceful efforts of the missionaries and the government's desire to use the natives as a bulwark against the power of the English. To her alliance with the Algonquian tribes of the Great Lakes and the regions south and east of them, including New France and Acadia, France owed in great part her strength on this continent, while on the other hand the confederacy of the Iroquois, the natural enemies of the Algonquian peoples, contributed largely to her overthrow.

The most celebrated of the Indian allies of the French during their long struggle with the English in America was Pontiac, an Ottawa chief, born about 1720, probably on Maumee river, Ohio, about the mouth of the Auglaize. Though his paternity is not positively established, it seems likely that his father was an Ottawa chief and his mother a Chippewa woman. J. Wimer says that as early as 1746 he commanded the Indians—mostly Ottawa —who defended Detroit against the attack of the northern tribes. It is supposed he led the Ottawa and Chippewa warriors at Braddock's defeat. He first appears prominently in history at his meeting with Maj. Robert Rogers, in 1760, at the place where Cleveland, Ohio, now stands. The British had dispatched this officer to take possession of Detroit. Pontiac objected to the further invasion of the territory, but, learning that the French had been

Geronimo (*c.* 1834-1909). Medicine-man and prophet of the Apache. Stirred opposition to the American authorities

Black Hawk (1767-1838). Leader of the Sauk and Fox in the Black Hawk War of 1832

defeated in Canada, consented to the surrender of Detroit to the British and was the means of preventing an attack on the latter by a body of Indians at the mouth of the strait.

What gives him most prominence in history and forms the chief episode of his life is the plan he devised for a general uprising of the Indians and the destruction of the forts and settlements of the British. For a time he displayed a disposition to be on terms of friendship with the British and consented to acknowledge King George, but only as an "uncle," not as a superior. Failing to receive the recognition he considered his due as a great sovereign, and being deceived by the rumor that the French were preparing for the reconquest of their American possessions, he resolved to put his scheme into operation. He brought to his aid most of the tribes northwest of the Ohio, and planned a sudden and simultaneous attack on all the British posts on the Lakes—at St. Joseph, Ouiatenon, Michilimackinac, and Detroit—as well as on the Miami and Sandusky, and also an attack on the forts at Niagara, Presque Isle, Le Boeuf, Venango, and Fort Pitt (Du Quesne). He reserved the capture of Detroit for himself. The end of May, 1763, was the time set for each tribe to attack the nearest fort and, after killing the garrison, to fall on the adjacent settlements. In short order the posts at Sandusky, St. Joseph, Miami (Ft. Wayne), Ouiatenon, Michilimackinac, Presque Isle, Le Boeuf, and Venango fell, and the garrison in most cases suffered massacre; but the British successfully defeated the main points, Detroit and Fort Pitt, and forced the Indians to raise the siege. This was a severe blow to Pontiac, but what finally crushed his hopes was the receipt of a letter from M. Neyon, commander of Fort Chartres, advising him to desist from further warfare, as peace had been concluded between France and Great Britian. However, unwilling to abandon entirely his hope of driving back the British, he attempted to incite the tribes along the Mississippi to join in another effort. Unsuccessful in this, he finally made peace at Detroit, August 17, 1765. In 1769 he attended a drinking carousal at Cahokia, Illinois, where he was murdered by a Kaskaskia Indian. Pontiac, if not fully the equal of the great Tecumseh, stands closely second to him in strength of mind and breadth of comprehension.

The history of the Government's relations with the Indians is a checkerboard of good and evil, errors of intent and errors of mistaken kindness, mixed with enlightened fairness. It could not probably have been otherwise. In any case the net result has been to drive the Indian off the unfenced land and corral him in reservations, to wean him from the paths and faiths of his race, and to make of him an "American."

Soon after the Colonies had secured their independence, they set about the "winning of the West," a policy which involved not only the acquisition of territory by purchase and conquest from France, Spain, and Mexico, but likewise the conquest of the powerful Indian tribes who roamed the plains and haunted the forests of the vast region which lay beyond the original thirteen States. The conflict brought out many notable Indian leaders, men of intelligence, force and, of course, courage, who would do honor to any people. Destiny sentenced them to employ these qualities in behalf of a cause that could not win, but in so doing she added the dignity of tragedy to their fame. Of none is this more true than of Tecumseh, Shooting Star, celebrated chief and son of chiefs of the Shawnee.

Tecumseh came inevitably by his implacable enmity to the white invader. Born in 1768, the death of his father followed shortly in the battle of Point Pleasant in 1774. The Kentuckians destroyed his native village of Piqua on Mad River, about six miles southwest of the present Springfield, Ohio, in 1780. His guardian and elder brother fell in battle with the whites on the Tennessee frontier in 1788 or 1789. Still another brother was killed by Tecumseh's side at Wayne's victory in 1794. While still a young man Tecumseh distinguished himself in the border wars of the period, but was noted also for his humane character, evinced by persuading his tribe to discontinue the practice of torturing prisoners.

Together with his brother, Tenskwatawa the Prophet, he was an ardent opponent of the advance of the white man, and denied the right of the Government to make land purchases from any single tribe, on the ground that the territory, especially in the Ohio valley country, belonged to all the tribes in common. On the refusal of the Government to recognize this principle, he undertook the formation of a great confederacy of all the western and southern tribes for the purpose of holding the Ohio river as the permanent boundary between the two races. In pursuance of this object he or his agents visited every tribe from Florida to the head of the Missouri river. While Tecumseh was organizing the work in the south, his plans were brought to disastrous overthrow by the premature battle of Tippecanoe under the direction of the Prophet, November 7, 1811.

On the breaking out of the War of 1812, Tecumseh at once led his forces to the support of the British, and was rewarded with a regular commission as brigadier-general, having under his command some 2,000 warriors of the allied tribes. He fought at Frenchtown, The Raisin, Fort Meigs, and Fort Stephenson, and covered Proctor's retreat after Perry's decisive victory on Lake Erie, until declining to retreat farther, he compelled Proctor to make a stand on the Thames River, near the present Chatham, Ontario. In the bloody battle which ensued, the allied British and Indians were completely defeated by Harrison, Tecumseh himself falling in the front of his warriors, October 5, 1813, being then in his forty-fifth year. With a presentiment of death he had discarded his general's uniform before the battle and dressed himself in his Indian deerskin.

From all that is said of Tecumseh in contemporary record, there is no reason to doubt the verdict of Trumbull that he was the most extraordinary Indian character in United States history. There is no true portrait of him in existence, the one commonly given as such in Lossing's "War of 1812," and reproduced in Appleton's "Cyclopedia of American Biography" and Mooney's "Ghost Dance," being a composite result based on a pencil sketch made about 1812, on which were mounted his cap, medal, and uniform.

In contrast to Tecumseh stands Pushmataha the man who was largely responsible for the failure of Tecumseh's mission to the Choctaw in 1811, when he attempted to persuade them to join in an uprising against the Americans. This noted Choctaw, though he opposed the great Shawnee Chief, presents by no means an unheroic figure. Of unknown ancestry, he was born on Noxuba Creek in Noxubee County, Mississippi, in 1764. The bravery he manifested in war with the Osage gained for him a chieftaincy before he had reached twenty.

During the War of 1812 most of the Choctaw became friendly to the United States through the opposition of Pushmataha and John Pitchlynn to a neutral course, Pushmataha being alleged to have said, on the last day of a ten day's council: "The Creeks were once our friends. They have joined the English and we must now follow different trails. When our fathers took the hand of Washington, they told him the Choctaw would always be friends of his nation, and Pushmataha can not be false to their promises. I am now ready to fight against both the English and the Creeks." He was at the head of 500 warriors during the war, engaging in 24 fights and serving under Jackson's eye in the Pensacola campaign. In 1813, with about 150 Choctaw warriors, he joined General Claiborne and distinguished himself in the attack

Sequoya (*c.* 1760-1843). Inventor of the Cherokee alphabet

Osceola (*c.* 1803-1838). Leader of the Seminole in their war with the United States

and defeat of the Creeks under Weatherford at Kantchati, or Holy Ground, on the Alabama River, Alabama. While aiding the United States troops he was so rigid in his discipline that he soon succeeded in converting his wild warriors into efficient soldiers, while for his energy in fighting the Creeks and Seminole he became popularly known to the whites as "The Indian General."

Pushmataha signed the treaties of November 16, 1805; October 24, 1816; and October 18, 1820. In negotiating the last treaty, at Doak's Stand, "he displayed much diplomacy and showed a business capacity equal to that of General Jackson, against whom he was pitted, in driving a sharp bargain." In 1824 he went to Washington to negotiate another treaty in behalf of his tribe.

Following a brief visit to Lafayette, then at the capital, Pushmataha became ill and died within twenty-four hours. In accordance with his request he was buried with military honors, a procession of 2,000 persons, military and civilian, accompanied by President Jackson, following his remains to Congressional Cemetery. A shaft bearing the following inscriptions was erected over his grave: "Pushmataha a Choctaw chief lies here. This monument to his memory is erected by his brother chiefs who were associated with him in a delegation from their nation, in the year 1824, to the General Government of the United States." "Push-ma-taha was a warrior of great distinction; he was wise in council; eloquent in an extraordinary degree; and on all occasions, and under all circumstances, the white man's friend." "He died in Washington, on the 24th of December, 1824, of the croup, in the 60th year of his age." General Jackson frequently expressed the opinion that Pushmataha was the greatest and the bravest Indian he had every known, and John Randolph of Roanoke, in pronouncing a eulogy on him in the Senate, uttered the words regarding his wisdom, his eloquence, and his friendship for the whites that afterward were inscribed on his monument.

He was deeply interested in the education of his people, and it is said devoted $2,000 of his annuity for fifteen years toward the support of the Choctaw school system. As mingo of the Oklahannali, Pushmataha was succeeded by Nittakechi, "Day-prolonger." Several portraits of Pushmataha are extant, including one in the Redwood Library at Newport, Rhode Island. The first portrait, painted by C. B. King at Washington in 1824, shortly before Pushmataha's death, was burned in the Smithsonian fire of 1865.

The Americans purchased the consolidation of practically every advance they made in the West by a war, in addition to the constant border fighting and massacres. Open war came usually as a climax to the guerrilla fighting and represented the last stand of the Indians in a certain area. The Black Hawk War, of 1832, was typical of these forlorn outbursts. Added interest attaches to it because of the participation in it of one Abraham Lincoln, Captain of Illinois Volunteers.

This war took its name from Black Hawk, a subordinate Chief of the Sauk and Fox Indians. Born at a Sauk village at the mouth of the Rock River, Illinois, in 1767, he distinguished himself as a warrior when only fifteen. Four years later he led two hundred Sauk and Foxes in a desperate engagement with an equal number of Osage, destroying half of his opponents, killing five men and a woman with his own hands. In a subsequent raid on the Cherokee his party killed twenty-eight with a loss of but seven. But the dead included his own father, who was guardian of the tribal medicine, and his loss led Black Hawk to refrain from war during the five years following and to endeavor to increase his supernatural power. At the end of that time he led an attack against the Osage, destroyed a camp of forty lodges, with the exception of two women, and himself slew nine persons. On a subsequent expedition against the Cherokee in revenge for his father's death he found only five enemies, four men and a woman. The latter he carried off, but the men he released deeming it no honor to kill so few. During the War of 1812 he fought with the British.

By the treaty of November 3, 1804, concluded at St. Louis, the Sauk and the Foxes had agreed to surrender all their lands on the east side of the Mississippi, but had been left undisturbed therein until the country should be thrown open to settlement. After the conclusion of the War of 1812, however, the stream of settlers pushed westward once more and began to pour into the old Sauk and Fox territory. The majority of the Sauk, including the famous orator, Keokuk, bowing to the inevitable, soon moved across the Mississippi into what is now Iowa; but Black Hawk declined to leave, maintaining that when he had signed the treaty of St. Louis he had been deceived regarding its terms. At the same time he entered into negotiations with the Winnebago, Potawatomi, and Kickapoo to enlist them in concerted opposition to the threatened aggressions.

By the year 1832 serious friction had developed. An order to General Atkinson to demand from the Sauk and the Foxes the chief members of a band who had massacred some Menominee the year before, precipitated hostilities. Black Hawk led a band estimated at 2,000, of whom 500 were warriors. The undisciplined militia proved ineffectual and Black Hawk turned loose his followers on the frontier settlements. He attacked Apple River fort, but was repulsed and fought a sanguinary battle with Major Dement's battalion. During the next two months, volunteers and regulars harried the Indians to cover, inflicting heavy casualties. The Sioux cut off a good many and the Winnebago captured Black Hawk and his principal warrior, Neapope, after the final rout in August. Black Hawk was then sent East and confined for more than a month at Fortress Monroe, Virginia, when he was taken on a tour through the principal eastern cities, everywhere proving an object of the greatest interest. In 1837 he accompanied Keokuk on a second trip to the East, after which he settled on the Des Moines River near Iowaville, there to die on October 3, 1838.

The Sioux have written their name indelibly in the bloody epic of the white man's conquest of the West. The present generation knows more of them, perhaps, than of other tribes because their warlike activities came nearer in time. Sitting Bull, who led the rebellion of 1876, in which Custer was killed, is the best known, but Red Cloud outranks him and all other Sioux chiefs in merit and power. Red Cloud led the Oglala Teton Sioux of Pine Ridge Reservation, the largest band of the Sioux nation. His career extended over the better part of a century, from 1822 to 1909. He was a member of the Snake family, the most distinguished and forceful of his tribe, and rose to prominence by his own force of character, having no claim to hereditary chiefship. Red Cloud's father died of drunkenness brought about by the introduction of unlimited liquor into the tribe.

When in 1865 the Government undertook to build a road from Fort Laramie, Wyoming, on the North Platte, by way of Powder River to the gold regions of Montana, Red Cloud headed the opposition for his tribe, on the ground that the influx of travel along the trail would destroy the best remaining buffalo ground of the Indians. The first small detachment of troops sent out to begin construction work were intercepted by Red Cloud with a large party of Oglala Sioux and Cheyenne, and held practically as prisoners for more than two weeks, but finally were allowed to proceed when it seemed to the chief that they might be massacred by his young men. In the fall of the same year commissioners were sent to treat with the Oglala for permission to build the road, but Red Cloud forbade the negotiations and refused to attend the council.

On June 30, 1866, another council for the same purpose was called at Fort Laramie, Red Cloud this time attending and repeating his refusal to endanger the hunting grounds of his people. While he was speaking, a strong force of troops under General Carrington arrived, and on being told, in reply to a question, that they had come to build forts and open the road to Montana, he seized his rifle and with a final defiant message left the council with his entire following. Another protest to Carrington himself proving ineffectual, Red Cloud surrounded the troops and working force at Fort Kearny with perhaps 2,000 warriors and harassed them so constantly that not even a load of hay could be brought in from the prairie except under the protection of a strong guard. On December 21, 1866, an entire detachment of eighty-one men under Captain Fetterman was cut off and every man killed. On August 1, 1867, another severe engagement occurred near the post.

In all this time not a single wagon had been able to pass over the road, and in 1868 another commission was appointed to come to terms with Red Cloud, who demanded as an ultimatum the abandonment of the three army posts in the region and of all further attempts to open the Montana road. A treaty was finally made on this basis, defining the limits of the Sioux country as claimed by the Sioux, Red Cloud refusing to sign or even to be present until the garrisons had actually been withdrawn, thus winning a complete victory for the position which he had taken from the beginning. He finally affixed his signature at Fort Laramie, November 6, 1868. From that date he seems to have kept his promise to live at peace with the whites, although constantly resisting the innovations of civilization. He took no active part in the Sioux war of 1876, although he is accused of having secretly aided and encouraged the hostiles. Being convinced of the hopelessness of attempting to hold the Black Hills after the discovery of gold in that region, he joined in the agreement of cession in 1876. In the outbreak of 1890-91 also he remained quiet, being then an old man and partially blind, and was even said to have been threatened by the hostiles on account of his loyal attitude toward the Government.

As a warrior Red Cloud stood first among his people, claiming eighty *coups* or separate deeds of bravery in battle. As a general and statesman he ranked equally high, several times serving as a delegate to Washington. His attitude was always that of a patriot from the Indian standpoint. Unlike Indians generally, he had but one wife, with whom he lived from early manhood. Personally he is described by one well acquainted with him as a most courtly chief and a natural-born gentleman, with a bow as graceful as that of a Chesterfield. For some years before his death he was blind and decrepit, and lived in a house built for him by the Government.

Sitting Bull, born in 1834 and so a slightly younger contemporary of Red Cloud, seems to have been less constructive in his quarrels with the whites. He inherited from his father, a sub-chief, leadership of the Hunkpapa Teton Sioux. When he was fourteen he accompanied his father on the warpath against the Crows and counted his first *coup* on the body of a fallen enemy. On the return of the party his father made a feast, gave away many horses, and announced that his son had won the right to be known henceforth by his own name. He rapidly acquired influence in his own band, being especially skillful in the character of peacemaker. He took an active part in the Plains wars of the '60's, and first became widely known to the whites in 1866, when he led a memorable raid against Fort Buford. Sitting Bull was on the warpath with his band of followers from various tribes almost continuously from 1869 to 1876, either raiding the frontier posts or making war on the Crows or the Shoshoni, especially the former. His autographic pictorial record in the Army Medical Museum at Washington refers chiefly to contests with the Crows and to horse stealing.

His refusal to return to a reservation in 1876 led General

Sheridan to begin against him and his followers the campaign which led to the surprise and annihilation of Custer's troop on Little Bighorn River, Montana, in June. During this battle, in which 2,500 to 3,000 Indian warriors engaged, Sitting Bull was in the hills "making medicine," and his accurate foretelling of the battle enabled him "to come out of the affair with higher honor than he possessed when he went into it" (McLaughlin). After this fight the hostiles separated into two parties. Sitting Bull, in command of the western party, was attacked by General Miles and routed; a large number of his followers surrendered, but the remainder of the band, including Sitting Bull himself, escaped to Canada. There they remained until 1881, when he surrendered at Fort Buford, under promise of amnesty, and was confined at Fort Randall until 1883.

Although he had surrendered and gone upon a reservation, Sitting Bull continued unreconciled. It was through his influence that the Sioux refused to sell their land in 1888; and it was at his camp at Standing Rock agency and at his invitation that Kicking Bear organized the first Ghost Dance on the reservation. The demand for his arrest was followed by an attempt on the part of some of his people to rescue him, during which he was shot and killed by Sergeants Red Tomahawk and Bullhead of the Indian police, December 15, 1890. His son, Crow Foot, and several others, with six of the Indian police, were also killed in the struggle.

Although a chief by inheritance, it was rather Sitting Bull's success as an organizer and his later reputation as a sacred dreamer that brought him into prominence. According to McLaughlin, "his accuracy of judgment, knowledge of men, a student-like disposition to observe natural phenomena, and a deep insight into affairs among Indians and such white people as he came into contact with, made his stock in trade, and he made 'good medicine!' " He stood well among his own people, and was respected for his generosity, quiet disposition, and steadfast adherence to Indian ideals. He had two wives at the time of his death (one of whom was known as Pretty Plume), and was the father of nine children.

The recognition of the rights of his people which Red Cloud, the Sioux, obtained by the intelligent use of force, Standing Bear, the Ponca, obtained by a passive resistance which won him the sympathy of the nation and effected a change in Government policy toward the Indians. Little was known of Standing Bear, chief of the Ponca, until the removal of his people from northern Nebraska to Indian Territory, on the excuse that the reservation confirmed to them by treaty had been included in the land granted to the Sioux.

When the order for removal was given, January 15, 1877, Standing Bear strongly opposed it, but in February he and nine other chiefs were taken South to choose a reservation. They followed the official, but would not select a place. Their wearisome journey brought them to Arkansas City, Kansas, whence they asked to be taken home. Being refused, they started back afoot, with a few dollars among them and a blanket each. In forty days they had walked 500 miles, reaching home April 2, to find the official there unwilling to listen to protests and determined to remove the people. He called the military, and the tribe, losing hope, abandoned their homes in May. Standing Bear could get no response to his demand to know why he and his people were arrested and treated as criminals when they had done no wrong.

The change of climate brought great suffering to the Ponca; within the year a third of the tribe had died and most of the survivors were ill or disabled. A son of Standing Bear died. Craving to bury the lad at his old home, the chief determined to defy restraint. He took the bones of his son and with his immediate following turned northward in January, 1879, and in March arrived destitute at the Omaha Reservation. Asking to borrow land and seed,

PLATE 83

"Saturioua, King of Florida in North America, in the act of going to war." About 1564. By Jacques Le Moyne de Morgues, earliest known painter of North American Indians. Courtesy of Mr. David I. Bushnell, Junior

his request was granted, and the Ponca were about to put in a crop when soldiers appeared with orders to arrest Standing Bear and his party and return them to Indian Territory. On their way they camped near Omaha, where Standing Bear was interviewed by T. H. Tibbles, a newspaper correspondent, and accounts of the grievances appeared in the Omaha newspapers. The citizens became actively interested and opened a church, where to a crowded house the chief repeated his story. Messrs. Poppleton and Webster proffered legal services to the prisoners, and in their behalf took out a writ of *habeas corpus*. The United States denied the prisoners' right to the writ on the ground that they were "not persons within the meaning of the law." On April 18 Judge Dundy decided that "an Indian is a person within the meaning of the law of the United States," and therefore had a right to the writ when restrained in violation of law; that "no rightful authority exists for removing by force any of the prisoners to the Indian Territory," and therefore "the prisoners must be discharged from custody."

Standing Bear and his band returned to northern Nebraska. In the winter of 1879–80, accompanied by Susette La Flesche ("Bright Eyes") and Francis La Flesche, as interpreters, with T. H. Tibbles, Standing Bear visited the cities of the East, where, by relating his story of wrongs suffered, he won attention and sympathy. Many people wrote to the President and to other executive officials of the Government, and to members of Congress, protesting against the unjust treatment of the Indians. In the spring of 1880 the Senate appointed a committee to investigate the Ponca removal, the report of which confirmed the story of Standing Bear, and a satisfactory adjustment was effected. Better lands were given those Ponca who chose to remain in Indian Territory; payment was made to all who had lost property, and a home was provided for Standing Bear and his followers at their old reservation. Here, in September, 1908, after having been instrumental in bringing about a change of Governmental policy toward all Indians and their homes, the chief died at the age of 79 and was buried among the hills overlooking the village site of his ancestors.

The turbulent Indian element in the Southwest was furnished by the Apache. Although they have been a hostile people, not only to the whites but to other Indians, since the Spaniards first made them known to history, the most serious modern outbreaks seem to have been due to mismanagement on the part of civil authorities. The insurrection led by Cochise, a Chiricahua Apache chief, illustrates this. Although constantly at war with the Mexicans, he gave no trouble to the Americans until after he went, in 1861, under a flag of truce, to the camp of a party of soldiers to deny that his tribe had abducted a white child. The denial angered the commanding officer and he ordered the visiting chiefs seized and bound because they would not confess. The troops killed one and caught four; but Cochise, cutting through the side of a tent, made his escape with three bullets in his body. He began immediate hostilities to avenge his companions, who were hanged by the Federal troops. The Indians forced the troops to retreat and laid waste white settlements in Arizona. Soon afterward the recall of the troops to take part in the Civil War led to the abandonment of the military posts. This convinced the Apache that they need only fight to prevent Americans from settling in their country. Cochise and Mangas Coloradas defended Apache Pass in southeastern Arizona against the Californians, who marched under General Carleton to reopen communication between the Pacific Coast and the East. The howitzers of the California volunteers put the Apache to flight. When United States troops returned to resume the occupancy of the country after the close of the Civil War, a war of extermination was carried on against the Apache. Cochise did not surrender till September, 1871. When orders came to transfer his people from Cañada Alamosa to the new Tularosa Reservation, in New Mexico, he escaped with a band of 200 in the spring of 1872, and his example was followed by 600 others. After the Chiricahua Reservation was established in Arizona, in the summer of 1872, he came in and there died in peace, June 8, 1874.

The case of Geronimo, a medicine-man and prophet of the Chiricahua Apache differed somewhat from that of Cochise. He acquired notoriety through his opposition to the authorities and by systematic and sensational advertising; he was born about 1834 at the headwaters of the Gila River, New Mexico, near old Fort Tulerosa. His father was Taklishim, "The Gray One," who was not a chief, although his father (Geronimo's grandfather) assumed to be a chief without heredity or election. Geronimo's mother was known as Juana.

Taking astute advantage of the nearness of the Mexican border, Geronimo repeatedly headed marauding bands of Apache, now in Mexico, now in the United States. Several times he was captured by troops and confined to the San Carlos Reservation, but the Indians found causes of discontent, some relating to irrigation, others to restrictions on the making of intoxicants. During 1884-85, Geronimo gathered a band of hostiles, who terrorized the inhabitants of southern Arizona and New Mexico, as well as of Sonora and Chihuahua, in Mexico. General Crook proceeded against them with instructions to capture or destroy the chief and his followers. In March, 1886, a truce was made, followed by a conference at which the terms of surrender were agreed on; but Geronimo and his followers having again fled to the Sierra Madre across the Mexican frontier, and General Miles having been placed in command, active operations were renewed and their surrender was ultimately effected in the following August. The entire band, numbering about 340, including Geronimo and Nachi, the hereditary chief, were deported as prisoners of war, first to Florida and later to Alabama, being finally settled at Fort Sill, Oklahoma.

The West Coast produced at least one master military leader in the person of Chief Joseph, leader of the Nez Percés in the hostilities of 1877. His mother was a Nez Percé, his father a Cayuse who received the name Joseph from his teacher, the missionary Spalding, the companion of Dr. Whitman in his mission to the Idaho country in the late thirties of the nineteenth century. Joseph was a man of fine presence and impressive features. His record stamps him as one of the most remarkable Indians within the borders of the Union. The treaty of 1863, by which the whites obtained a right to the Wallowa Valley, the ancient home of Joseph's band in northeastern Oregon, was not recognized by Joseph and the Indians sympathizing with him, who continued to dwell there in spite of more and more frequent collisions between the Indians and the whites. The removal of these Indians to the Lapwai Reservation in Idaho, after the failure of a commission the previous year, was proceeding to a peaceful settlement when outrageous acts on the part of the white settlers caused the Nez Percés to break loose and attack the settlements.

War was declared. After several engagements, in which the whites lost severely, Joseph displayed remarkable generalship in a retreat worthy to be remembered with that of Xenophon's ten thousand. In spite of the fact that in front of him was Colonel Miles, behind, General Howard, on his flank Colonel Sturgis and his Indian scouts, Joseph brought his little band, incommoded with women and children, to within fifty miles of the Canadian border, their objective point, when they were cut off by fresh troops in front and forced to surrender conditionally on October 5, 1877. Not only the conduct of the Nez Percés during this retreat of more than 1,000 miles, but also the military and tactical skill displayed by their leader, won unstinted praise from their conquerors.

The whites ignored the promises made to Joseph and his people, removing them, 431 in number, to Fort Leavenworth, Kansas, and afterward to the Indian Territory, where they remained for several years, always yearning for the mountains and valleys of Idaho. In 1883, a party of thirty-three women and children received permission to go back to their old home and were followed the next year by 118 others. Joseph and the remaining members of his band, however, numbering 150, were not permitted to return to Idaho, but were sent to the Colville Reservation, Washington. He lived to visit President Roosevelt and General Miles at Washington in March 1903, but died at Nespelim, on the Colville Reservation, Washington, September 21, 1904. According to the Indian agent, he had become reconciled to civilization in his last years, lending his aid in the education of the children of his tribe, and discouraging gambling and drunkenness.

While most of the Indian wars during the nineteenth century took place in the West, one sporadic outbreak in the East occurred in Florida. This was the Seminole War of 1835, in which Osceola, or "Black Drink Crier," led the Indians. Born on Tallapoosa River, in the Creek country, about 1803, Osceola was descended from a Scotch grandfather. According to report, his features and complexion betrayed the Caucasian strain. He was not a chief by descent, nor, so far as is known, by formal election, but took his place as leader and acknowledged chieftain by reason of his abilities as a warrior and commander during the memorable struggle of his people with the United States. Secreting the women, children, and old men of his tribe in the depths of a great swamp, where the white troops were for a long time unable to find them, Osceola turned his energy to the work of harassing the Government forces. Major Dade and his detachment, the first to attack him, were cut off, only two or three wounded men escaping. Beginning with General

Gaines, one officer after another succeeded to command of the army sent against this intrepid warrior and his followers. These were successively baffled, owing largely to the physical difficulties to be overcome in the Seminole country, until General Jesup, maddened by the public cry for more energetic action, seized Osceola and his attendants while holding a conference under a flag of truce—an act condemned as inexcusable treachery by the same public that had urged him on. The loss of freedom, and brooding over the manner in which he had been betrayed, broke the spirit of the youthful chief, who died a prisoner in Fort Moultrie, Florida, in January, 1838. Not until 1926 did the Seminole tribe formally accept peace with the United States.

Though circumstances forced the majority of great Indian leaders into war, there were some among them who pursued more peaceful paths to glory. Chief among these stands Sequoya, the inventor of the Cherokee alphabet, who was born in the Cherokee town of Taskigi, Tennessee, about 1760, and died near San Fernando, Tamaulipas, Mexico, in August, 1843. He was the son of a white man and a Cherokee woman of mixed blood, daughter of a chief in Echota, and grew up in the tribe quite unacquainted with English or civilized arts. He became a hunter and trader in furs. He also showed ability as a craftsman in silverwork, and proved himself an ingenious natural mechanic. His inventive powers found chance for development in consequence of an accident that befell him while hunting and rendered him a cripple for life.

The importance of the arts of writing and printing as instruments and weapons of civilization began to impress Sequoya in 1809, and he studied, undismayed by the discouragement and ridicule of his fellows, to elaborate a system of writing suitable to the Cherokee language. In 1821 he submitted his syllabary to the chief men of the nation, and on their approval the Cherokee of all ages set about to learn it with such zeal that after a few months thousands were able to read and write their language. In 1822, Sequoya visited Arkansas to introduce writing in the western division of the Cherokee, among whom he took up his permanent abode in 1823. Parts of the Bible were printed in Cherokee in 1824, and in 1828 *The Cherokee Phoenix*, a weekly newspaper in Cherokee and English, began to appear.

Sequoya was sent to Washington in 1828 as an envoy of the Arkansas band in whose affairs he bore a conspicuous part, and when the eastern Cherokee joined the old settlers in the West his influence and counsel were potent in the organization of the reunited nation in Indian Territory. When, in his declining years, he withdrew from active political life, speculative ideals once again possessed his mind. He visited tribes of various stocks in a fruitless search for the elements of a common speech and grammar. He sought also to trace a lost band of the Cherokee that, according to tradition, had crossed the Mississippi before the Revolution and wandered to some mountains in the West. While pursuing this quest in the Mexican Sierras, he met his death.

The Indian of today has small need for a native alphabet. The rising generation, like the children of European immigrants, prefer as a rule to acquire the English language and to forget their native tongue. The Government provides a sound English education for its wards on the reservations, Unfortunately it has not yet supplied an adequate field for the exercise of the intellectual faculties thus developed.

The presence of the red men in our midst constitutes, indeed, a problem less menacing but scarcely less perplexing than in colonial times. Education has long been regarded as its only solution, but so far the tendency to confuse education with mere "book learning" has limited its applicability to the needs of the Indian. Even in colonial days, benevolent spirits like Roger Williams,

John Eliot, and Eleazer Whitlock, in New England, and a few like-minded scholars in the southern colonies, sought to educate and to Christianize the natives, with a view to making them peaceful and useful neighbors and ultimately incorporating them into the citizenship of America. To this end a number of institutions of learning were established. Harvard, Dartmouth, and the College of William and Mary all began, in whole or in part, as colleges for Indian youths. The royal charter of Dartmouth College (1769) specifically states that it is to be "for the education and instruction of youths of the Indian tribes in this land," and "for civilizing and Christianizing the children of pagans." That of Harvard looked to "the education of the English and Indian youth in knowledge and godliness." The success of these deliberately planned educational institutions for the benefit of the Indian was slight indeed, as shown by the record of Harvard, which during the colonial period had but one Indian graduate, Caleb Cheeshateauniuck, of whom scarcely more than his unpronounceable name is known.

The ever westward march of pioneers involved, as we have seen, the tribes of the Great Plains and later those of the Rockies and the West Coast in the struggle between the races. After white supremacy was assured and the destiny of the Colonies was merged in the destiny of the United States, it became the policy of the Government to confine the remnants of the tribes to reservations. In return for lands abandoned the Indians received large sums of money, but owing to their lack of business knowledge profited little by the transaction.

In spite of the dishonesty and injustice which are apparently inseparable from the reservation system, it seemed the only practicable plan by which the Indians might be provided with homes and with land for cultivation and at the same time kept under the control of the Government. The policy had already been followed in Canada under both the French and English, and also

PLATE 84

"The Creek house in its best state of native improvement in 1790." After Schoolcraft

to some extent in the Colonies. It was adopted by the United States in 1786. The setting apart of the reservations by solemn treaty was later modified by Congress and simplified from time to time, being finally placed in the control of the President, who now has the power of making such allotments of land by executive order.

In accordance with a plan, adopted at an early date, of removing all eastern tribes to reservations west of the Mississippi, a large territory, including the present Oklahoma and the greater portion of what is now Kansas, was set apart under the name "Indian Territory" as a permanent home for the tribes to be removed from the settled portions of the United States. Most of the northern portion of the territory was acquired by treaty purchase from the Osage and the Kansa. A series of treaties was then inaugurated by which, before the close of 1840, almost all the principal eastern tribes and tribal remnants had been removed to the Indian Territory, the five important southern tribes—Cherokee, Creek, Choctaw, Chickasaw, and Seminole—being guaranteed autonomy under the style of "Nations." By subsequent legislation Kansas was detached from the Territory, most of the emigrant tribes within the bounds of Kansas being again removed to new reservations south of the boundary line. By other and later treaties lands within the same Territory were assigned to the actual native tribes—Kiowa, Comanche, Wichita, Cheyenne, etc.—whose claims had been entirely overlooked in the first negotiations, which considered only the Osage and Kansa along the eastern border. Other tribes were brought in at various periods from Texas, Nebraska, and farther north, to which were added, as prisoners of war, The Modoc of California (1873), the Nez Percés of Oregon and Idaho (1878), and the Chiricahua Apache of Arizona (1889), until the Indian population of the Territory comprised some forty officially recognized tribes. There are also some small State reservations in Maine, New York, Virginia, South Carolina, and Texas.

The Government was now faced with the problem of the education of its wards. The aborigines of North America had their own systems of education through which children were instructed in their coming labors and obligations, embracing not only the whole round of economic pursuits—hunting, fishing, handicraft, agriculture, and household work—but speech, fine art, customs, etiquette, social obligations, and tribal lore. By unconscious absorption and by constant teaching the boy and girl became the accomplished man and woman.

The Eskimo, for instance, exercised the greatest care in the education of their girls and boys, setting them difficult problems in canoeing, sledding, and hunting, showing them how to solve them, and asking boys how they would meet a given emergency. But everywhere there existed the closest association, for education, of parents with children, who learned the names and uses of things in nature. From earliest youth they played at serious business, girls attending to household duties, boys following men's pursuits. Children were furnished with appropriate toys; they became little basket makers, weavers, potters, water carriers, cooks, archers, stone workers, watchers of crops and flocks, the range of instruction being limited only by tribal custom. In a similar manner the intangible properties of the tribe were communicated to them—its customs, laws, beliefs, its traditional and mythic lore.

On the coming of the whites, a new era of secular education, designed and undesigned, began. All the natives, young and old, were pupils, and all the whites who came in contact with them were instructors, whether purposely or through the influence of their example and patronage. The undesigned instruction can not be measured, but its effect was profound. The Indian passed at once into the iron age; the stone period, except in ceremony, was at an end. So radical was the change in the eastern tribes that it is difficult now to illustrate their true life in museum collections.

After the establishment of the United States Government the following Christian bodies either instituted secular day and boarding schools among the Indians or continued those already in existence, and these schools have borne a large part in Indian education: Roman Catholic and Moravian, from colonial times; Friends (Orthodox), 1795; Baptist, 1807; American Board of Commissioners for Foreign Missions (Congregational), 1810; Episcopal, 1815; Methodist Episcopal, 1816; Presbyterian (North), 1833; Old School Presbyterian, 1837; Methodist Episcopal (South), 1844; Congregational American Missionary Association, 1846; Reformed Dutch, 1857; Presbyterian (South), 1857; Friends (Hicksite), 1869; United Presbyterian, 1869; Unitarian, 1886. Miss Alice C. Fletcher affirms that the missionary labors among the Indians have been as largely educational as religious. Until 1870 all Government aid for educational purposes passed through the hands of the missionaries.

A committee on Indian affairs was appointed in the Continental Congress, July 12, 1775, with General Schuyler as chairman, and in the following year a standing committee was created. Money was voted to support Indian students at Dartmouth and Princeton colleges. From the creation of the War Department in 1789, Indian affairs remained in the hands of its Secretary until 1849, when the Department of the Interior was established and the Indian Bureau transferred to it. General Knox, Washington's Secretary of War, urged industrial education, and the President agreed with him. In his message of 1801 President Adams noted the success of continued efforts to introduce among the Indians modern implements and methods of agriculture and the domestic arts.

The first petition of an Indian for schools among his

tribe was made by David Folsom, a Choctaw, in 1816. The Ottawa, in the treaty of 1817, and in their address to President Monroe in 1822, stipulated for industrial and literary education. In 1819 Congress made a first appropriation of $10,000 for Indian education, the superintendents and agents to be nominated by the President. In 1823 there were twenty-one schools receiving Government aid, and the number was increased to thirty-eight in 1825. The first contract school was established on the Tulalip Reservation, Washington, in 1869, but not until 1873 were Government schools proper provided. At first only day schools existed; later boarding schools were established on the reservations, and finally remote from them. The training in all these schools aimed to bring the Indians nearer to civilized life, with a view to ultimate citizenship.

In recent years the policy of the Government has tended toward the division in severalty among the Indian proprietors of the tribal reservations. Many of the tribes have reached so high a grade of civilization as to render this practicable. In such cases the Indian rapidly merges into the citizen of the United States and ceases to be a separated element.

By the act of June 2, 1924, all Indians within United States territory, not previously citizens, were made so. During the World War the Indians were very forward in patriotic enterprises. About 10,000 served in the armed forces of the United States, nearly three quarters of them being volunteers. Others served in Red Cross and other war work. The Indian soldiers generally were attached to white organizations, and as a rule were highly commended by their officers.

An interesting picture of Indian progress is given by the following figures:

	1911	*1925*
Indian population in United States....	322,715	349,595
Children eligible to school............	63,411	77,597
Children attending school............	39,397	67,438

"Public granary" of the Florida Indians. From Jacques Le Moyne, 1564

A fortified Indian town in Florida. From Le Moyne, 1564

The Government itself maintains nearly 300 schools for Indians, but about 34,000 of their children are enrolled in the public schools of the various States. Many Indians are students at State universities and other institutions of learning, qualifying for various professions. Others have already attained eminence.

The transition from the Stone Age to the Age of Electricity which the Indians have been forced to make so rapidly has necessarily been accompanied by many evils. It has been already pointed out that contact with the white man's civilization, particularly those phases to be found in frontier life, tended to debase and demoralize the natives. The forced removal from their old haunts and homes, the necessary change in their manner of life, the abandonment of their old and tried traditions for the white man's unknown God, all this sudden uprooting and transplanting could not but bring many a heavy grief, especially to the hearts of the older people, who found "a sorrow's crown of sorrow is remembering happier things." Then, too, they reaped a doleful harvest of disease and death, which for a time threatened their very existence.

Slow as the betterment of these conditions must be, it is confidently to be looked for. The old order is inevitably passing and with it will go also the reservation system with its iniquities and makeshift policies. The Indian must eventually merge, with other racial elements, into that hypothetical and cosmopolitan being, the American of the future.

REFERENCES

Bancroft, George. History of the United States. Vols. i–xi. Boston, 1838–75.

Bancroft, Hubert Howe. The works of. Vols. i–xxxix. San Francisco, 1886–90.

Bandelier, Adolph F. Historical introduction to studies among the sedentary Indians of New Mexico. Papers Archaeol. Inst. Amer. (Amer. Ser.) Vol. i. Boston, 1881.

—— Documentary history of the Zuñi Tribe. J. Amer. Ethnol. Archaeol. Vol. 3, 1892.

Barrett, S. M., editor. Geronimo's story of his life. New York, 1906.

Bartram, William. Travels through North and South Carolina, Georgia, East and West Florida, the Cherokee country, the extensive territories of the Muscogulges or Creek Confederacy, and the country of the Choctaws. Philadelphia, 1791.

Drake, Samuel G. Indian biography, containing the lives of more than two hundred Indian Chiefs. Boston, 1832.

Handbook of American Indians North of Mexico. Edited by Frederick Webb Hodge. In two parts. Bur. Amer. Ethnol. Bull. 30, Part 1, 1907; Part 2, 1910.

Hariot, Thomas. A briefe and true report of the new found land of Virginia. Francfort, 1590. (Same. New York, 1871.)

—— Narrative of the first English plantation of Virginia. 1588 and 1590. (Reprint. London, 1893.)

Hennepin, Louis. Description de la Louisiane nouvellement découverte au sud oüest de la Nouvelle France. Paris, 1683. (Same, trans. by John G. Shea. New York, 1880.)

—— A new discovery of a vast country in America extending above four thousand miles between New France and New Mexico. London, 1698. (Same. 2 vols. Chicago, 1903.)

Marquette, Jacques. Discovery of some new countries and nations in northern America. London, 1698.

Parkman, Francis. France and England in North America. Vols. i–viii. Boston, 1867–92.

—— History of the conspiracy of Pontiac. Boston, 1868.

—— La Salle and the discovery of the Great West. 12th ed. Boston, 1883.

Roosevelt, Theodore. The winning of the West. Vols. i–ii. New York, 1889.

Schoolcraft, Henry R. Historical and statistical information, respecting the history, condition and prospects of the Indian tribes of the United States. Parts i–vi. Philadelphia, 1851–57.

Smith, John. The generall historie of Virginia, New England, and the Summer Iles. (Vol. ii of the True Travels, Adventures and Observations of Captaine John Smith.) Richmond, 1819.

Spanish Explorers in the Southern United States. [Narratives of de Vaca and Castañeda edited by Frederick W. Hodge. Narrative of de Soto edited by Theodore H. Lewis.] New York, 1907.

Swanton, John R. Indian tribes of the lower Mississippi Valley. Bur. Amer. Ethnol. Bull. 43. Washington, 1911.

—— Early History of the Creek Indians and Their Neighbors. Bur. Amer. Ethnol. Bull. 73. Washington, 1922.

APPENDIX

Indian Stocks and Tribes

Among the tribes that by reason of ancient fame or present strength are most interesting are the following:

NAME	FORMER STRENGTH	RECENT STRENGTH	FORMER LOCATION	PRESENT LOCATION
*Algonquian Stock.**				
Abnaki (including Passamaquoddy and Penobscot)	3,000	1,200	Maine and vicinity	Quebec; Maine
Arapahoe	3,000	2,000	Great Central Plains	Oklahoma; Wyoming
Blackfoot	15,000	1,000	Great Northern Plains	Canada; Montana
Cheyenne	3,500	3,300	Minnesota	Oklahoma; Montana
Chippewa	25,000	18,000	Great Lakes	Canada; Great Lakes
Cree and Muskegon	15,000	15,000	Canada	Canada
Delaware and Munsee	(?)8,000	1,800	Del.; N. J.; N. Y.; Penn.	Canada; Oklahoma
Illinois	8,000	50	Illinois	Oklahoma
Kickapoo	2,000	800	Wisconsin	Kansas; Oklahoma; Mexico
Menominee	3,000	1,900	Wisconsin	Wisconsin
Miami	4,500	400	Wisconsin	Indiana; Oklahoma
Micmac	3,500	4,000	Nova Scotia; New Brunswick; Prince Edward Island	Nova Scotia; New Brunswick; Prince Edward Island
Ottawa and Algonkin	6,000	(?)7,000	Eastern Canada	Eastern Canada; Michigan; Oklahoma
Pottawatomi	4,000	2,000	Wisconsin; Michigan	Ontario; Kansas; Michigan; Oklahoma; Wisconsin

* The famous Algonquian tribes, the Mohegan, Narraganset, Niantic, and Pequot, with whom the New England colonists had so much contact in the seventeenth century, are now practically extinct.

INDIAN STOCKS AND TRIBES

NAME	FORMER STRENGTH	RECENT STRENGTH	FORMER LOCATION	PRESENT LOCATION
Powhatan	150	*	Virginia	Virginia
Sauk and Fox	6,500	1,000	Michigan	Kansas; Iowa; Oklahoma
Shawnee	3,000	600	Tennessee; Kentucky	Oklahoma
Athapascan Stock				
Apache	5,000	4,500	New Mexico	Arizona; New Mexico; Oklahoma
Carrier	8,000	900	British Columbia	British Columbia
Chipewyan	2,250	1,520	Northwest Canada	Northwest Canada
Hupa		550	California	California
Kutchin	5,500	3,300	Northwest Canada; Alaska	Northwest Canada; Alaska
Navaho	8,000	30,000	Arizona; New Mexico	Arizona; New Mexico
Slave	1,250	1,000	Great Bear Lake	Northwest Canada
Caddoan Stock				
Caddo	8,500	600	Louisiana; Texas	Oklahoma
Pawnee	10,000	600	Nebraska	Oklahoma
Wichita	3,200	310	Oklahoma	Oklahoma
Eskimauan Stock				
Aleut	16,000	1,060	Aleutian Islands, Alaska	Aleutian Islands, Alaska
Eskimo	75,900	30,000	Arctic Coasts	Arctic Coasts
Iroquoian Stock				
Cherokee	22,000	25,000	Southern Appalachians	Oklahoma; Tennessee

* A few hundred mixed bloods.

NAME	FORMER STRENGTH	RECENT STRENGTH	FORMER LOCATION	PRESENT LOCATION
Huron	18,000	850	Ontario	Quebec; Oklahoma
Iroquois (including Cayuga, Mohawk, Oneida, Onondaga, and Seneca)	5,500	17,630	New York	Canada; Oklahoma; New York; Wisconsin
Tuscarora	5,000	800	North Carolina	Canada; New York
Muskhogean Stock				
Chickasaw	8,000	5,000	Mississippi	Oklahoma
Choctaw	15,000	18,000	Mississippi	Louisiana; Oklahoma; Mississippi
Creek and Seminole*	18,000	13,500	Alabama; Georgia	Oklahoma
Natchez	4,500	(?)5	Mississippi	Oklahoma
Piman Stock				
Papago	6,000	5,800	Arizona	Arizona; Mexico
Pima	4,000	5,500	Arizona	Arizona
Salishan Stock				
Bellacoola	1,400	300	British Columbia	British Columbia
Cowichan	12,500	2,700	British Columbia	British Columbia
Flathead	600	600	Montana	Montana
Kalispel	1,200	900	Idaho; Washington	Montana; Washington
Nisqualli, Puyallup, etc	1,200	800	Washington	Washington
Shuswap	(?)4,500	2,100	British Columbia	British Columbia
Thompson Indians		1,800	British Columbia	British Columbia

* An offshoot of the Creek, dating from about 1750.

NAME	FORMER STRENGTH	RECENT STRENGTH	FORMER LOCATION	PRESENT LOCATION
Shoshonean Stock				
Comanche	7,000	1,400	Kansas	Oklahoma
Hopi	2,800	2,000	Arizona	Arizona
Paiute	7,500	5,600	Nevada; Utah	Nevada; Utah; Arizona
Shoshone	4,500	2,000	Idaho; Nevada; Wyoming	Idaho; Nevada; Wyoming
Ute	4,500	2,000	Utah; Colorado	Utah; Colorado
Siouan Stock				
Assiniboin	10,000	2,500	Lake Superior and northward	Montana; Alberta; Saskatchewan
Catawba	4,600	100	Carolinas	South Carolina
Crow	4,000	1,800	Dakota	Montana
Dakota (Sioux)	25,000	26,000	Minnesota	Dakotas and adjoining States
Hidatsa, etc	2,500	468	North Dakota	North Dakota
Mandan	3,600	263	North Dakota	North Dakota
Omaha	2,800	1,100	Missouri; Iowa	Nebraska
Osage	6,200	2,000	Arkansas; Missouri	Oklahoma
Winnebago	3,800	2,500	Wisconsin	Nebraska; Wisconsin
Various Stocks				
Haida	9,800	799	British Columbia	British Columbia; Alaska
Keresan	2,500	1,971	New Mexico	New Mexico
Kiowa	2,000	1,200	Colorado and northward	Oklahoma
Kwakiutl	4,500	376	British Columbia	British Columbia
Mission	(?)40,000	3,000	California	California

NAME	FORMER STRENGTH	RECENT STRENGTH	FORMER LOCATION	PRESENT LOCATION
Modoc	400	300	Oregon	Oregon; California
Mohave	3,500	1,600	California	Arizona
Nez Percés	4,000	1,600	Idaho; Oregon	Idaho; Washington
Nootka	6,000	2,100	Vancouver Island, B.C.	Vancouver Island, B.C.
Pomo		1,000	California	California
Tanoan	17,000	2,900	New Mexico	New Mexico
Tlingit tribes	10,000	5,450	Alaska	Alaska
Tsimshian	5,500	1,800	British Columbia	British Columbia
Yakima	3,000	1,500	Washington	Washington
Yuma	3,000	800	California	Arizona
Zuñi	2,500	1,500	New Mexico	New Mexico

INDEX

INDEX

INDEX

INDEX

INDEX

INDEX

INDEX